BURN THE ORPHANAGE

BURN THE ORPHANAGE
REIGN OF TERROR

SINA GRACE
CO-WRITER, ARTIST

DANIEL FREEDMAN
CO-WRITER

RENEE KEYES
COLORIST

RUS WOOTON
LETTERER

COVER
SINA GRACE & JOHN RAUCH

BACK COVER
BRANDON HUGHES

BURN THE ORPHANAGE CREATED BY SINA GRACE & DANIEL FREEDMAN
LOGO DESIGNED BY TIM DANIEL

IMAGE COMICS, INC.
Robert Kirkman – Chief Operating Officer
Erik Larsen – Chief Financial Officer
Todd McFarlane – President
Marc Silvestri – Chief Executive Officer
Jim Valentino – Vice-President

Eric Stephenson – Publisher
Ron Richards – Director of Business Development
Jennifer de Guzman – Director of Trade Book Sales
Kat Salazar – Director of PR & Marketing
Corey Murphy – Director of Retail Sales
Jeremy Sullivan – Director of Digital Sales
Emilio Bautista – Sales Assistant
Branwyn Bigglestone – Senior Accounts Manager
Emily Miller – Accounts Manager
Jessica Ambriz – Administrative Assistant
Tyler Shainline – Events Coordinator
David Brothers – Content Manager
Jonathan Chan – Production Manager
Drew Gill – Art Director
Meredith Wallace – Print Manager
Monica Garcia – Senior Production Artist
Addison Duke – Production Artist
Tricia Ramos – Production Assistant
IMAGECOMICS.COM

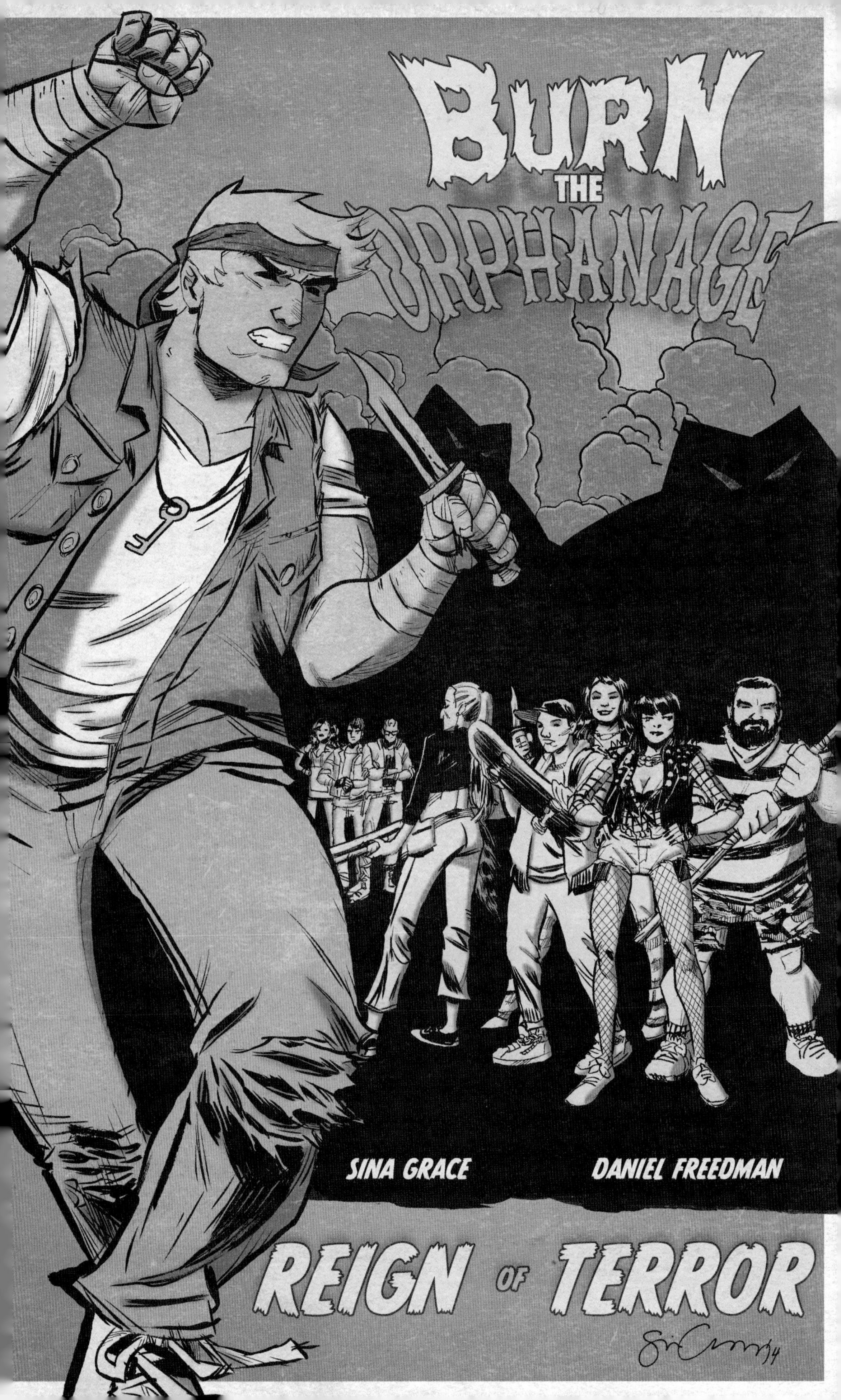
BURN THE ORPHANAGE
SINA GRACE
DANIEL FREEDMAN
REIGN OF TERROR

CHAPTER ONE

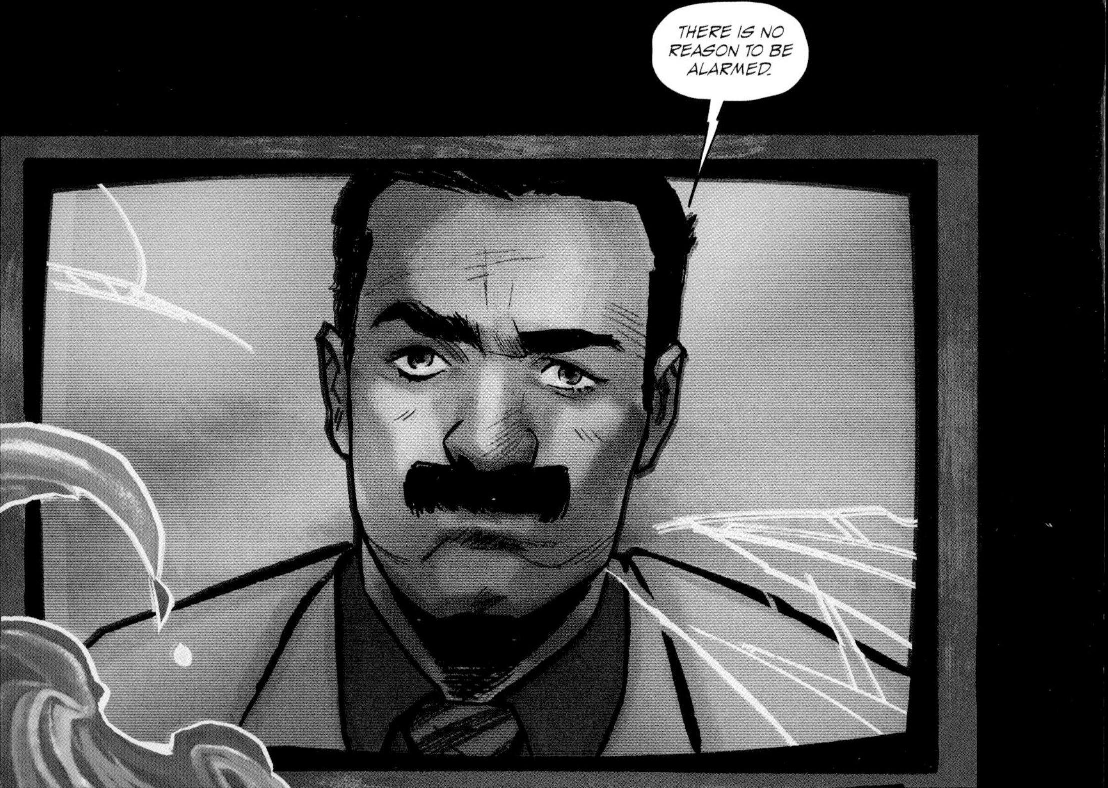
THERE IS NO REASON TO BE ALARMED.

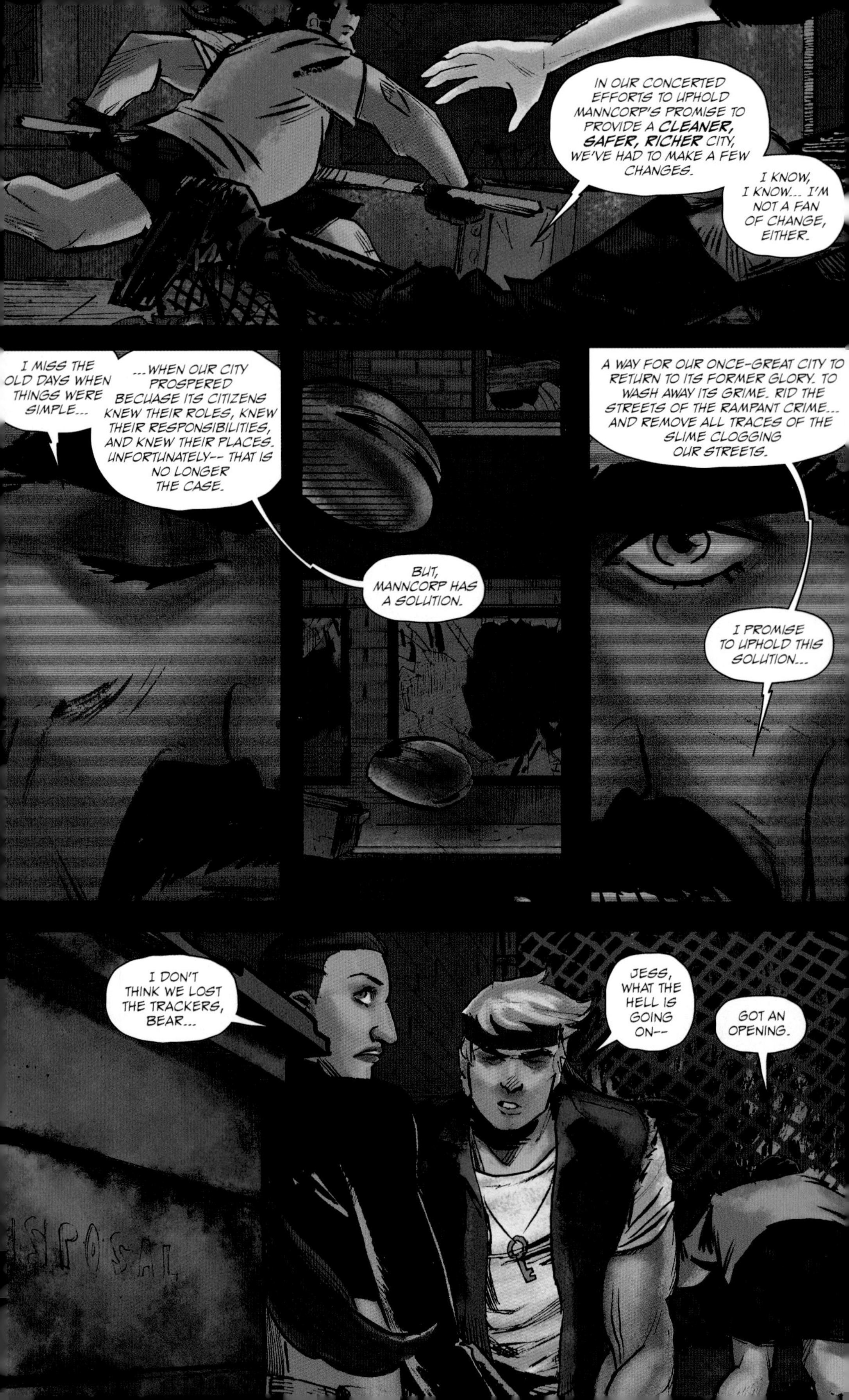
IN OUR CONCERTED EFFORTS TO UPHOLD MANNCORP'S PROMISE TO PROVIDE A CLEANER, SAFER, RICHER CITY, WE'VE HAD TO MAKE A FEW CHANGES.
I KNOW, I KNOW... I'M NOT A FAN OF CHANGE, EITHER.
I MISS THE OLD DAYS WHEN THINGS WERE SIMPLE...
...WHEN OUR CITY PROSPERED BECUASE ITS CITIZENS KNEW THEIR ROLES, KNEW THEIR RESPONSIBILITIES, AND KNEW THEIR PLACES. UNFORTUNATELY-- THAT IS NO LONGER THE CASE.
BUT, MANNCORP HAS A SOLUTION.
A WAY FOR OUR ONCE-GREAT CITY TO RETURN TO ITS FORMER GLORY. TO WASH AWAY ITS GRIME. RID THE STREETS OF THE RAMPANT CRIME... AND REMOVE ALL TRACES OF THE SLIME CLOGGING OUR STREETS.
I PROMISE TO UPHOLD THIS SOLUTION...
I DON'T THINK WE LOST THE TRACKERS, BEAR...
JESS, WHAT THE HELL IS GOING ON--
GOT AN OPENING.

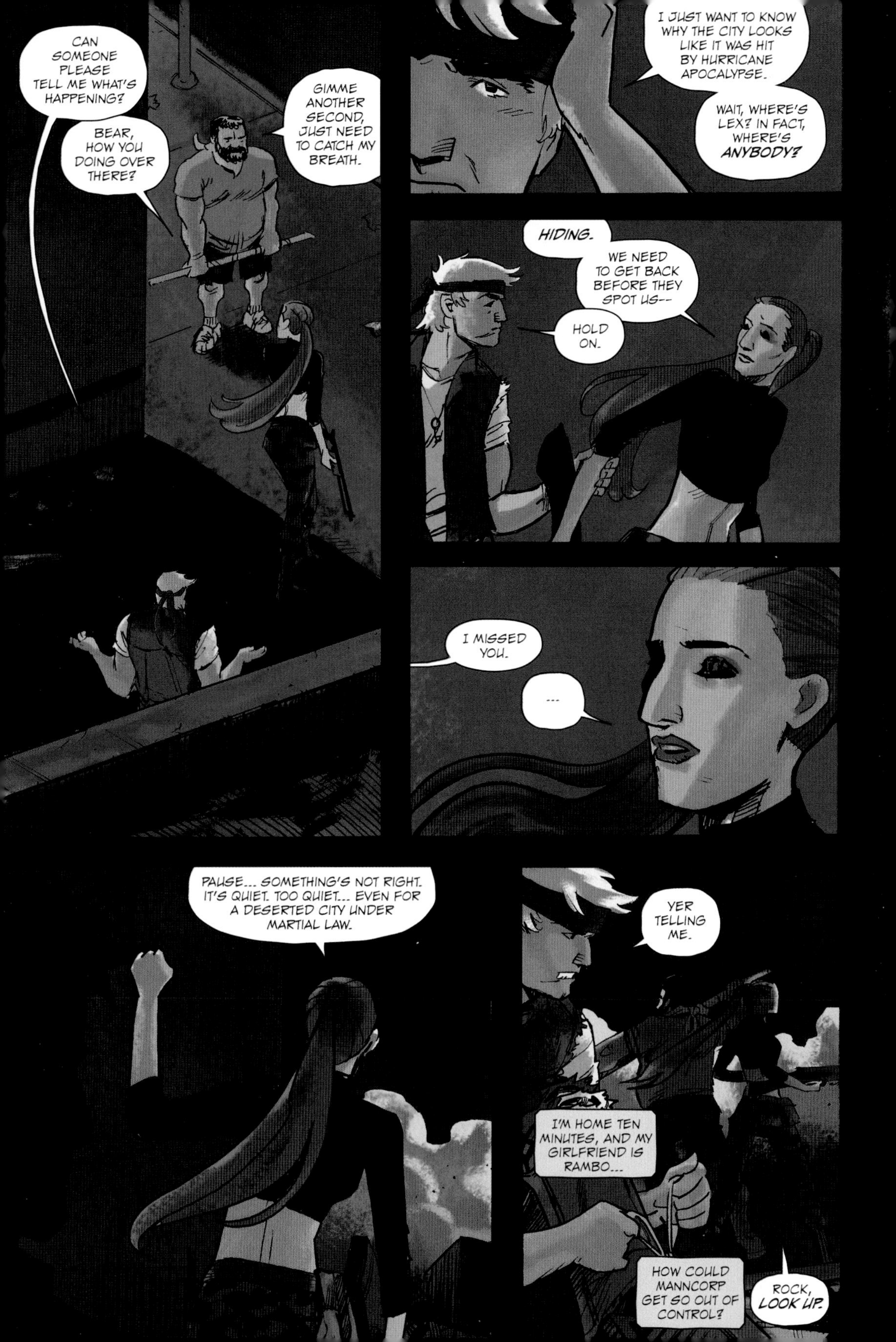
CAN SOMEONE PLEASE TELL ME WHAT'S HAPPENING?
BEAR, HOW YOU DOING OVER THERE?
GIMME ANOTHER SECOND, JUST NEED TO CATCH MY BREATH.
I JUST WANT TO KNOW WHY THE CITY LOOKS LIKE IT WAS HIT BY HURRICANE APOCALYPSE.
WAIT, WHERE'S LEX? IN FACT, WHERE'S ANYBODY?
HIDING.
WE NEED TO GET BACK BEFORE THEY SPOT US--
HOLD ON.
I MISSED YOU.
...
PAUSE... SOMETHING'S NOT RIGHT. IT'S QUIET. TOO QUIET... EVEN FOR A DESERTED CITY UNDER MARTIAL LAW.
YER TELLING ME.
I'M HOME TEN MINUTES, AND MY GIRLFRIEND IS RAMBO...
HOW COULD MANNCORP GET SO OUT OF CONTROL?
ROCK, LOOK UP.

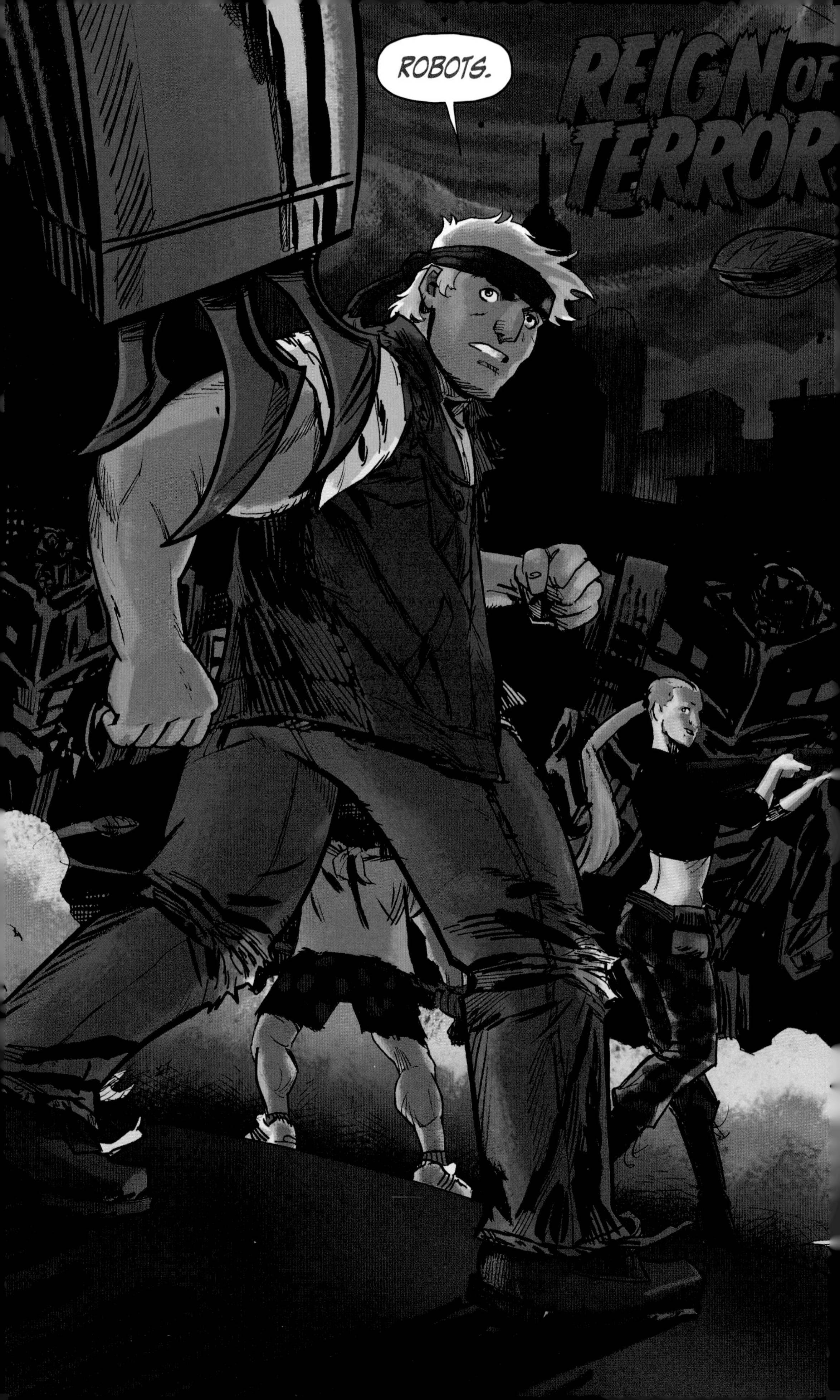
ROBOTS.
REIGN OF TERROR

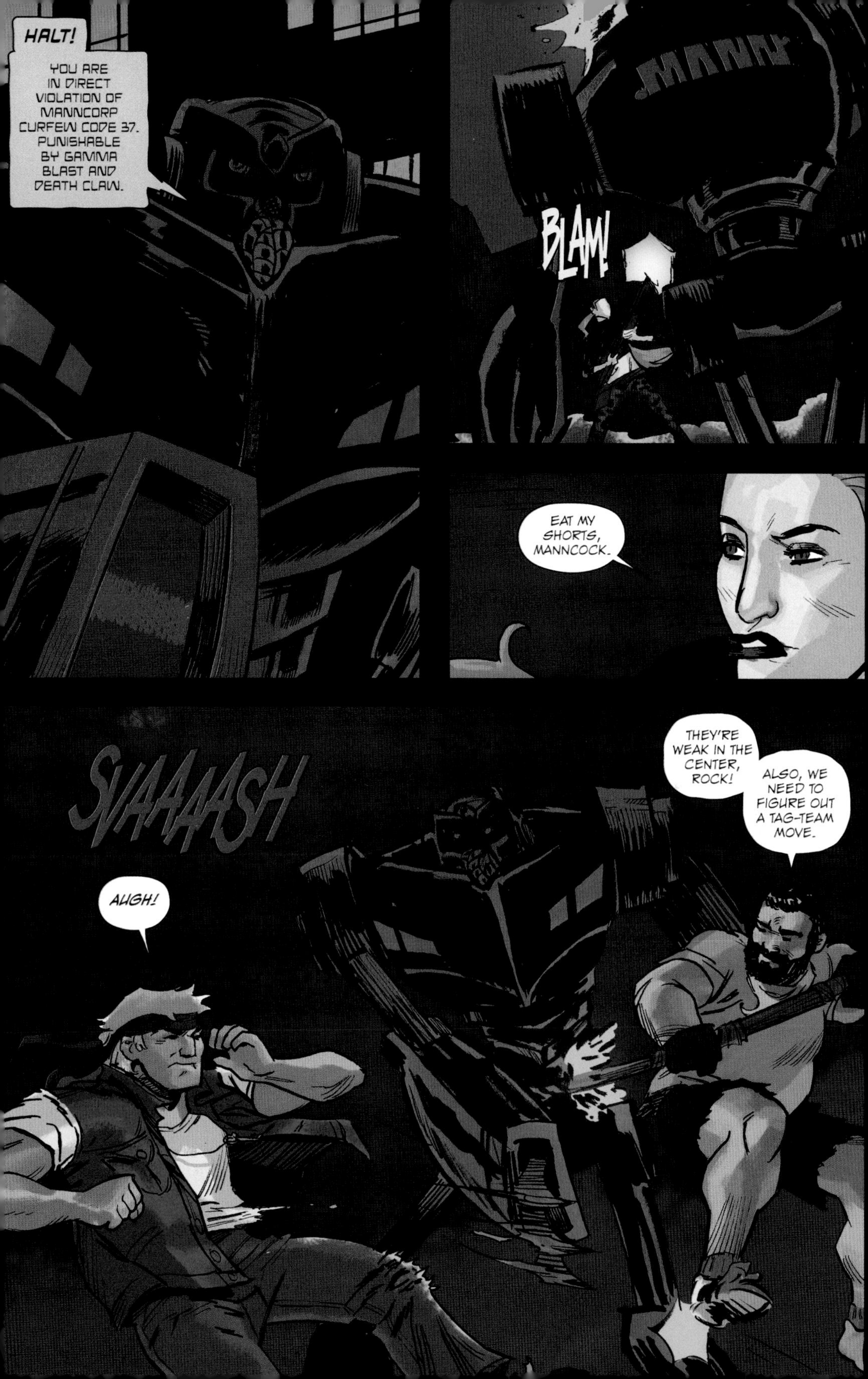
HALT!
YOU ARE IN DIRECT VIOLATION OF MANNCORP CURFEW CODE 37. PUNISHABLE BY GAMMA BLAST AND DEATH CLAW.
BLAM!
EAT MY SHORTS, MANNCOCK.
SVAAAASH
THEY'RE WEAK IN THE CENTER, ROCK!
ALSO, WE NEED TO FIGURE OUT A TAG-TEAM MOVE.
AUGH!

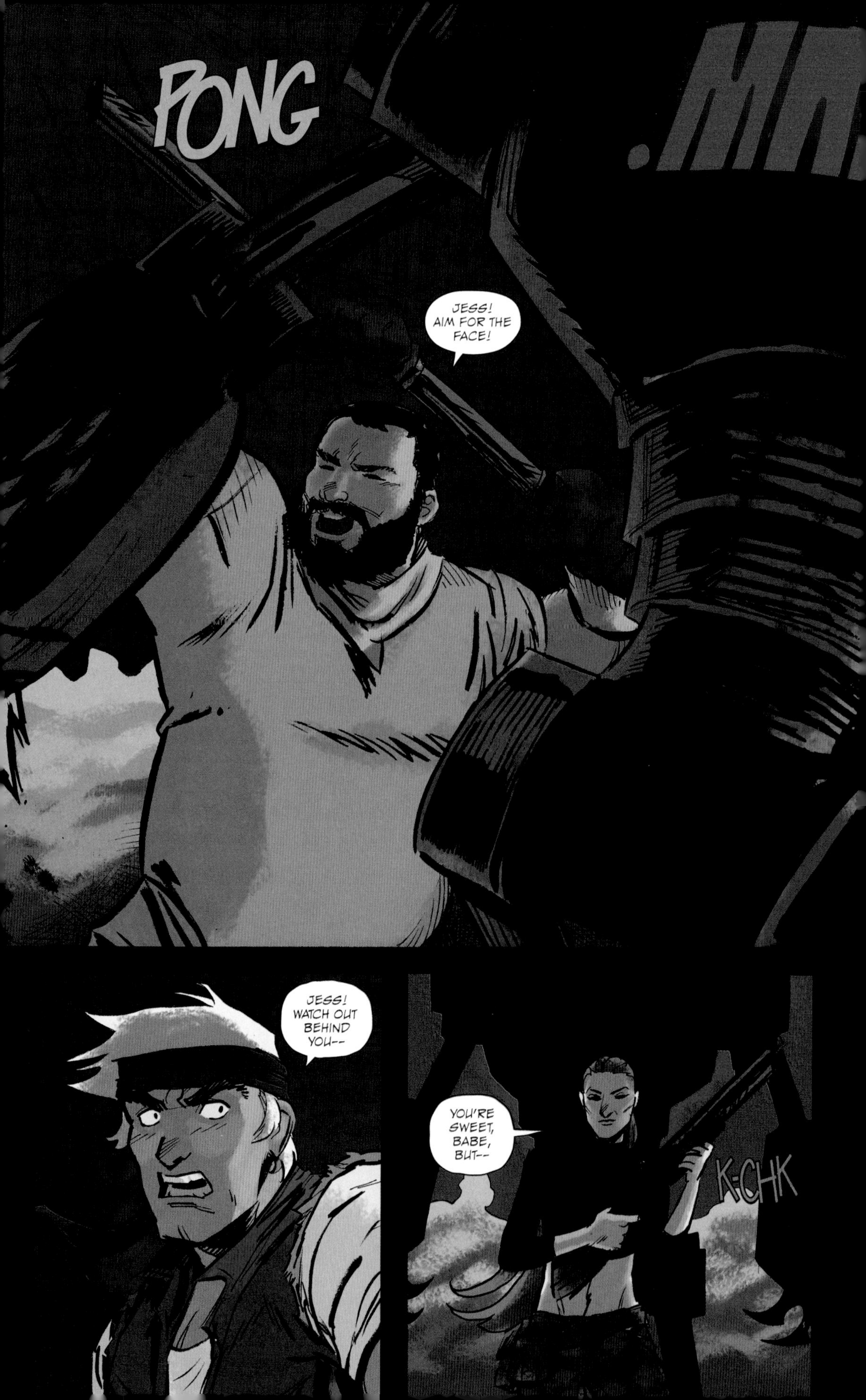
PONG
JESS! AIM FOR THE FACE!
JESS! WATCH OUT BEHIND YOU--
YOU'RE SWEET, BABE, BUT--
K-CHK

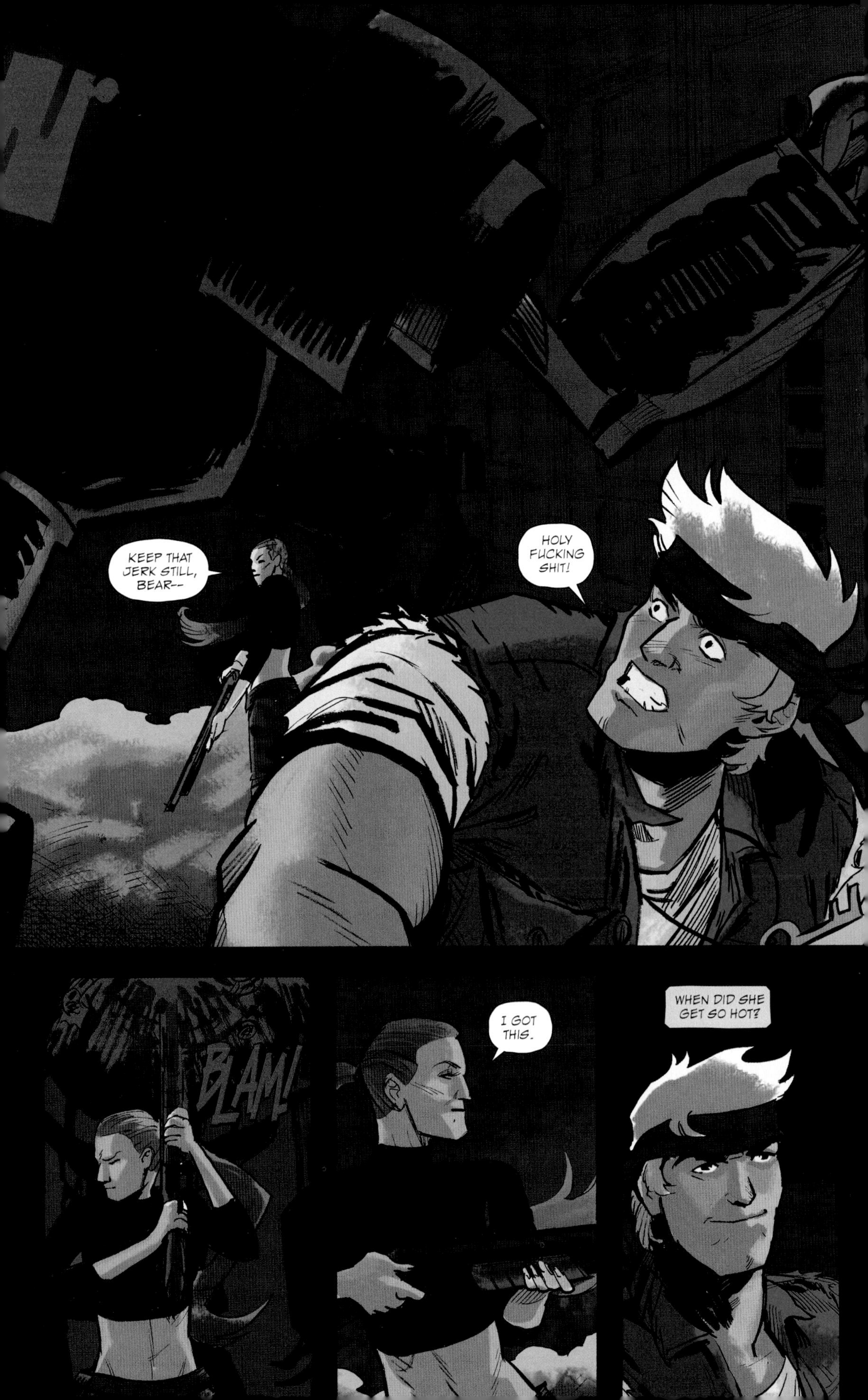
KEEP THAT JERK STILL, BEAR--
HOLY FUCKING SHIT!
BLAM
I GOT THIS.
WHEN DID SHE GET SO HOT?

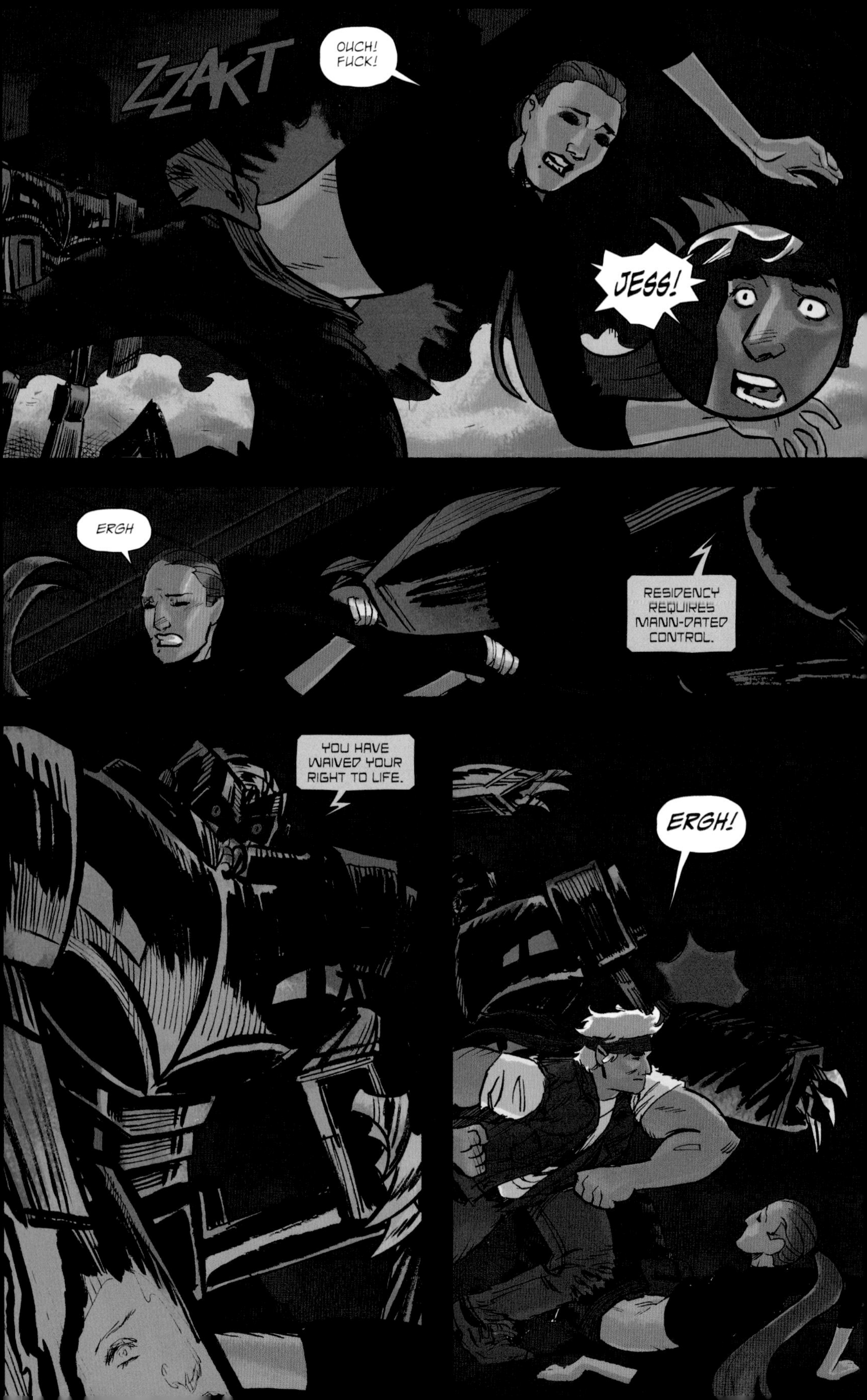
ZZAKT
OUCH! FUCK!
JESS!
ERGH
RESIDENCY REQUIRES MANN-DATED CONTROL.
YOU HAVE WAIVED YOUR RIGHT TO LIFE.
ERGH!

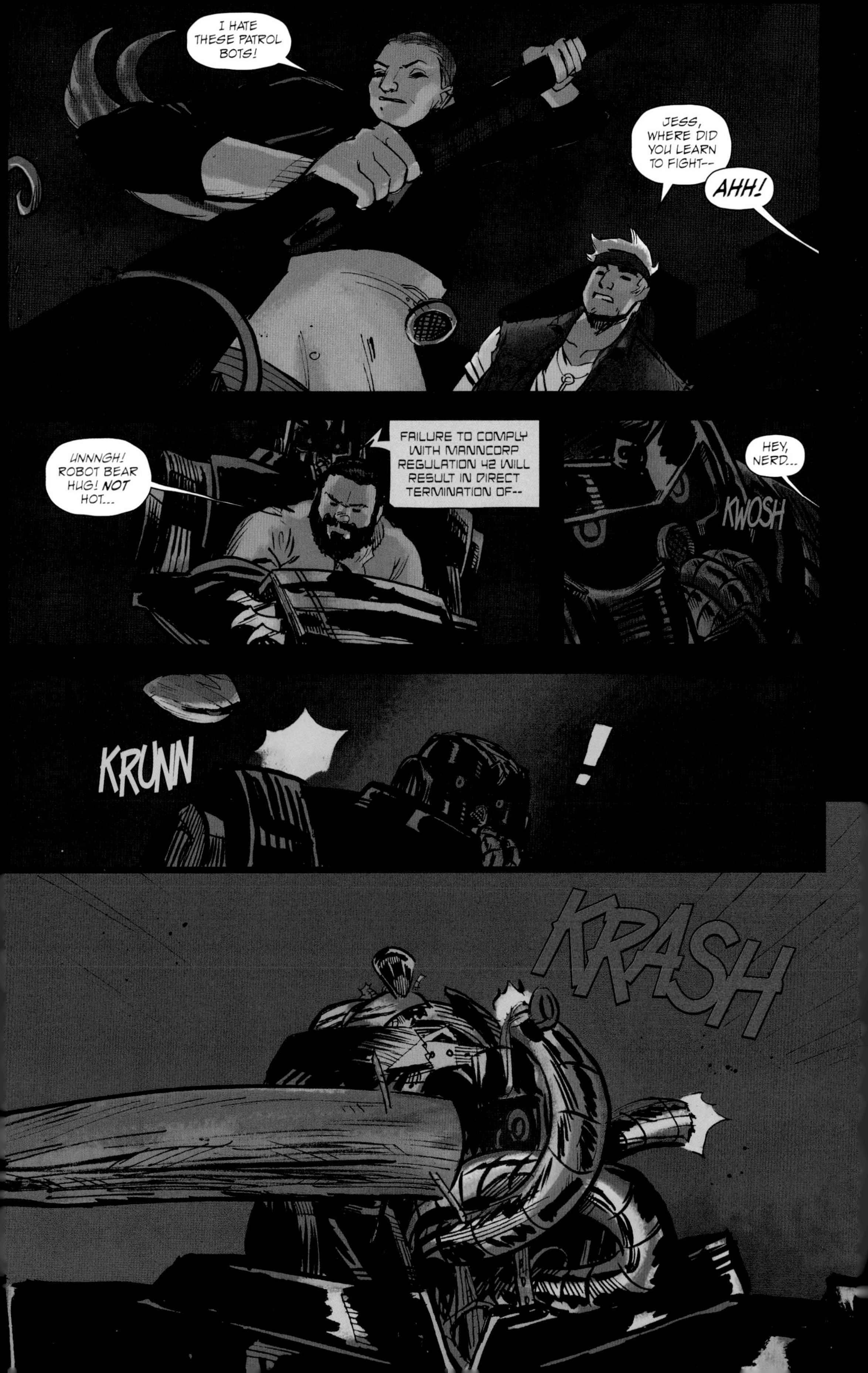

I HATE THESE PATROL BOTS!
JESS, WHERE DID YOU LEARN TO FIGHT--
AHH!
UNNNGH! ROBOT BEAR HUG! NOT HOT...
FAILURE TO COMPLY WITH MANNCORP REGULATION 42 WILL RESULT IN DIRECT TERMINATION OF--
HEY, NERD...
KWOSH
KRUNN
!
KRASH

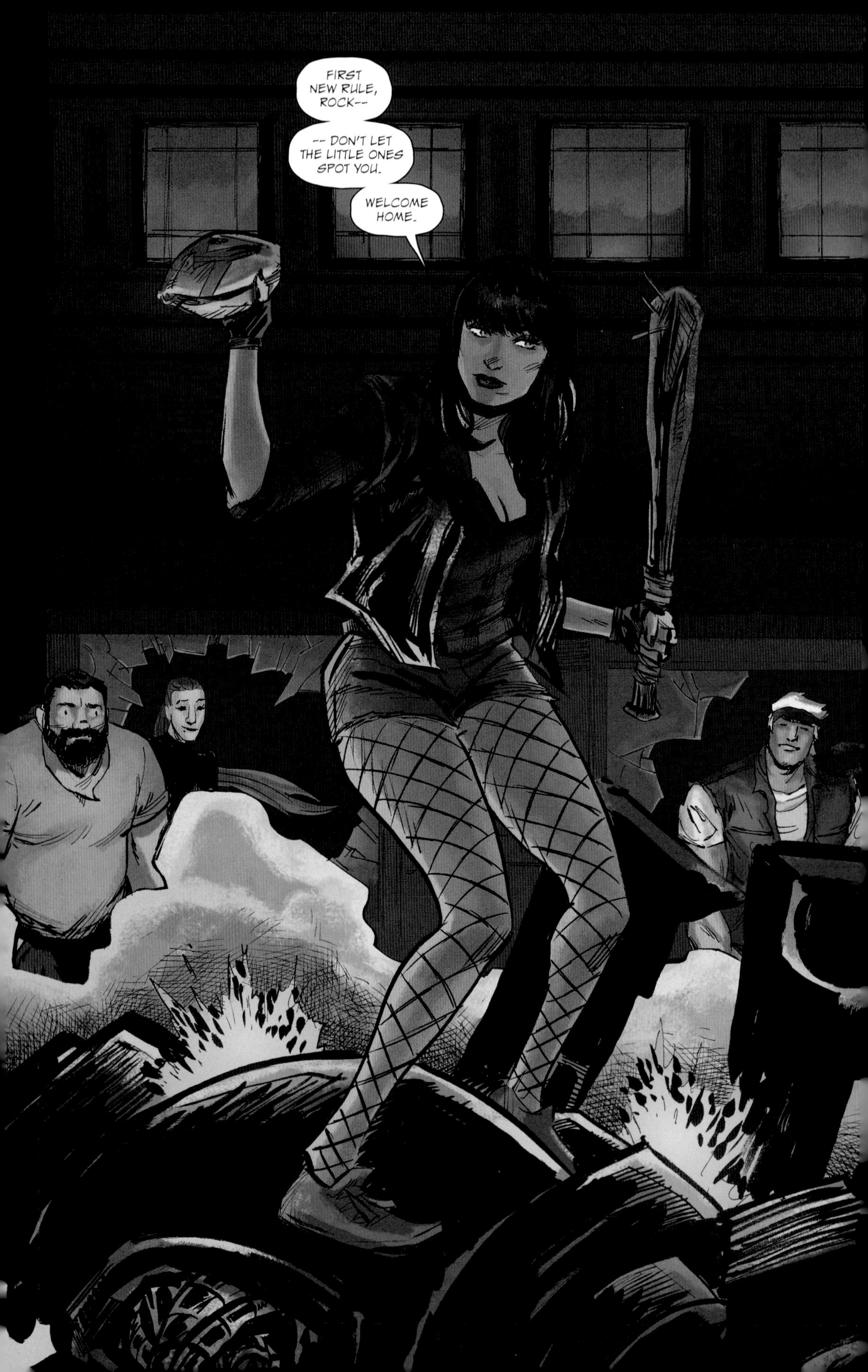
FIRST NEW RULE, ROCK--
-- DON'T LET THE LITTLE ONES SPOT YOU.
WELCOME HOME.

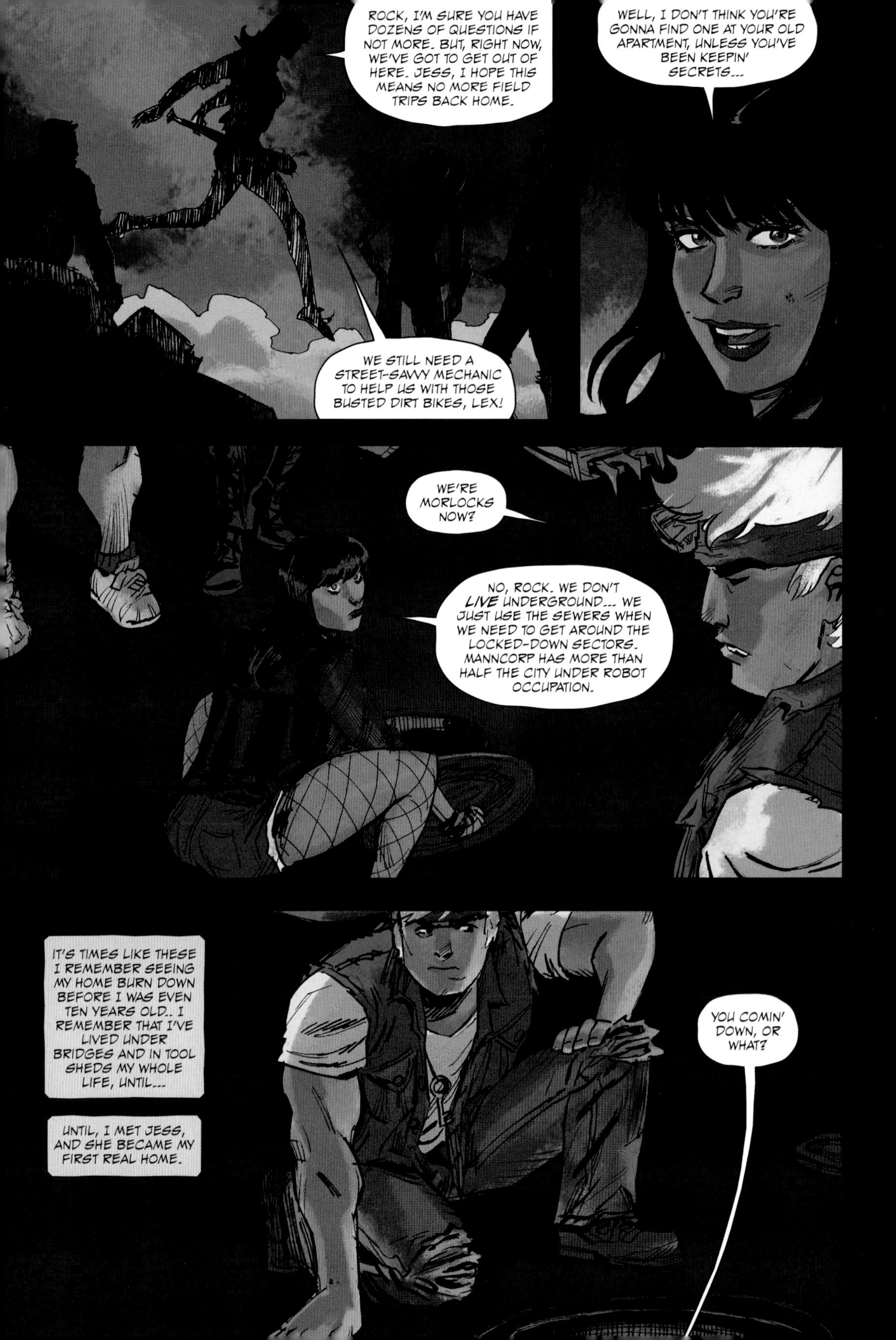
ROCK, I'M SURE YOU HAVE DOZENS OF QUESTIONS IF NOT MORE. BUT, RIGHT NOW, WE'VE GOT TO GET OUT OF HERE. JESS, I HOPE THIS MEANS NO MORE FIELD TRIPS BACK HOME.
WE STILL NEED A STREET-SAVVY MECHANIC TO HELP US WITH THOSE BUSTED DIRT BIKES, LEX!
WELL, I DON'T THINK YOU'RE GONNA FIND ONE AT YOUR OLD APARTMENT, UNLESS YOU'VE BEEN KEEPIN' SECRETS...
WE'RE MORLOCKS NOW?
NO, ROCK. WE DON'T *LIVE* UNDERGROUND... WE JUST USE THE SEWERS WHEN WE NEED TO GET AROUND THE LOCKED-DOWN SECTORS. MANNCORP HAS MORE THAN HALF THE CITY UNDER ROBOT OCCUPATION.
IT'S TIMES LIKE THESE I REMEMBER SEEING MY HOME BURN DOWN BEFORE I WAS EVEN TEN YEARS OLD.. I REMEMBER THAT I'VE LIVED UNDER BRIDGES AND IN TOOL SHEDS MY WHOLE LIFE, UNTIL...
UNTIL, I MET JESS, AND SHE BECAME MY FIRST REAL HOME.
YOU COMIN' DOWN, OR WHAT?

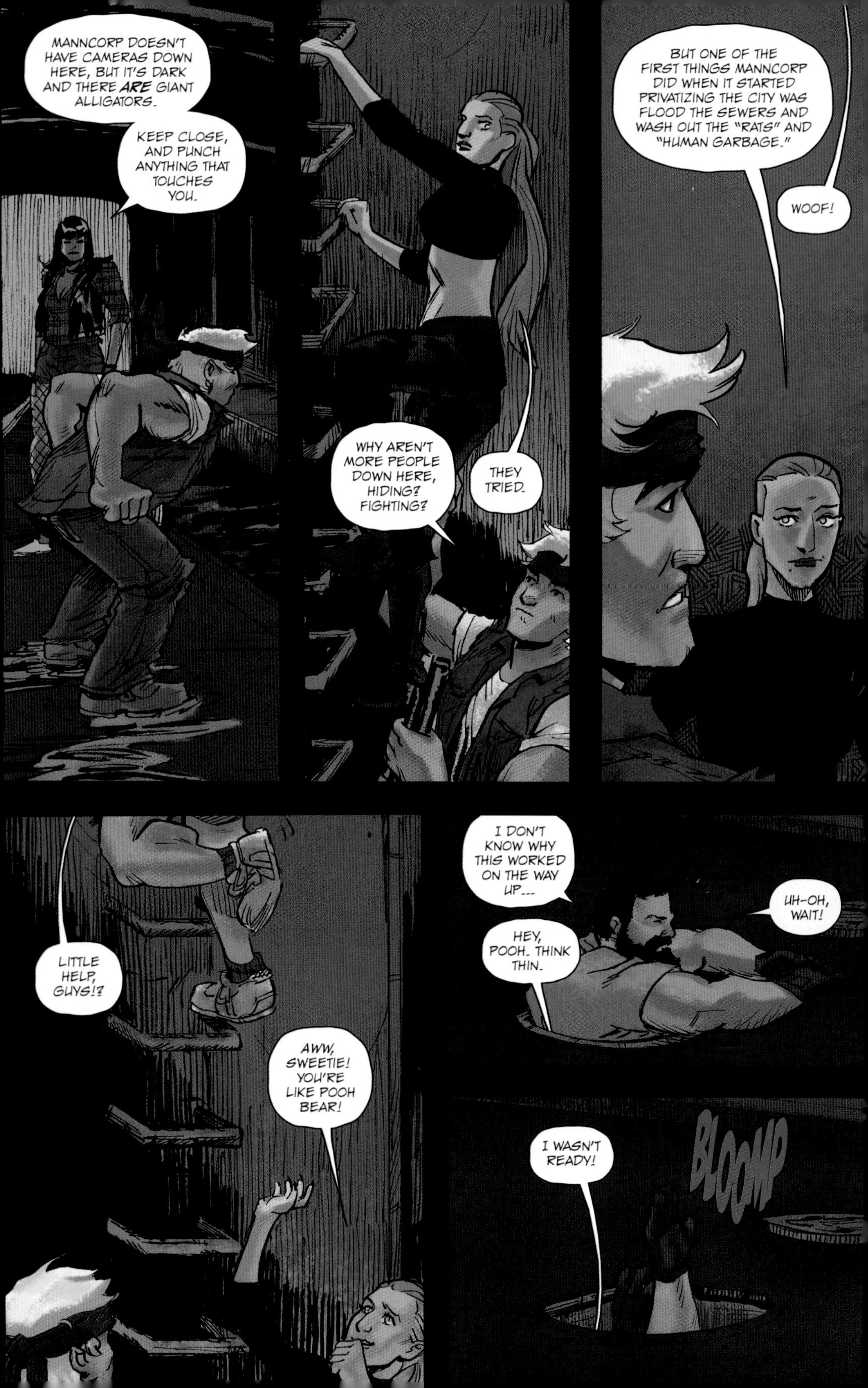
MANNCORP DOESN'T HAVE CAMERAS DOWN HERE, BUT IT'S DARK AND THERE *ARE* GIANT ALLIGATORS.
KEEP CLOSE, AND PUNCH ANYTHING THAT TOUCHES YOU.
WHY AREN'T MORE PEOPLE DOWN HERE, HIDING? FIGHTING?
THEY TRIED.
BUT ONE OF THE FIRST THINGS MANNCORP DID WHEN IT STARTED PRIVATIZING THE CITY WAS FLOOD THE SEWERS AND WASH OUT THE "RATS" AND "HUMAN GARBAGE."
WOOF!
LITTLE HELP, GUYS!?
AWW, SWEETIE! YOU'RE LIKE POOH BEAR!
I DON'T KNOW WHY THIS WORKED ON THE WAY UP...
HEY, POOH. THINK THIN.
UH-OH, WAIT!
I WASN'T READY!
BLOOMP

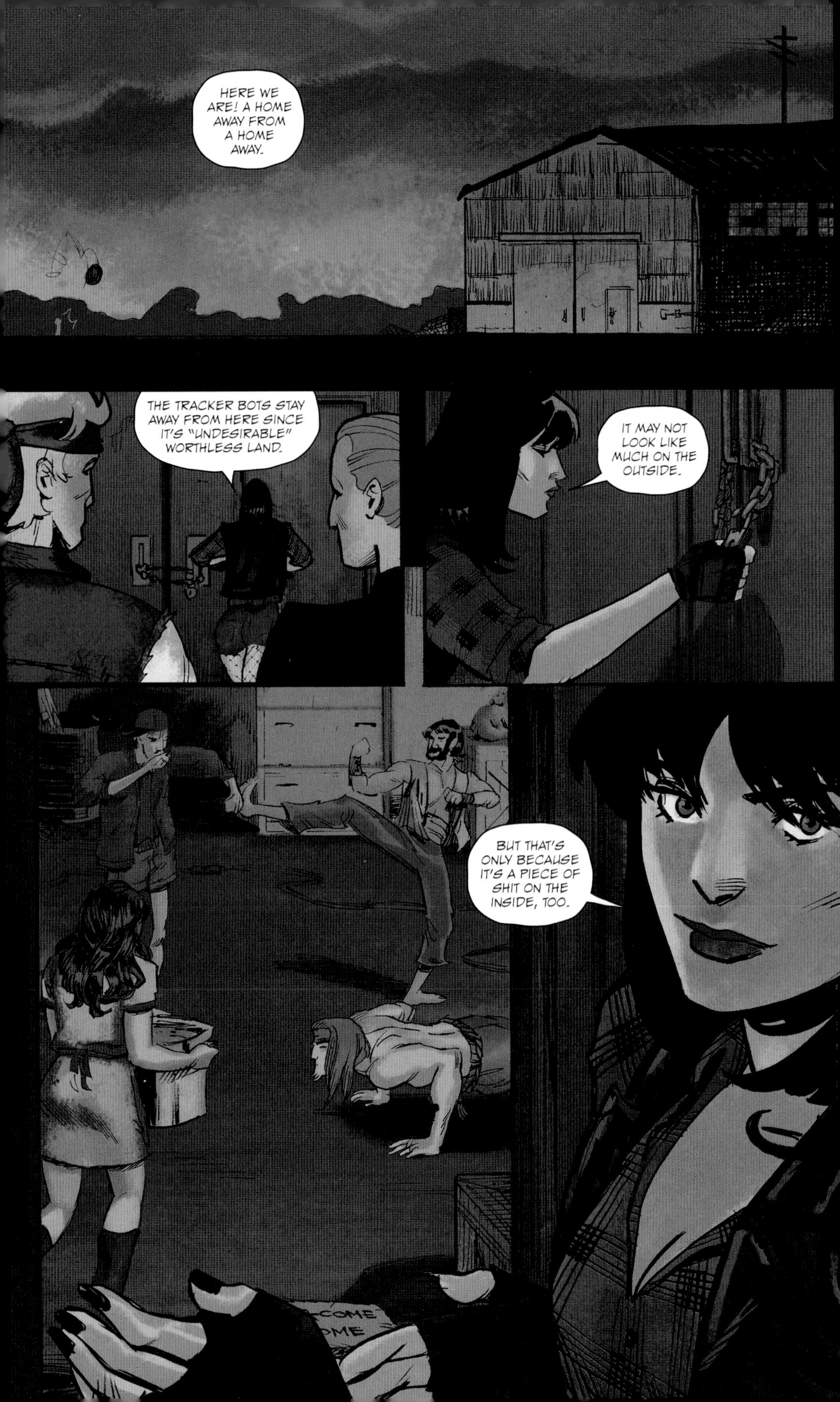
HERE WE ARE! A HOME AWAY FROM A HOME AWAY.
THE TRACKER BOTS STAY AWAY FROM HERE SINCE IT'S "UNDESIRABLE" WORTHLESS LAND.
IT MAY NOT LOOK LIKE MUCH ON THE OUTSIDE.
BUT THAT'S ONLY BECAUSE IT'S A PIECE OF SHIT ON THE INSIDE, TOO.

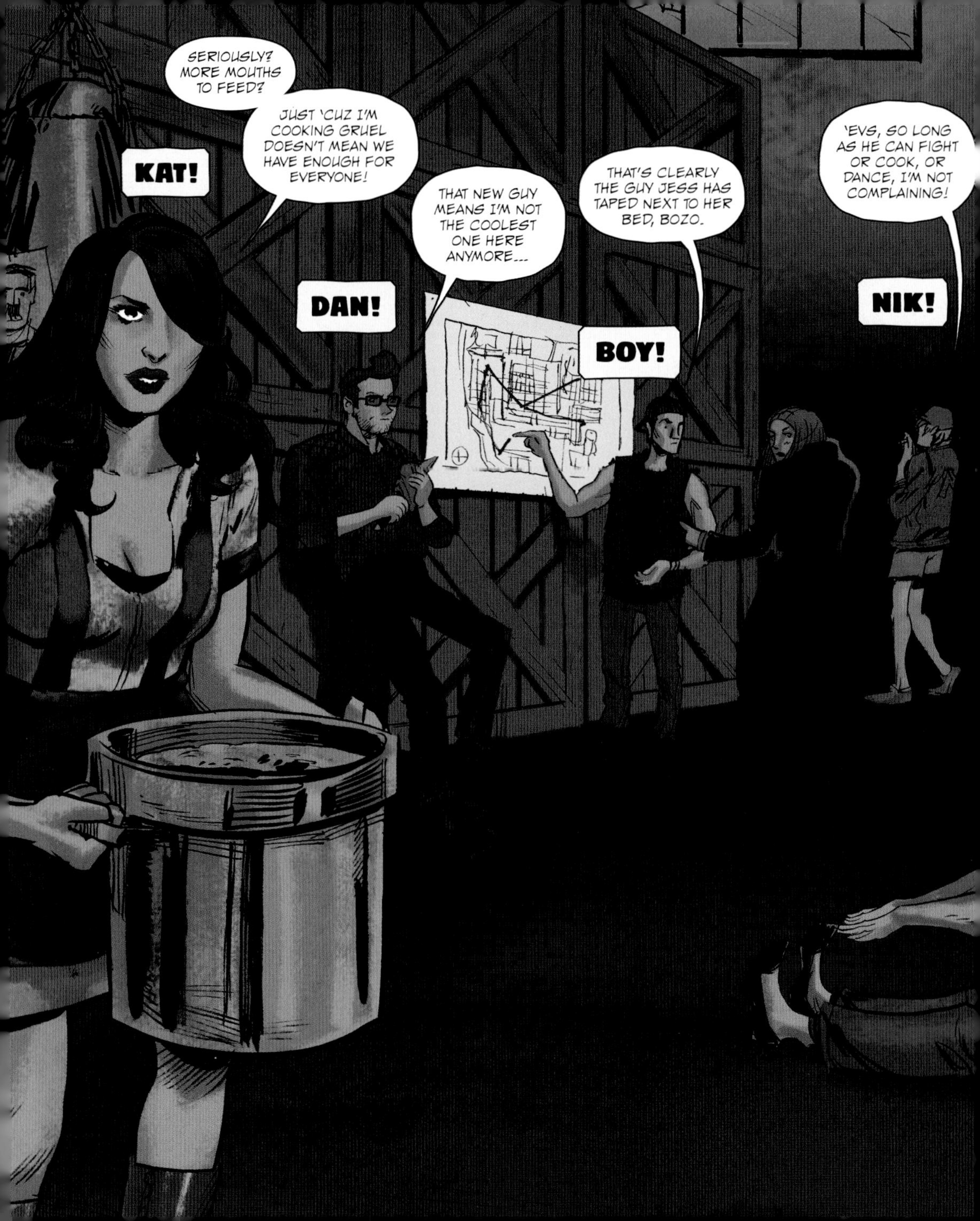
SERIOUSLY? MORE MOUTHS TO FEED?
JUST 'CUZ I'M COOKING GRUEL DOESN'T MEAN WE HAVE ENOUGH FOR EVERYONE!
KAT!
THAT NEW GUY MEANS I'M NOT THE COOLEST ONE HERE ANYMORE...
DAN!
THAT'S CLEARLY THE GUY JESS HAS TAPED NEXT TO HER BED, BOZO.
BOY!
'EVS, SO LONG AS HE CAN FIGHT OR COOK, OR DANCE, I'M NOT COMPLAINING!
NIK!

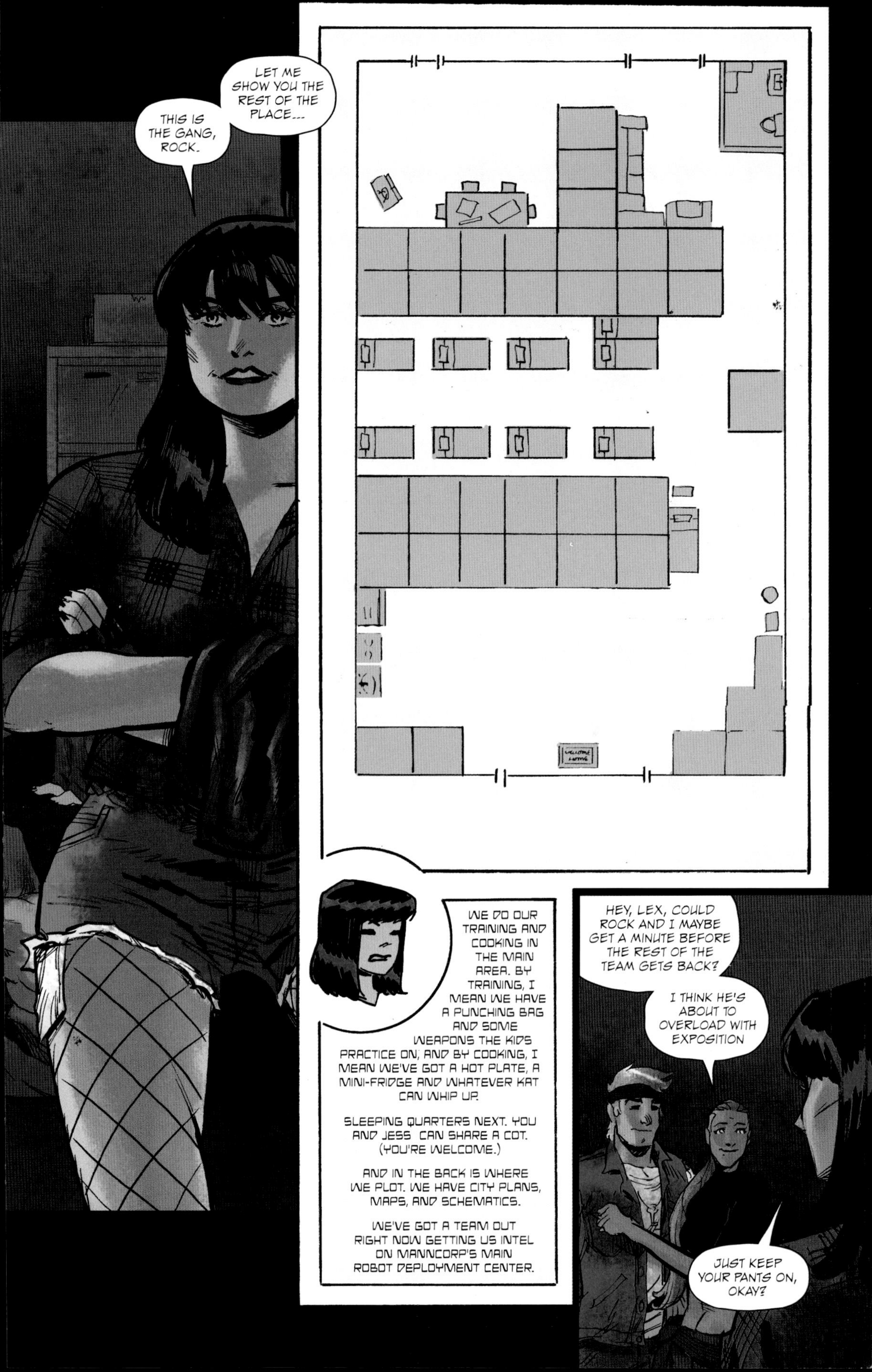
THIS IS THE GANG, ROCK.
LET ME SHOW YOU THE REST OF THE PLACE...
WE DO OUR TRAINING AND COOKING IN THE MAIN AREA. BY TRAINING, I MEAN WE HAVE A PUNCHING BAG AND SOME WEAPONS THE KIDS PRACTICE ON; AND BY COOKING, I MEAN WE'VE GOT A HOT PLATE, A MINI-FRIDGE AND WHATEVER KAT CAN WHIP UP.
SLEEPING QUARTERS NEXT. YOU AND JESS CAN SHARE A COT. (YOU'RE WELCOME.)
AND IN THE BACK IS WHERE WE PLOT. WE HAVE CITY PLANS, MAPS, AND SCHEMATICS.
WE'VE GOT A TEAM OUT RIGHT NOW GETTING US INTEL ON MANNCORP'S MAIN ROBOT DEPLOYMENT CENTER.
HEY, LEX, COULD ROCK AND I MAYBE GET A MINUTE BEFORE THE REST OF THE TEAM GETS BACK?
I THINK HE'S ABOUT TO OVERLOAD WITH EXPOSITION
JUST KEEP YOUR PANTS ON, OKAY?

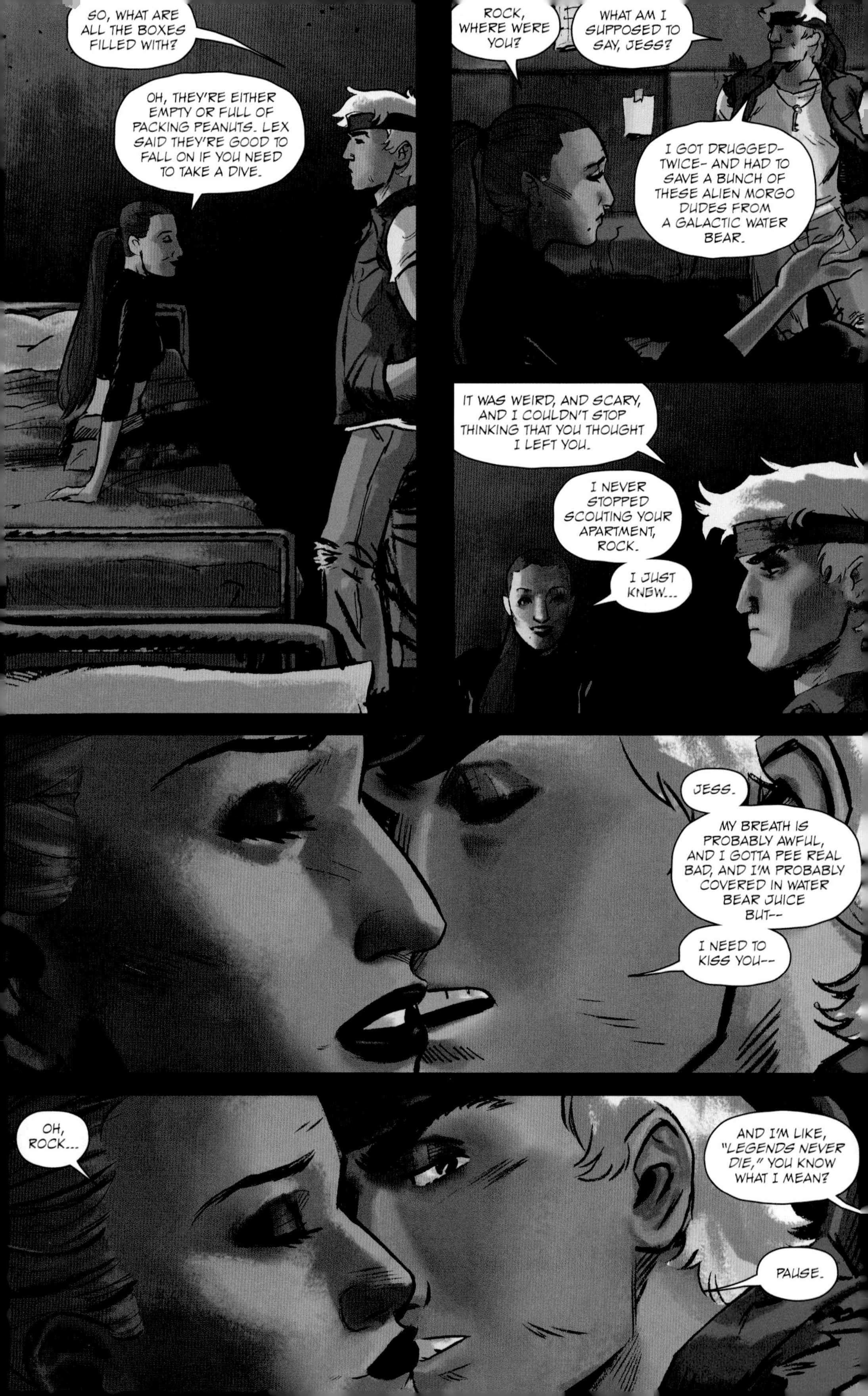
SO, WHAT ARE ALL THE BOXES FILLED WITH?
OH, THEY'RE EITHER EMPTY OR FULL OF PACKING PEANUTS. LEX SAID THEY'RE GOOD TO FALL ON IF YOU NEED TO TAKE A DIVE.
ROCK, WHERE WERE YOU?
WHAT AM I SUPPOSED TO SAY, JESS?
I GOT DRUGGED-TWICE- AND HAD TO SAVE A BUNCH OF THESE ALIEN MORGO DUDES FROM A GALACTIC WATER BEAR.
IT WAS WEIRD, AND SCARY, AND I COULDN'T STOP THINKING THAT YOU THOUGHT I LEFT YOU.
I NEVER STOPPED SCOUTING YOUR APARTMENT, ROCK.
I JUST KNEW...
JESS.
MY BREATH IS PROBABLY AWFUL, AND I GOTTA PEE REAL BAD, AND I'M PROBABLY COVERED IN WATER BEAR JUICE BUT--
I NEED TO KISS YOU--
OH, ROCK...
AND I'M LIKE, "LEGENDS NEVER DIE," YOU KNOW WHAT I MEAN?
PAUSE.

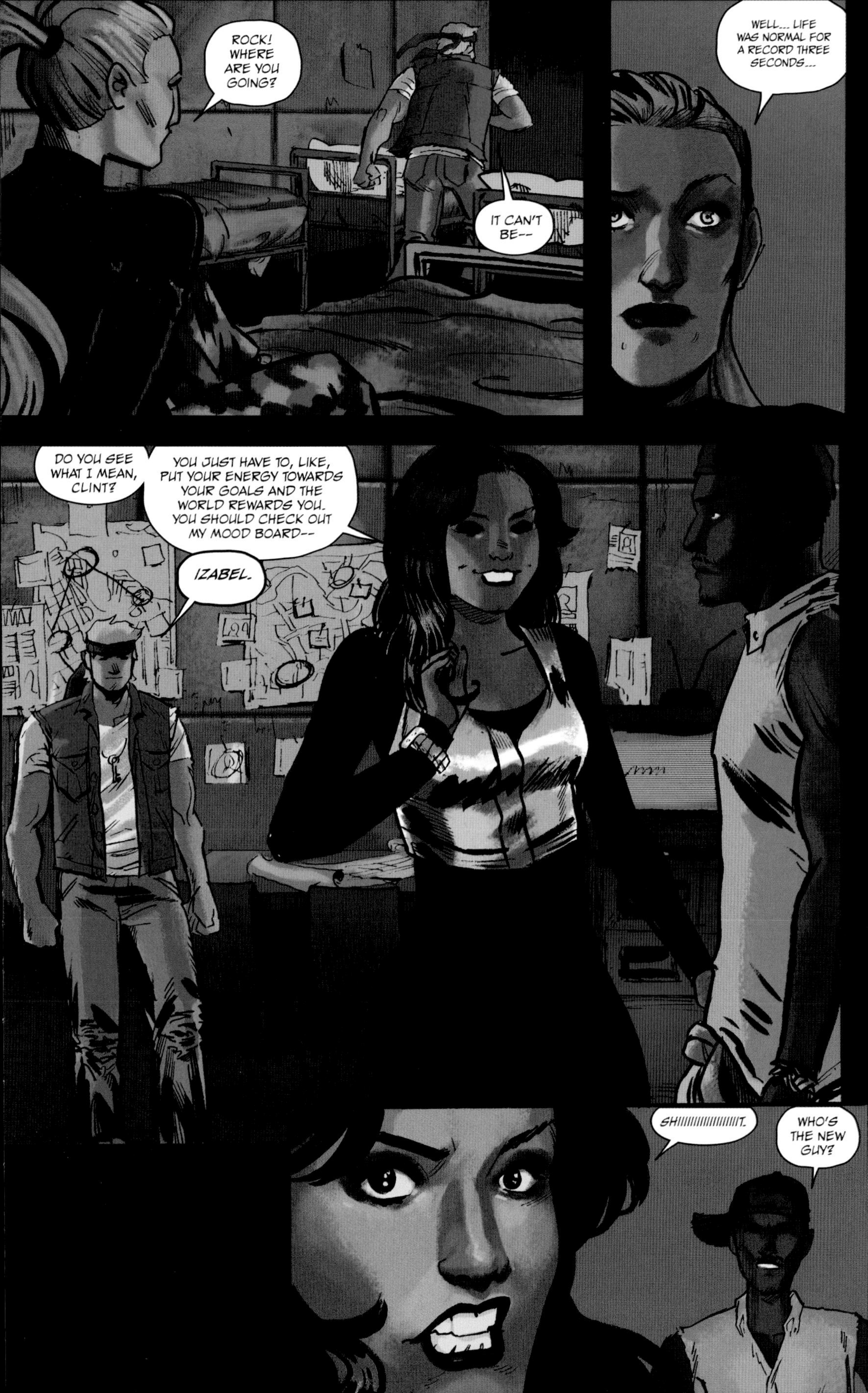
ROCK! WHERE ARE YOU GOING?
IT CAN'T BE--
WELL... LIFE WAS NORMAL FOR A RECORD THREE SECONDS...
DO YOU SEE WHAT I MEAN, CLINT?
YOU JUST HAVE TO, LIKE, PUT YOUR ENERGY TOWARDS YOUR GOALS AND THE WORLD REWARDS YOU. YOU SHOULD CHECK OUT MY MOOD BOARD--
IZABEL.
SHIIIIIIIIIIIIIIIIIIT.
WHO'S THE NEW GUY?

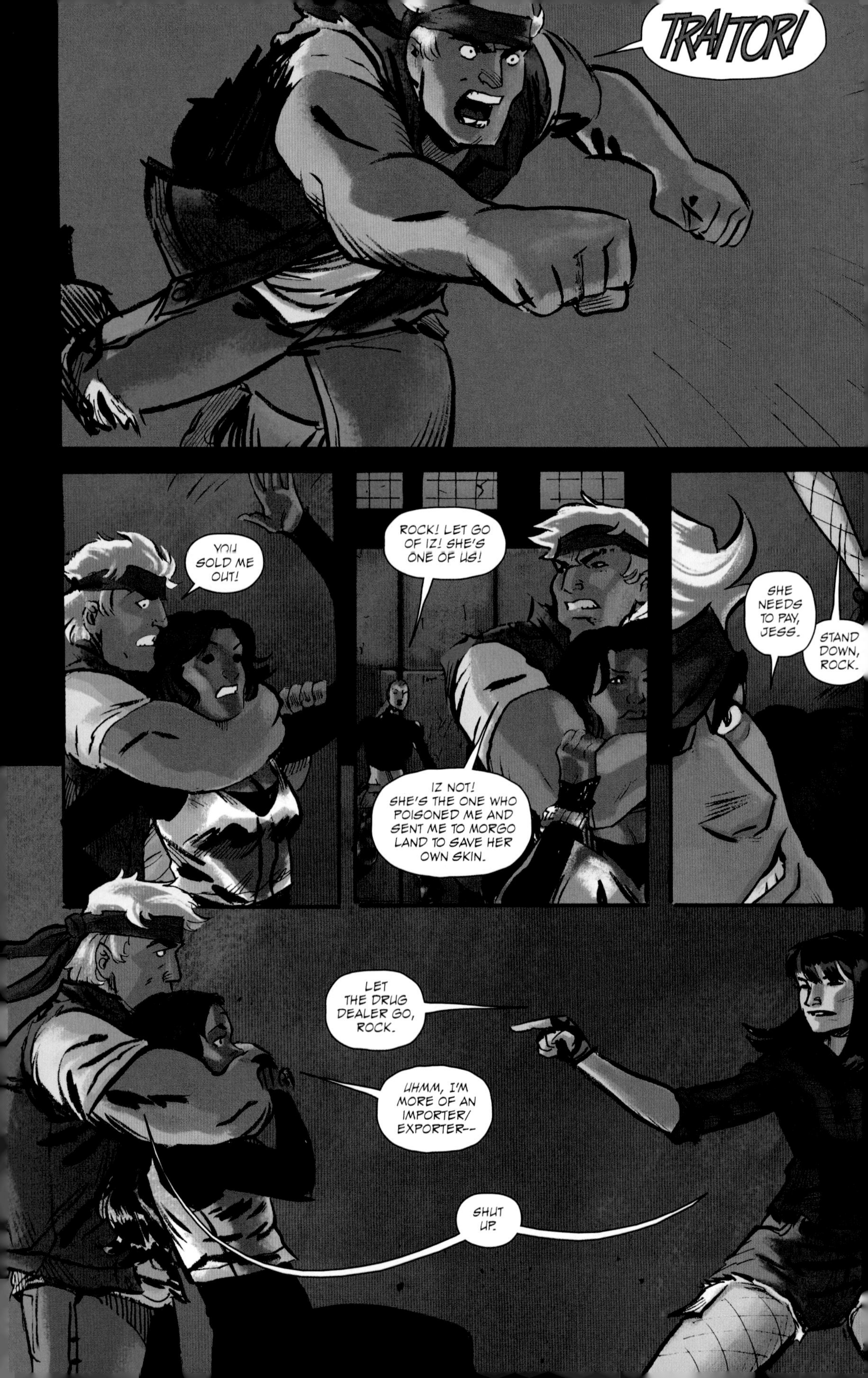
TRAITOR!
YOU SOLD ME OUT!
ROCK! LET GO OF IZ! SHE'S ONE OF US!
IZ NOT! SHE'S THE ONE WHO POISONED ME AND SENT ME TO MORGO LAND TO SAVE HER OWN SKIN.
SHE NEEDS TO PAY, JESS.
STAND DOWN, ROCK.
LET THE DRUG DEALER GO, ROCK.
UHMM, I'M MORE OF AN IMPORTER/ EXPORTER--
SHUT UP.

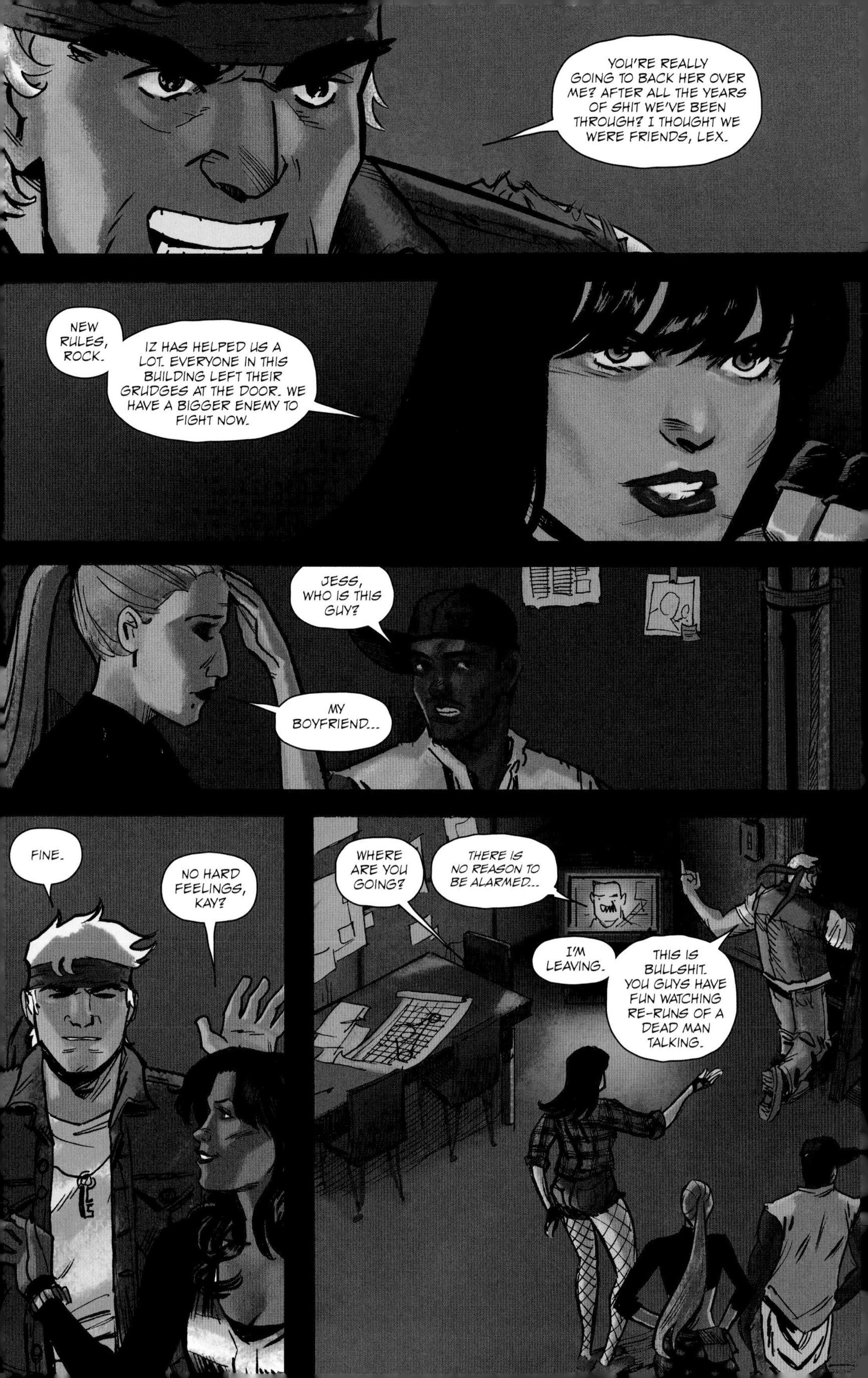

YOU'RE REALLY GOING TO BACK HER OVER ME? AFTER ALL THE YEARS OF SHIT WE'VE BEEN THROUGH? I THOUGHT WE WERE FRIENDS, LEX.
NEW RULES, ROCK.
IZ HAS HELPED US A LOT. EVERYONE IN THIS BUILDING LEFT THEIR GRUDGES AT THE DOOR. WE HAVE A BIGGER ENEMY TO FIGHT NOW.
JESS, WHO IS THIS GUY?
MY BOYFRIEND...
FINE.
NO HARD FEELINGS, KAY?
WHERE ARE YOU GOING?
THERE IS NO REASON TO BE ALARMED...
I'M LEAVING.
THIS IS BULLSHIT. YOU GUYS HAVE FUN WATCHING RE-RUNS OF A DEAD MAN TALKING.

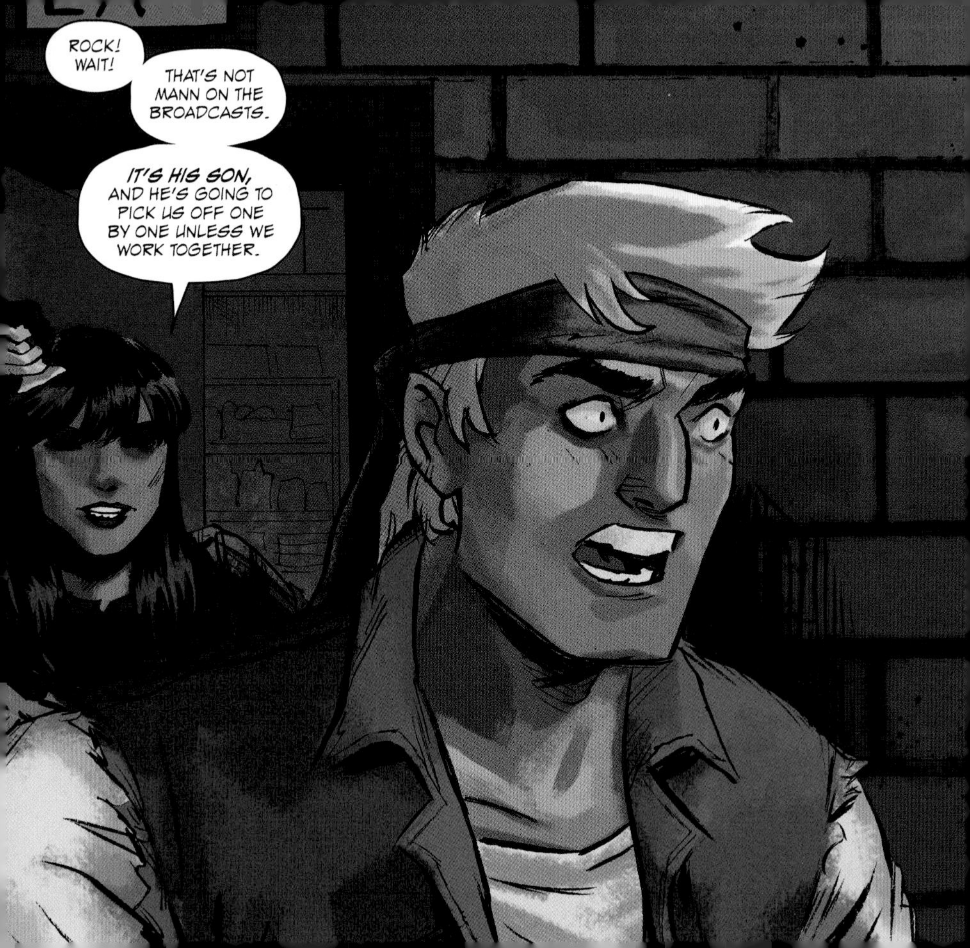
ROCK! WAIT!
THAT'S NOT MANN ON THE BROADCASTS.
IT'S HIS SON, AND HE'S GOING TO PICK US OFF ONE BY ONE UNLESS WE WORK TOGETHER.

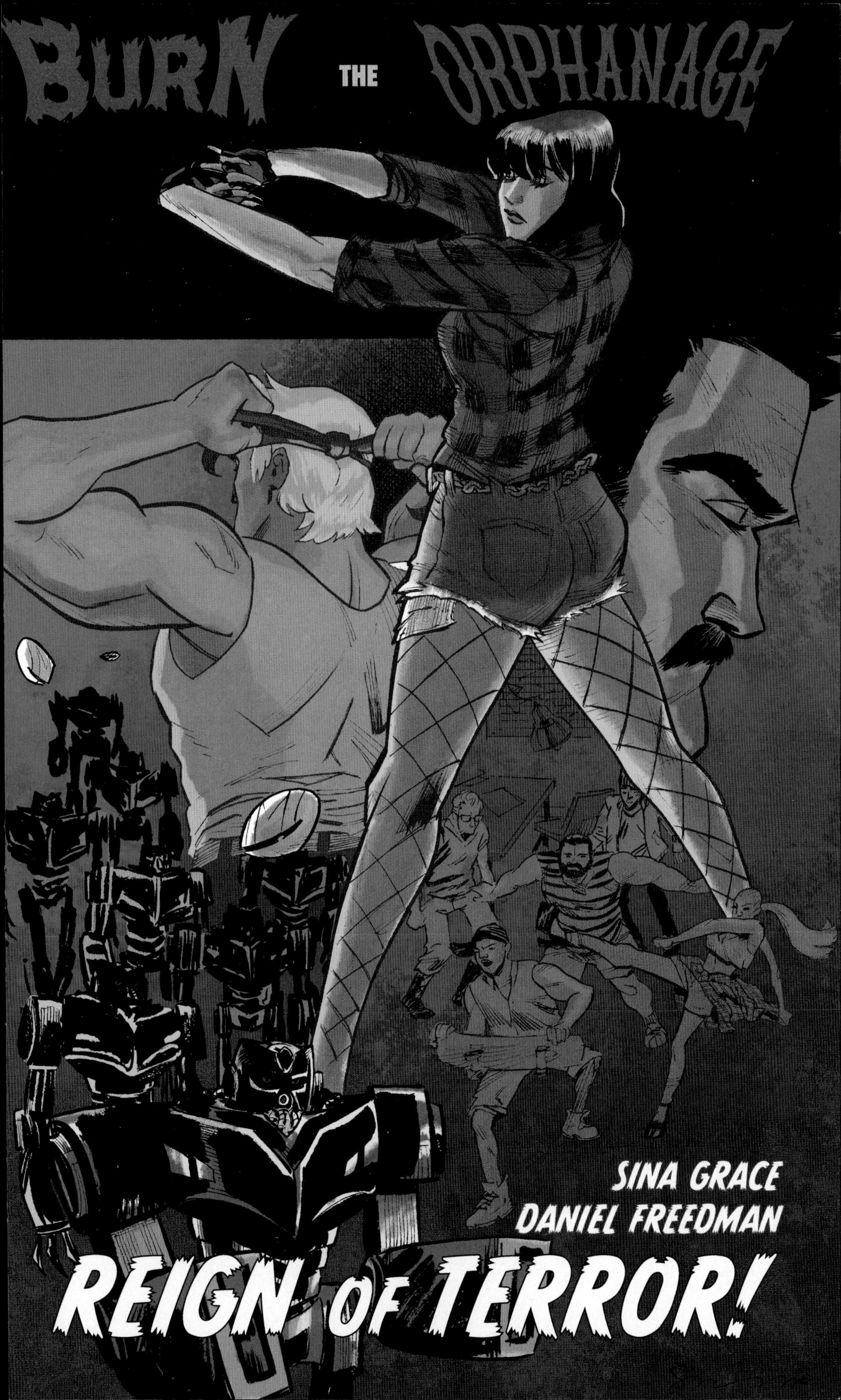
BURN THE ORPHANAGE
SINA GRACE
DANIEL FREEDMAN
REIGN OF TERROR!

CHAPTER TWO

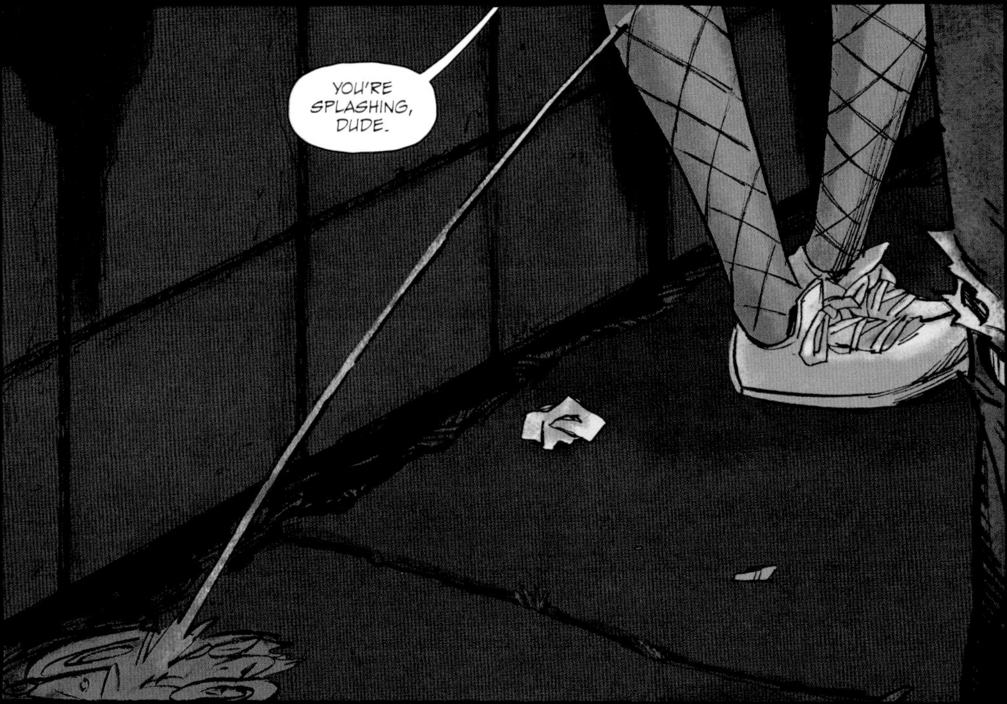
YOU'RE SPLASHING, DUDE.

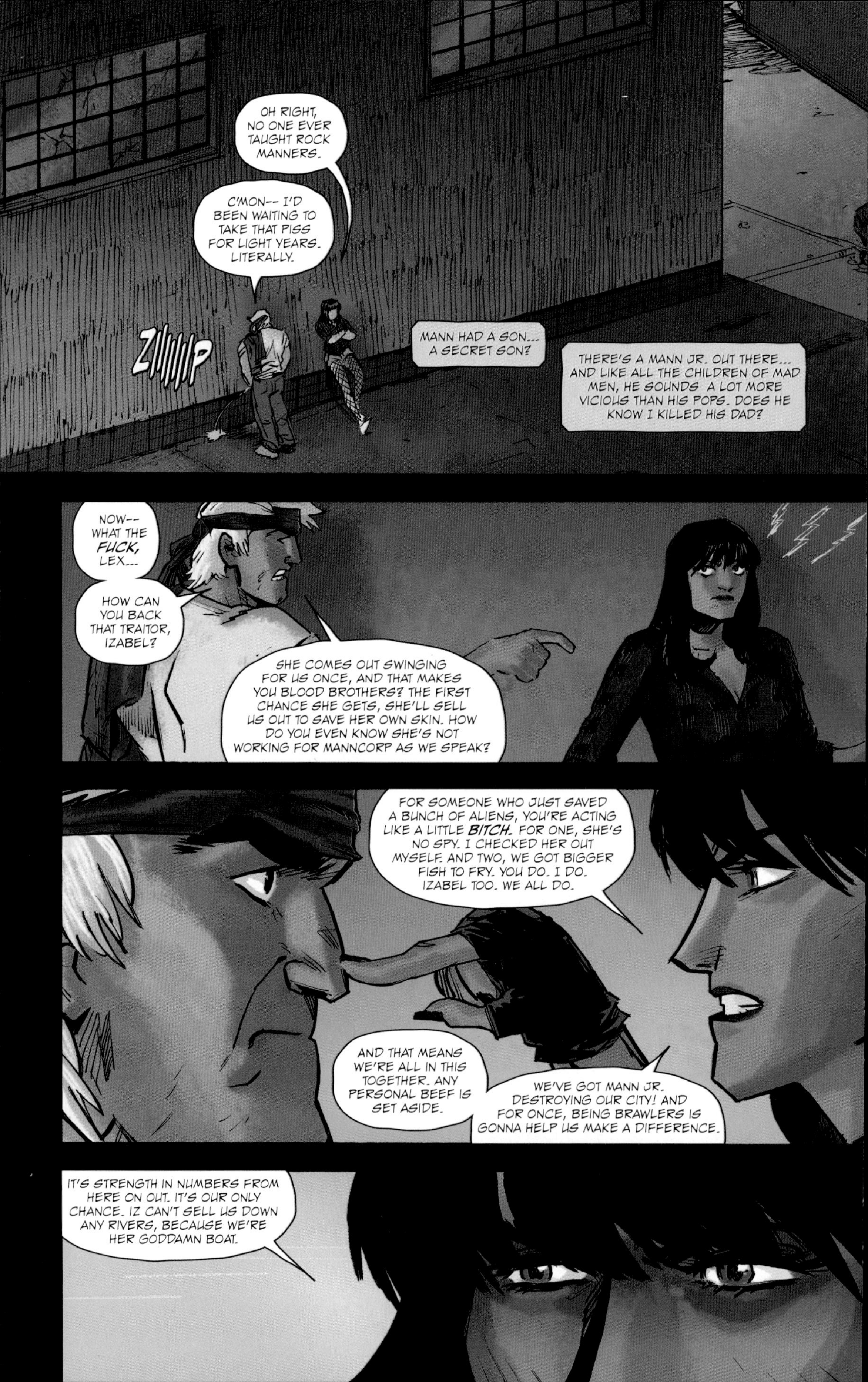
OH RIGHT, NO ONE EVER TAUGHT ROCK MANNERS.
C'MON-- I'D BEEN WAITING TO TAKE THAT PISS FOR LIGHT YEARS. LITERALLY.
ZIIIIP
MANN HAD A SON... A SECRET SON?
THERE'S A MANN JR. OUT THERE... AND LIKE ALL THE CHILDREN OF MAD MEN, HE SOUNDS A LOT MORE VICIOUS THAN HIS POPS. DOES HE KNOW I KILLED HIS DAD?
NOW-- WHAT THE *FUCK,* LEX...
HOW CAN YOU BACK THAT TRAITOR, IZABEL?
SHE COMES OUT SWINGING FOR US ONCE, AND THAT MAKES YOU BLOOD BROTHERS? THE FIRST CHANCE SHE GETS, SHE'LL SELL US OUT TO SAVE HER OWN SKIN. HOW DO YOU EVEN KNOW SHE'S NOT WORKING FOR MANNCORP AS WE SPEAK?
FOR SOMEONE WHO JUST SAVED A BUNCH OF ALIENS, YOU'RE ACTING LIKE A LITTLE *BITCH.* FOR ONE, SHE'S NO SPY. I CHECKED HER OUT MYSELF. AND TWO, WE GOT BIGGER FISH TO FRY. YOU DO. I DO. IZABEL TOO. WE ALL DO.
AND THAT MEANS WE'RE ALL IN THIS TOGETHER. ANY PERSONAL BEEF IS SET ASIDE.
WE'VE GOT MANN JR. DESTROYING OUR CITY! AND FOR ONCE, BEING BRAWLERS IS GONNA HELP US MAKE A DIFFERENCE.
IT'S STRENGTH IN NUMBERS FROM HERE ON OUT. IT'S OUR ONLY CHANCE. IZ CAN'T SELL US DOWN ANY RIVERS, BECAUSE WE'RE HER GODDAMN BOAT.

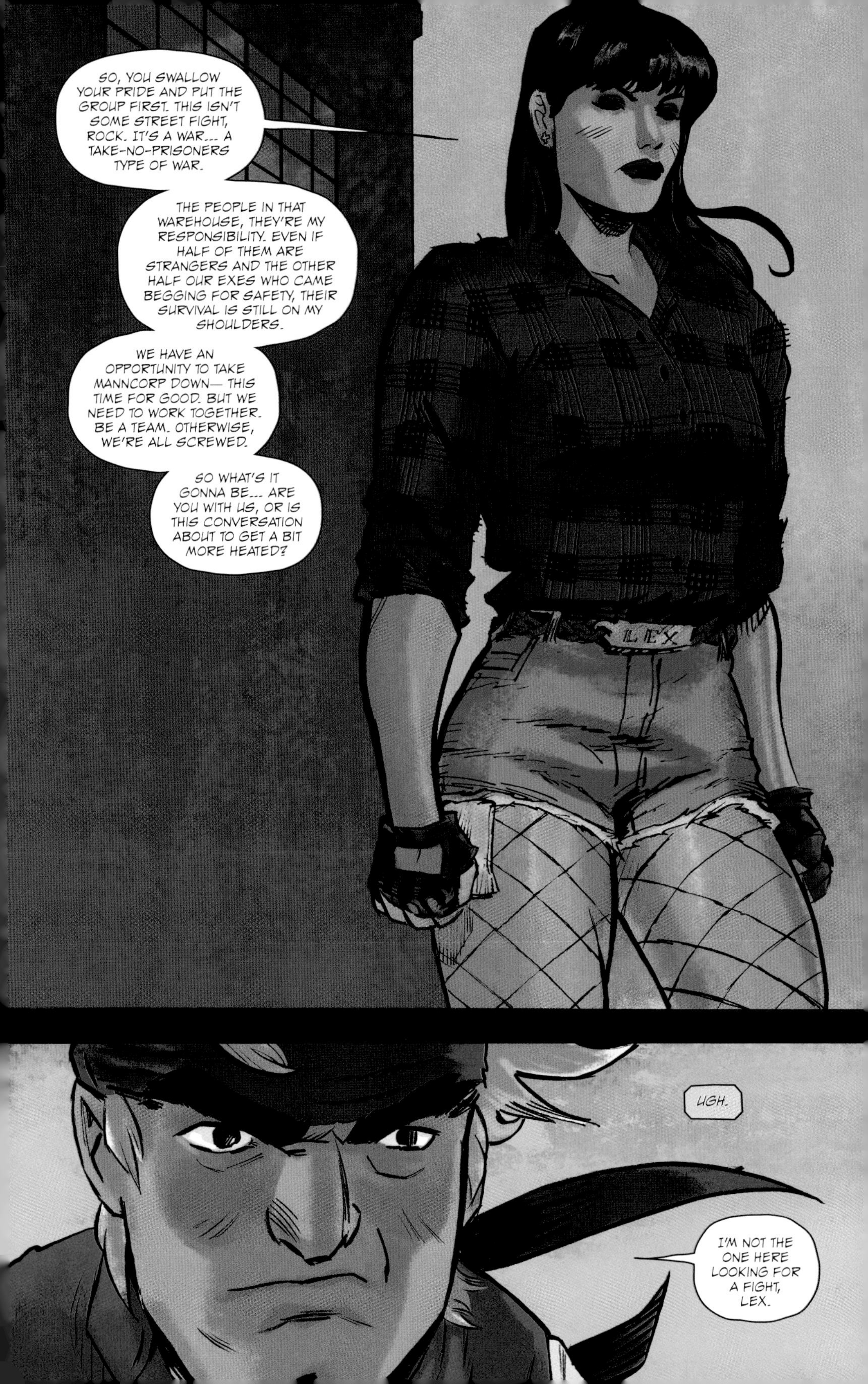
SO, YOU SWALLOW YOUR PRIDE AND PUT THE GROUP FIRST. THIS ISN'T SOME STREET FIGHT, ROCK. IT'S A WAR... A TAKE-NO-PRISONERS TYPE OF WAR.
THE PEOPLE IN THAT WAREHOUSE, THEY'RE MY RESPONSIBILITY. EVEN IF HALF OF THEM ARE STRANGERS AND THE OTHER HALF OUR EXES WHO CAME BEGGING FOR SAFETY, THEIR SURVIVAL IS STILL ON MY SHOULDERS.
WE HAVE AN OPPORTUNITY TO TAKE MANNCORP DOWN— THIS TIME FOR GOOD. BUT WE NEED TO WORK TOGETHER. BE A TEAM. OTHERWISE, WE'RE ALL SCREWED.
SO WHAT'S IT GONNA BE... ARE YOU WITH US, OR IS THIS CONVERSATION ABOUT TO GET A BIT MORE HEATED?
LEX
UGH.
I'M NOT THE ONE HERE LOOKING FOR A FIGHT, LEX.

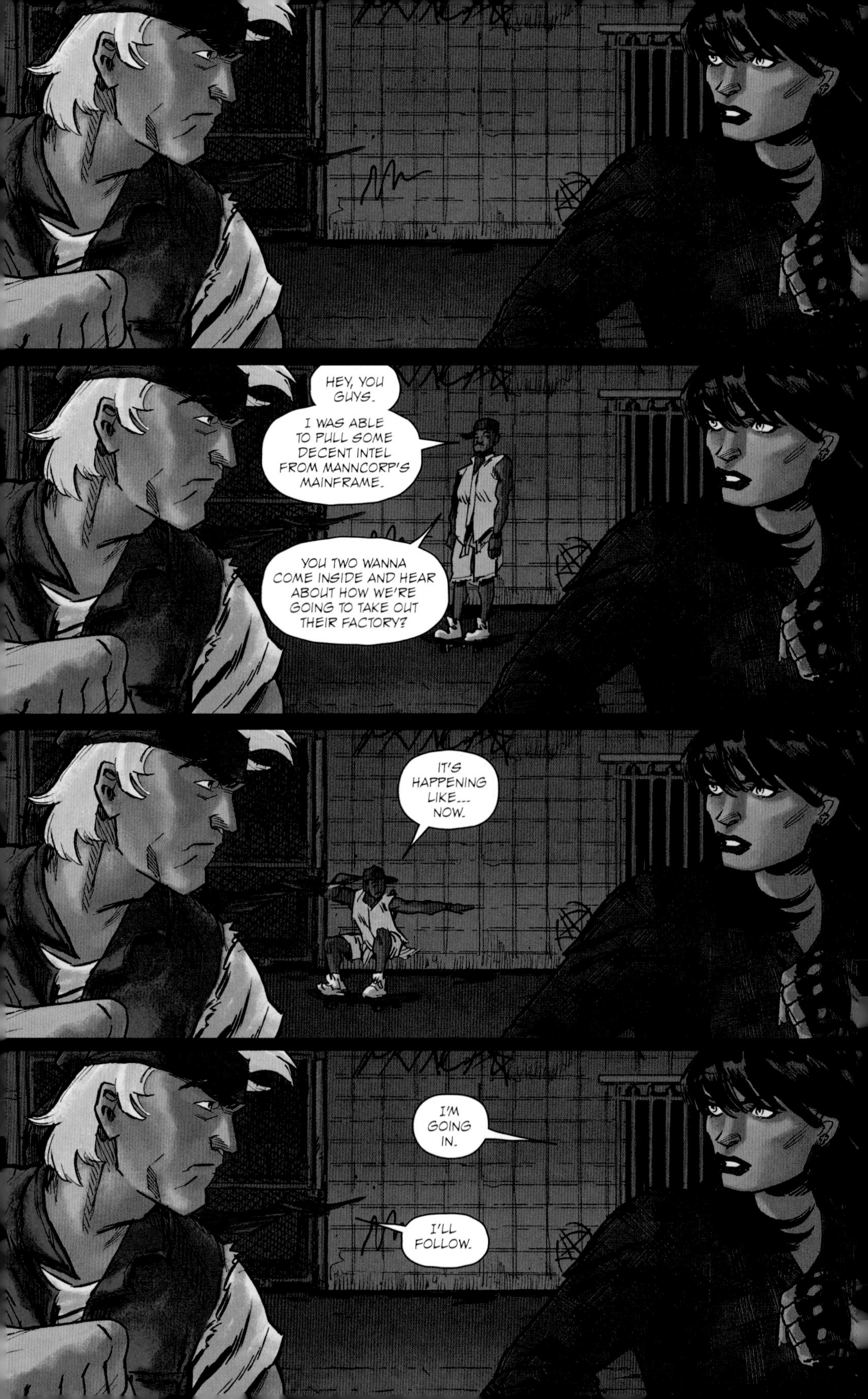
HEY, YOU GUYS.
I WAS ABLE TO PULL SOME DECENT INTEL FROM MANNCORP'S MAINFRAME.
YOU TWO WANNA COME INSIDE AND HEAR ABOUT HOW WE'RE GOING TO TAKE OUT THEIR FACTORY?
IT'S HAPPENING LIKE... NOW.
I'M GOING IN.
I'LL FOLLOW.

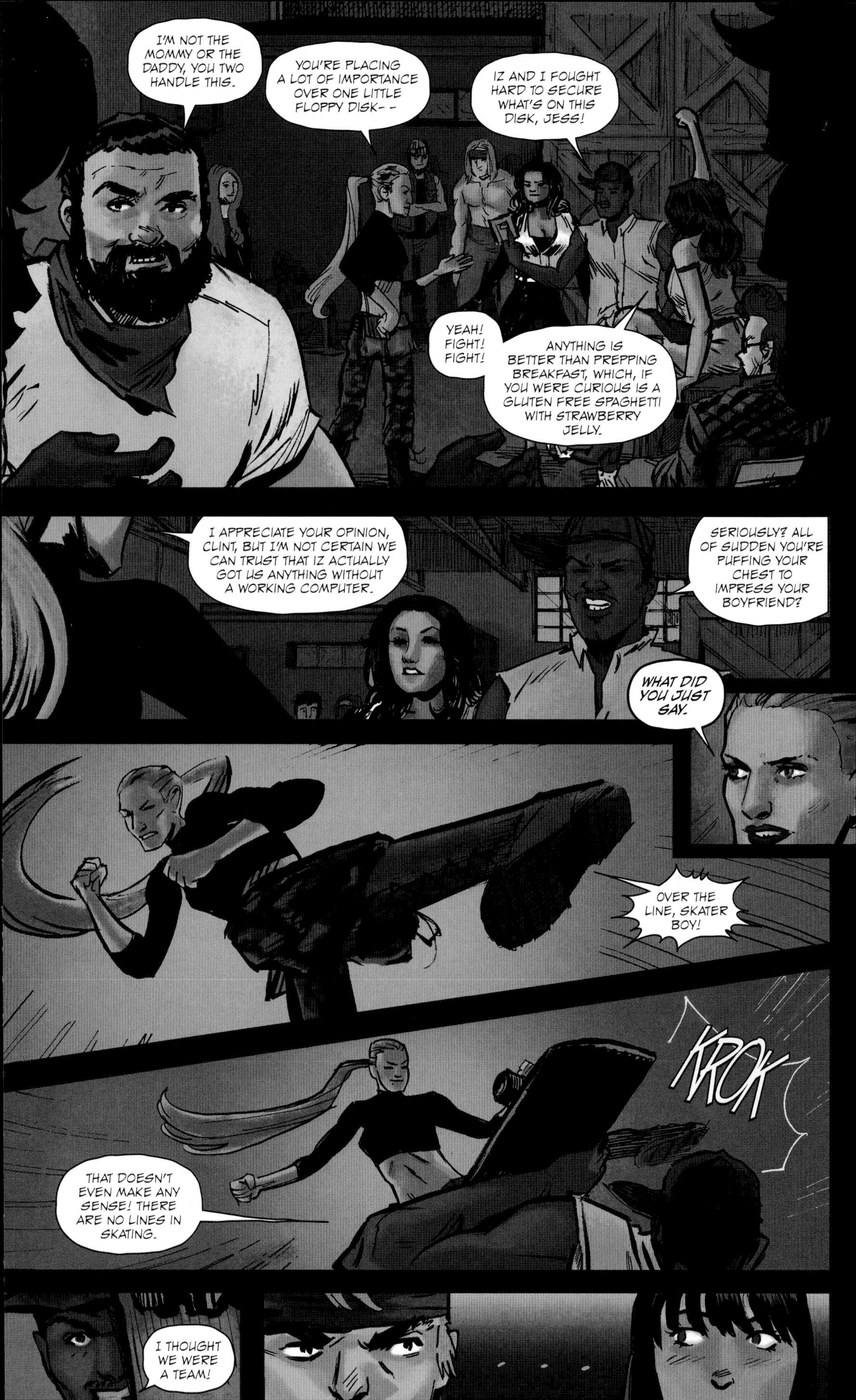
I'M NOT THE MOMMY OR THE DADDY, YOU TWO HANDLE THIS.
YOU'RE PLACING A LOT OF IMPORTANCE OVER ONE LITTLE FLOPPY DISK- -
IZ AND I FOUGHT HARD TO SECURE WHAT'S ON THIS DISK, JESS!
YEAH! FIGHT! FIGHT!
ANYTHING IS BETTER THAN PREPPING BREAKFAST, WHICH, IF YOU WERE CURIOUS IS A GLUTEN FREE SPAGHETTI WITH STRAWBERRY JELLY.
I APPRECIATE YOUR OPINION, CLINT, BUT I'M NOT CERTAIN WE CAN TRUST THAT IZ ACTUALLY GOT US ANYTHING WITHOUT A WORKING COMPUTER.
SERIOUSLY? ALL OF SUDDEN YOU'RE PUFFING YOUR CHEST TO IMPRESS YOUR BOYFRIEND?
WHAT DID YOU JUST SAY.
OVER THE LINE, SKATER BOY!
KROK
THAT DOESN'T EVEN MAKE ANY SENSE! THERE ARE NO LINES IN SKATING.
I THOUGHT WE WERE A TEAM!

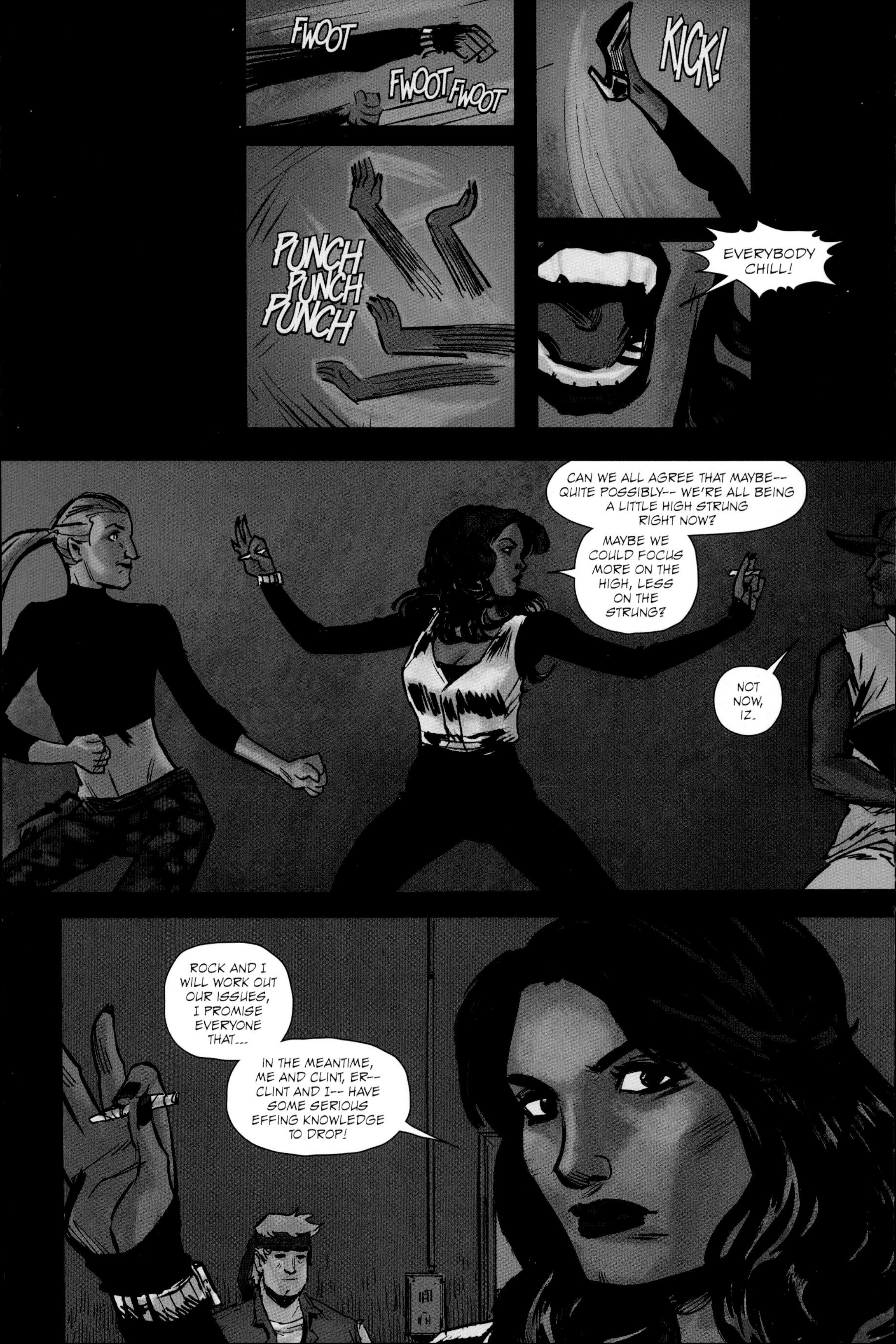
FWOOT
FWOOT FWOOT
KICK!
PUNCH PUNCH PUNCH
EVERYBODY CHILL!
CAN WE ALL AGREE THAT MAYBE-- QUITE POSSIBLY-- WE'RE ALL BEING A LITTLE HIGH STRUNG RIGHT NOW?
MAYBE WE COULD FOCUS MORE ON THE HIGH, LESS ON THE STRUNG?
NOT NOW, IZ.
ROCK AND I WILL WORK OUT OUR ISSUES, I PROMISE EVERYONE THAT...
IN THE MEANTIME, ME AND CLINT, ER-- CLINT AND I-- HAVE SOME SERIOUS EFFING KNOWLEDGE TO DROP!

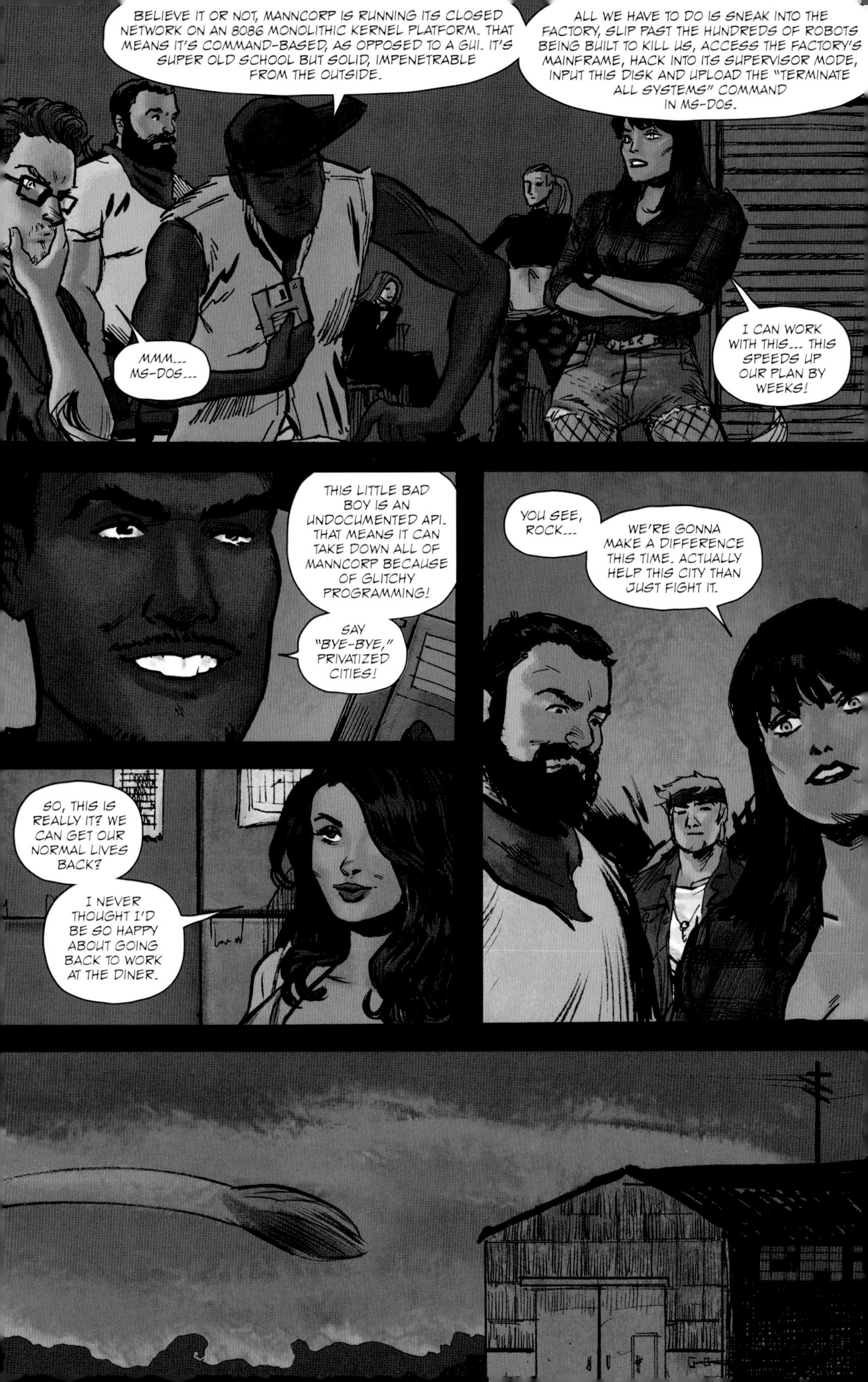
BELIEVE IT OR NOT, MANNCORP IS RUNNING ITS CLOSED NETWORK ON AN 8086 MONOLITHIC KERNEL PLATFORM. THAT MEANS IT'S COMMAND-BASED, AS OPPOSED TO A GUI. IT'S SUPER OLD SCHOOL BUT SOLID, IMPENETRABLE FROM THE OUTSIDE.
MMM... MS-DOS...
ALL WE HAVE TO DO IS SNEAK INTO THE FACTORY, SLIP PAST THE HUNDREDS OF ROBOTS BEING BUILT TO KILL US, ACCESS THE FACTORY'S MAINFRAME, HACK INTO ITS SUPERVISOR MODE, INPUT THIS DISK AND UPLOAD THE "TERMINATE ALL SYSTEMS" COMMAND IN MS-DOS.
I CAN WORK WITH THIS... THIS SPEEDS UP OUR PLAN BY WEEKS!
THIS LITTLE BAD BOY IS AN UNDOCUMENTED API. THAT MEANS IT CAN TAKE DOWN ALL OF MANNCORP BECAUSE OF GLITCHY PROGRAMMING!
SAY "BYE-BYE," PRIVATIZED CITIES!
YOU SEE, ROCK...
WE'RE GONNA MAKE A DIFFERENCE THIS TIME. ACTUALLY HELP THIS CITY THAN JUST FIGHT IT.
SO, THIS IS REALLY IT? WE CAN GET OUR NORMAL LIVES BACK?
I NEVER THOUGHT I'D BE SO HAPPY ABOUT GOING BACK TO WORK AT THE DINER.

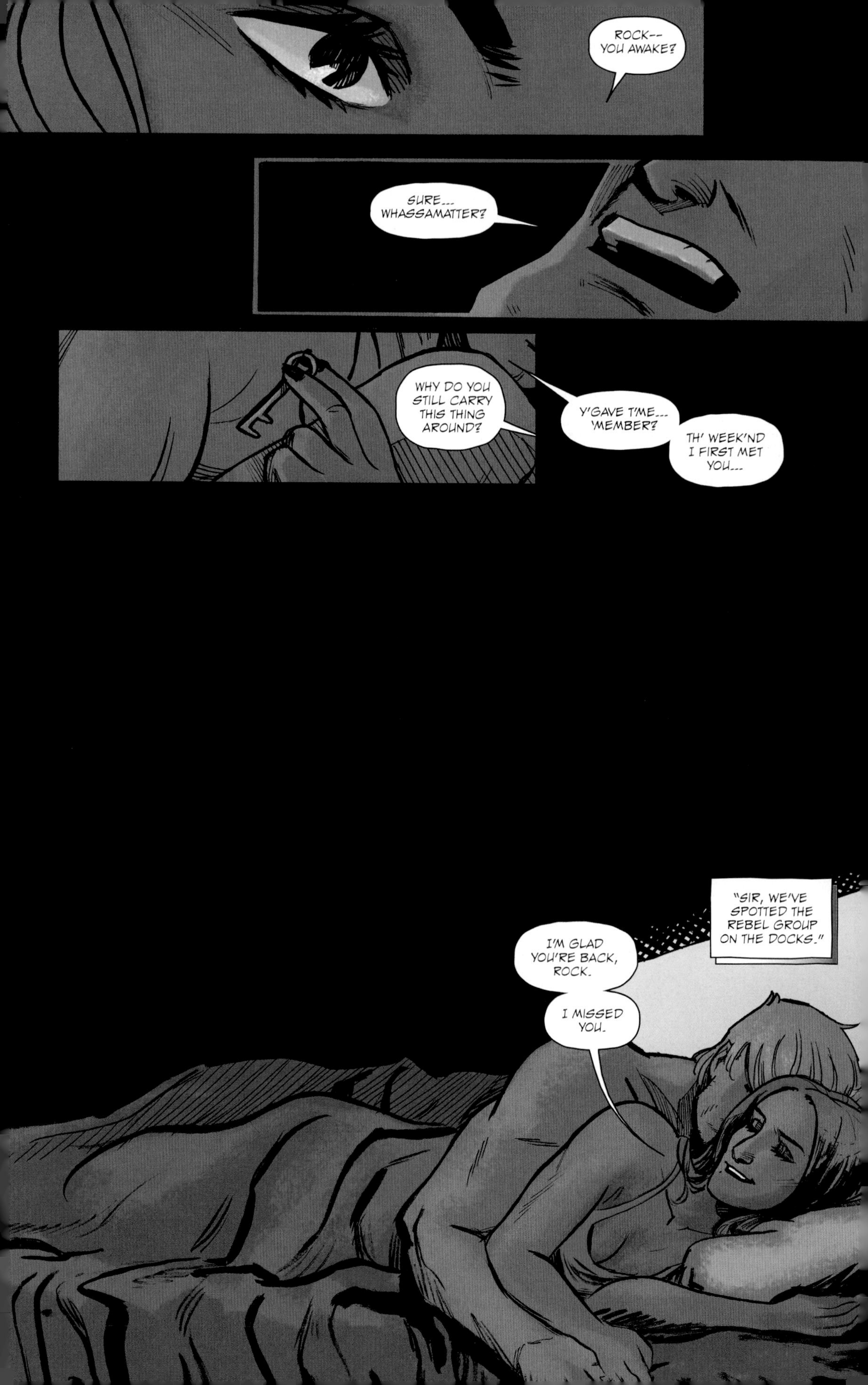
ROCK--
YOU AWAKE?
SURE...
WHASSAMATTER?
WHY DO YOU STILL CARRY THIS THING AROUND?
Y'GAVE T'ME... 'MEMBER?
TH' WEEK'ND I FIRST MET YOU...
"SIR, WE'VE SPOTTED THE REBEL GROUP ON THE DOCKS."
I'M GLAD YOU'RE BACK, ROCK.
I MISSED YOU.

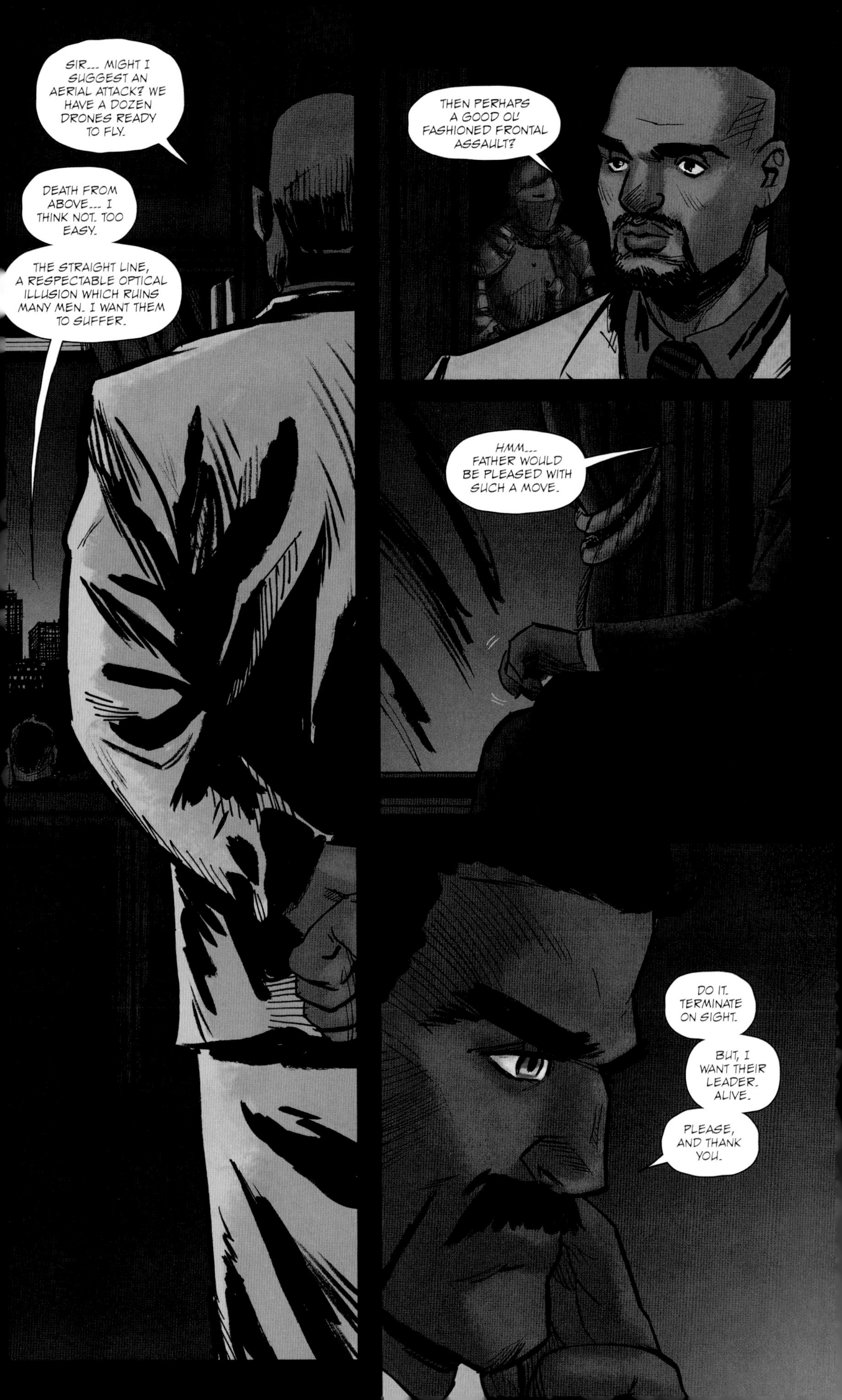
SIR... MIGHT I SUGGEST AN AERIAL ATTACK? WE HAVE A DOZEN DRONES READY TO FLY.
DEATH FROM ABOVE... I THINK NOT. TOO EASY.
THE STRAIGHT LINE, A RESPECTABLE OPTICAL ILLUSION WHICH RUINS MANY MEN. I WANT THEM TO SUFFER.
THEN PERHAPS A GOOD OL' FASHIONED FRONTAL ASSAULT?
HMM... FATHER WOULD BE PLEASED WITH SUCH A MOVE.
DO IT. TERMINATE ON SIGHT.
BUT, I WANT THEIR LEADER. ALIVE.
PLEASE, AND THANK YOU.

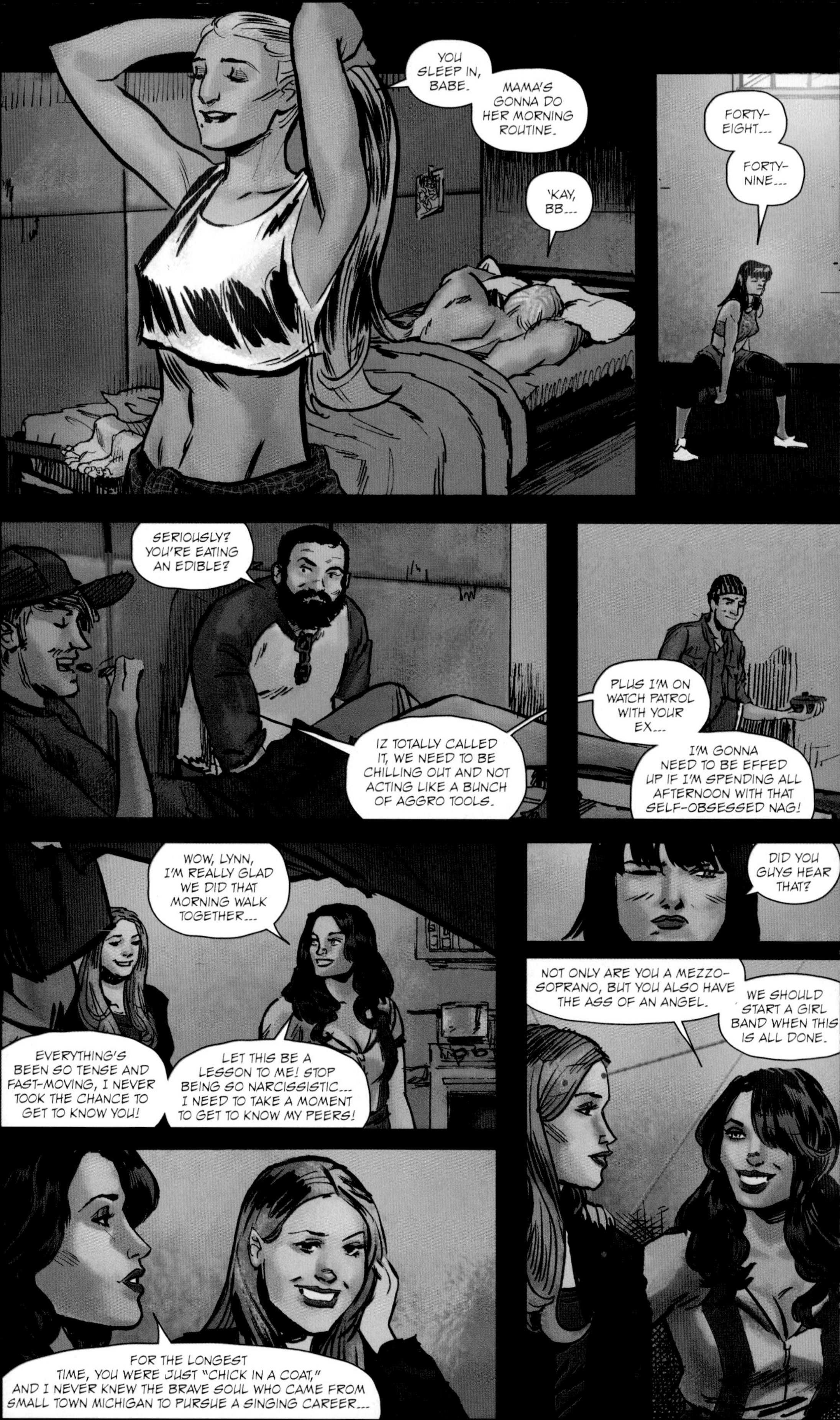
YOU SLEEP IN, BABE.
MAMA'S GONNA DO HER MORNING ROUTINE.
'KAY, BB...
FORTY-EIGHT...
FORTY-NINE...
SERIOUSLY? YOU'RE EATING AN EDIBLE?
IZ TOTALLY CALLED IT, WE NEED TO BE CHILLING OUT AND NOT ACTING LIKE A BUNCH OF AGGRO TOOLS.
PLUS I'M ON WATCH PATROL WITH YOUR EX...
I'M GONNA NEED TO BE EFFED UP IF I'M SPENDING ALL AFTERNOON WITH THAT SELF-OBSESSED NAG!
WOW, LYNN, I'M REALLY GLAD WE DID THAT MORNING WALK TOGETHER...
EVERYTHING'S BEEN SO TENSE AND FAST-MOVING, I NEVER TOOK THE CHANCE TO GET TO KNOW YOU!
LET THIS BE A LESSON TO ME! STOP BEING SO NARCISSISTIC... I NEED TO TAKE A MOMENT TO GET TO KNOW MY PEERS!
DID YOU GUYS HEAR THAT?
FOR THE LONGEST TIME, YOU WERE JUST "CHICK IN A COAT," AND I NEVER KNEW THE BRAVE SOUL WHO CAME FROM SMALL TOWN MICHIGAN TO PURSUE A SINGING CAREER...
NOT ONLY ARE YOU A MEZZO-SOPRANO, BUT YOU ALSO HAVE THE ASS OF AN ANGEL.
WE SHOULD START A GIRL BAND WHEN THIS IS ALL DONE.

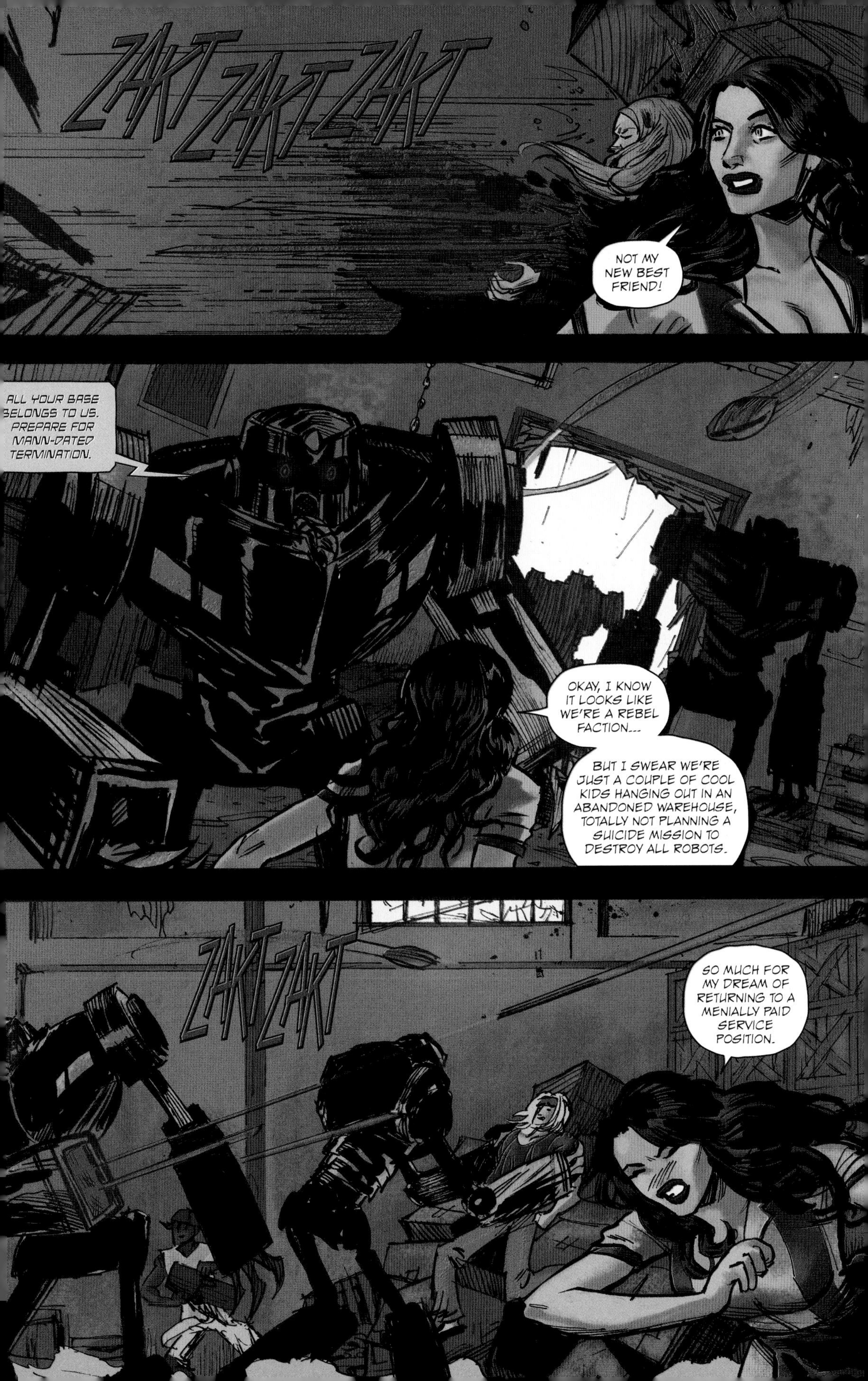
ZAKT ZAKT ZAKT
NOT MY NEW BEST FRIEND!
ALL YOUR BASE BELONGS TO US. PREPARE FOR MANN-DATED TERMINATION.
OKAY, I KNOW IT LOOKS LIKE WE'RE A REBEL FACTION...
BUT I SWEAR WE'RE JUST A COUPLE OF COOL KIDS HANGING OUT IN AN ABANDONED WAREHOUSE, TOTALLY NOT PLANNING A SUICIDE MISSION TO DESTROY ALL ROBOTS.
ZAKT ZAKT
SO MUCH FOR MY DREAM OF RETURNING TO A MENIALLY PAID SERVICE POSITION.

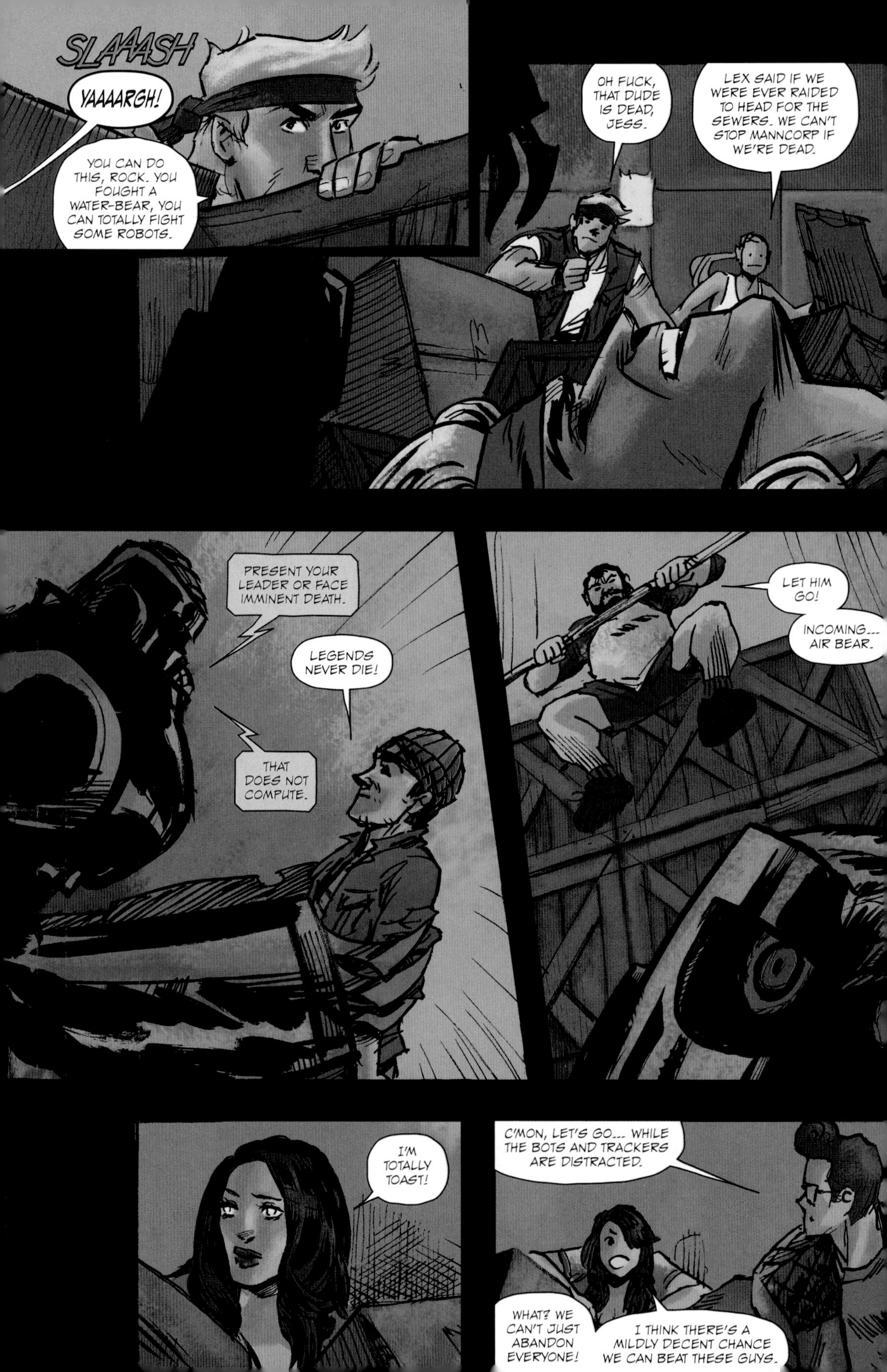
SLAAASH
YAAAARGH!
YOU CAN DO THIS, ROCK. YOU FOUGHT A WATER-BEAR, YOU CAN TOTALLY FIGHT SOME ROBOTS.
OH FUCK, THAT DUDE IS DEAD, JESS.
LEX SAID IF WE WERE EVER RAIDED TO HEAD FOR THE SEWERS. WE CAN'T STOP MANNCORP IF WE'RE DEAD.
PRESENT YOUR LEADER OR FACE IMMINENT DEATH.
LEGENDS NEVER DIE!
THAT DOES NOT COMPUTE.
LET HIM GO!
INCOMING... AIR BEAR.
I'M TOTALLY TOAST!
C'MON, LET'S GO... WHILE THE BOTS AND TRACKERS ARE DISTRACTED.
WHAT? WE CAN'T JUST ABANDON EVERYONE!
I THINK THERE'S A MILDLY DECENT CHANCE WE CAN BEAT THESE GUYS.

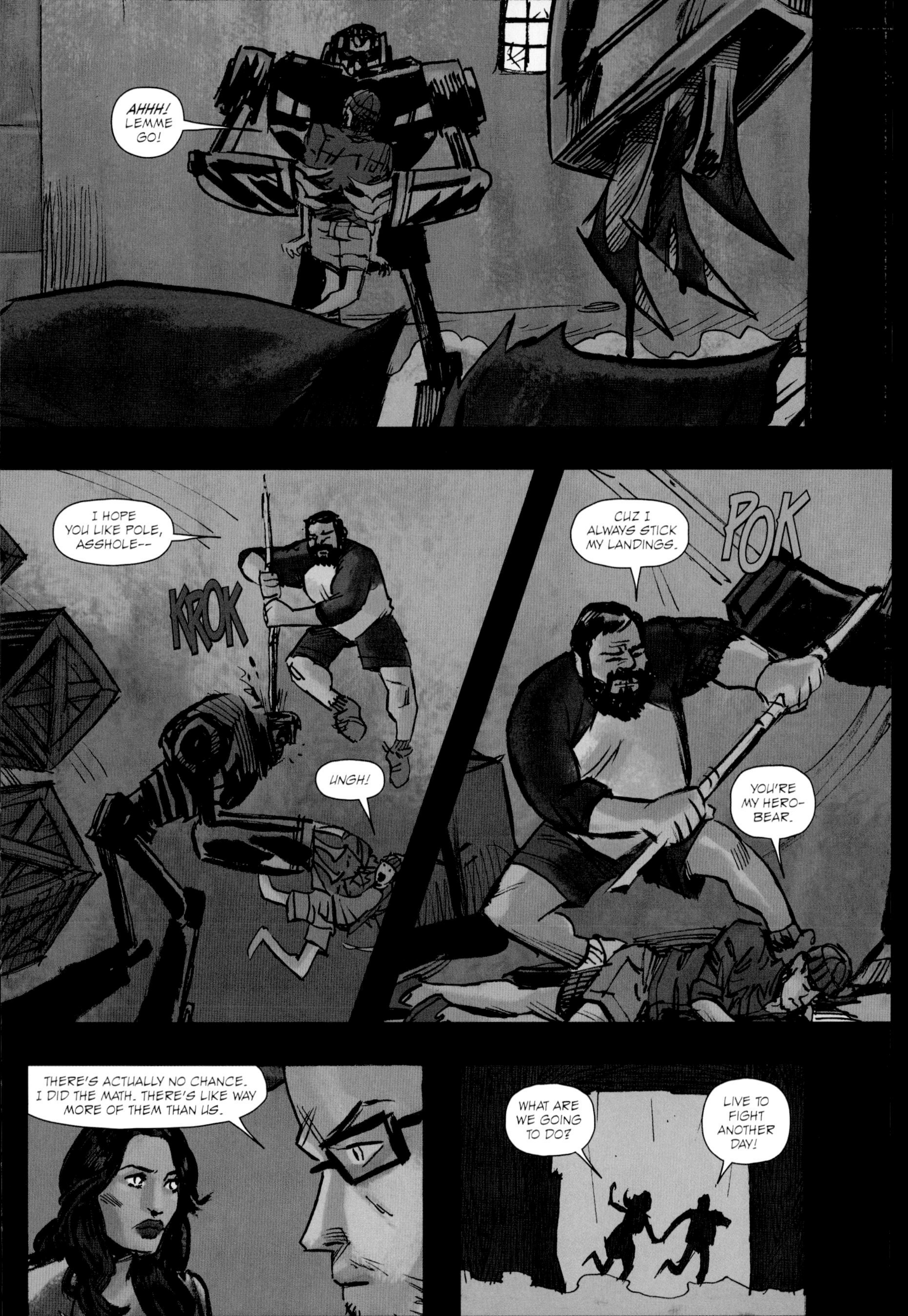
AHHH! LEMME GO!
I HOPE YOU LIKE POLE, ASSHOLE--
KROK
UNGH!
CUZ I ALWAYS STICK MY LANDINGS.
POK
YOU'RE MY HERO-BEAR.
THERE'S ACTUALLY NO CHANCE. I DID THE MATH. THERE'S LIKE WAY MORE OF THEM THAN US.
WHAT ARE WE GOING TO DO?
LIVE TO FIGHT ANOTHER DAY!

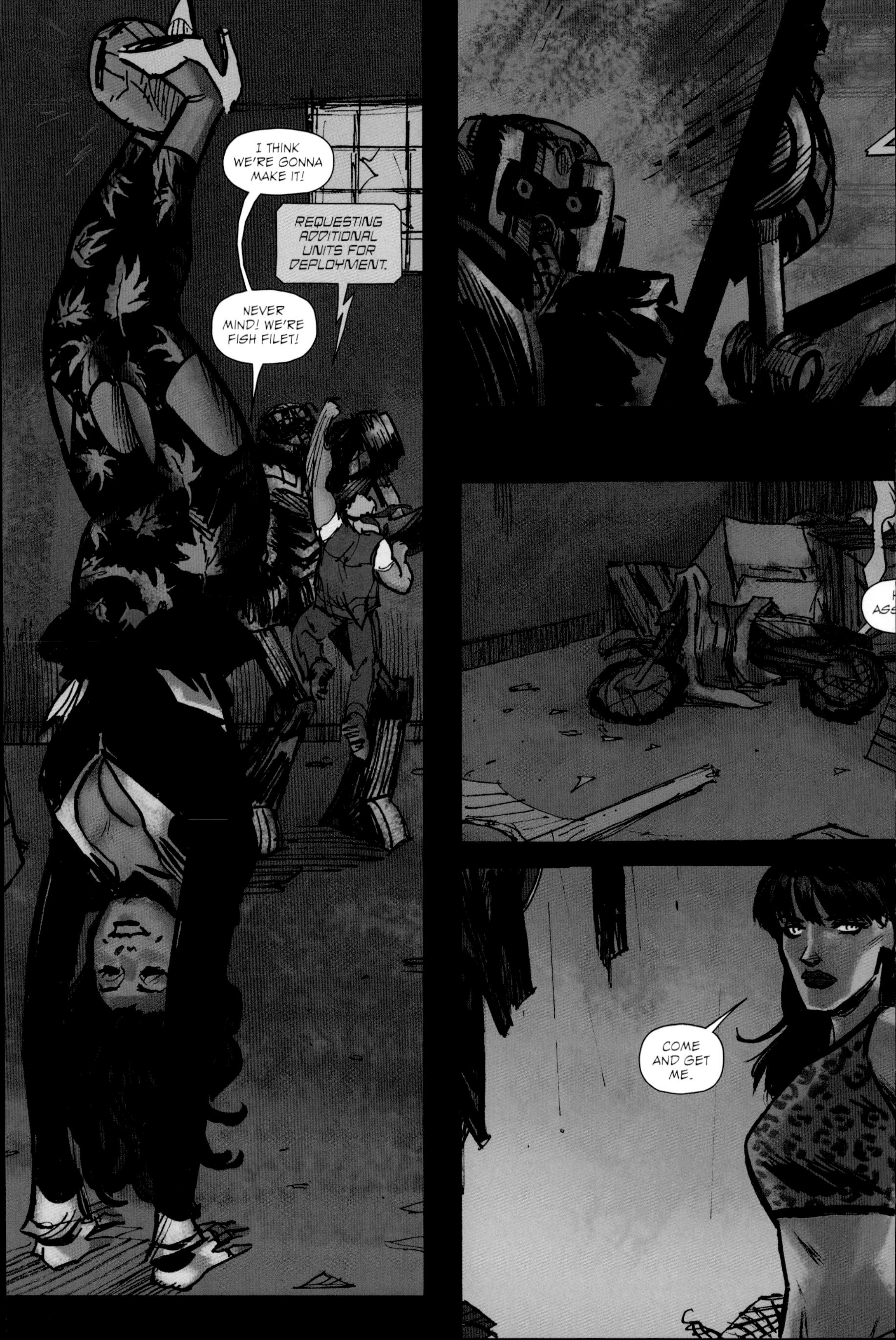
I THINK WE'RE GONNA MAKE IT!
REQUESTING ADDITIONAL UNITS FOR DEPLOYMENT.
NEVER MIND! WE'RE FISH FILET!
COME AND GET ME.

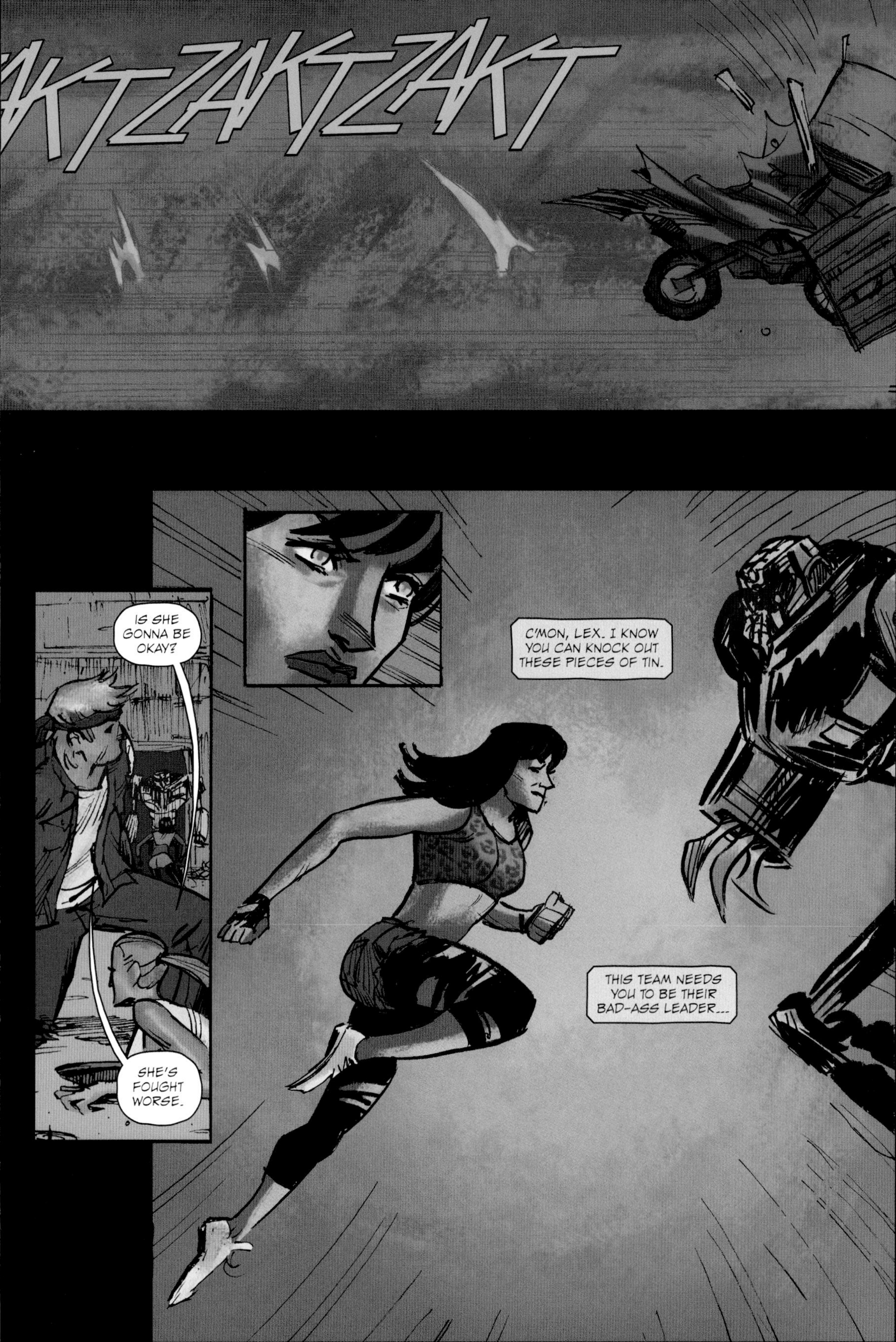

AKTZAKTZAKT
IS SHE GONNA BE OKAY?
SHE'S FOUGHT WORSE.
C'MON, LEX. I KNOW YOU CAN KNOCK OUT THESE PIECES OF TIN.
THIS TEAM NEEDS YOU TO BE THEIR BAD-ASS LEADER...

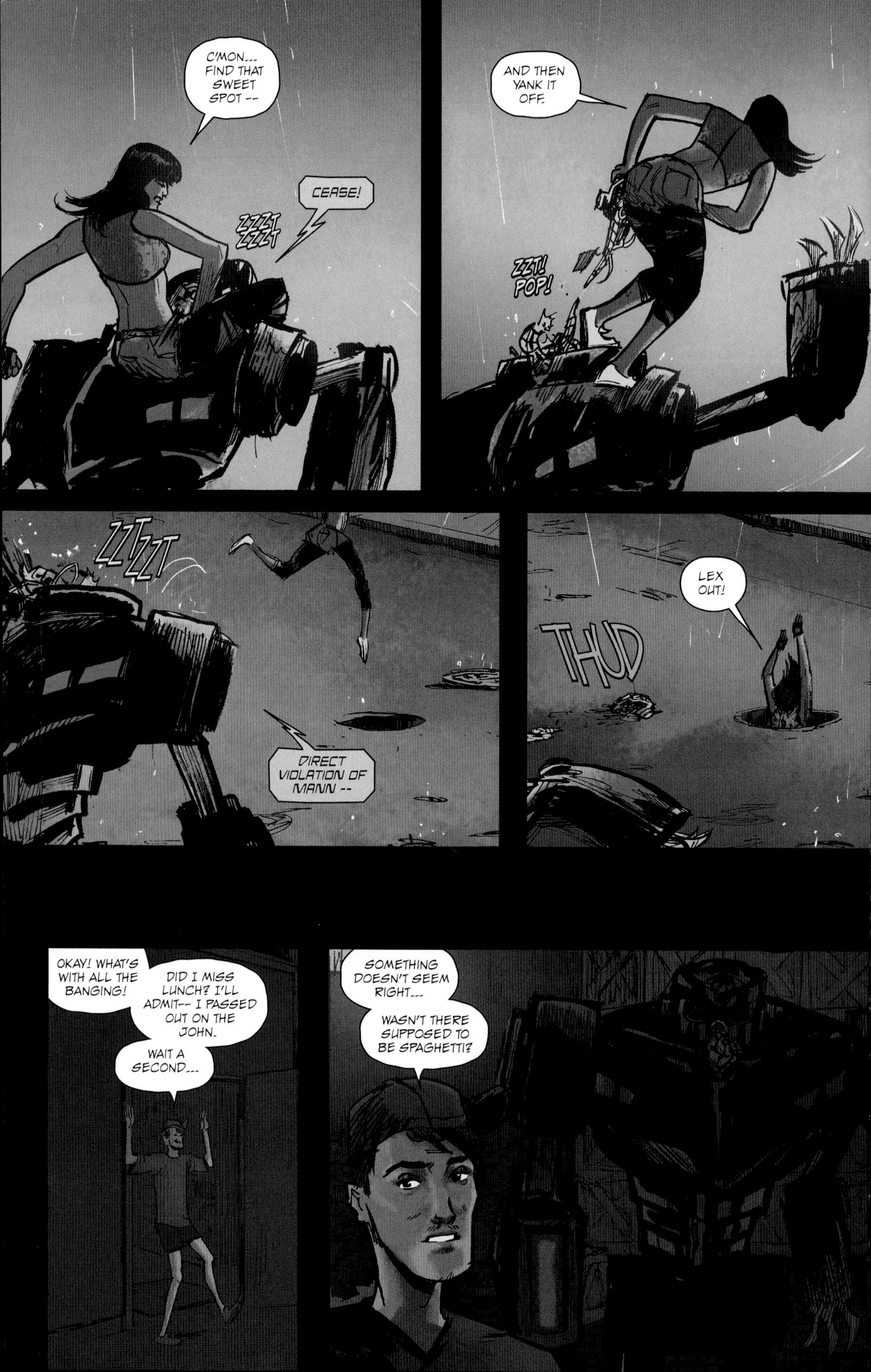

C'MON... FIND THAT SWEET SPOT --
CEASE!
ZZZT ZZZT
AND THEN YANK IT OFF.
ZZT! POP!
ZZT ZZZT
DIRECT VIOLATION OF MANN --
LEX OUT!
THUD
OKAY! WHAT'S WITH ALL THE BANGING!
DID I MISS LUNCH? I'LL ADMIT-- I PASSED OUT ON THE JOHN.
WAIT A SECOND...
SOMETHING DOESN'T SEEM RIGHT...
WASN'T THERE SUPPOSED TO BE SPAGHETTI?

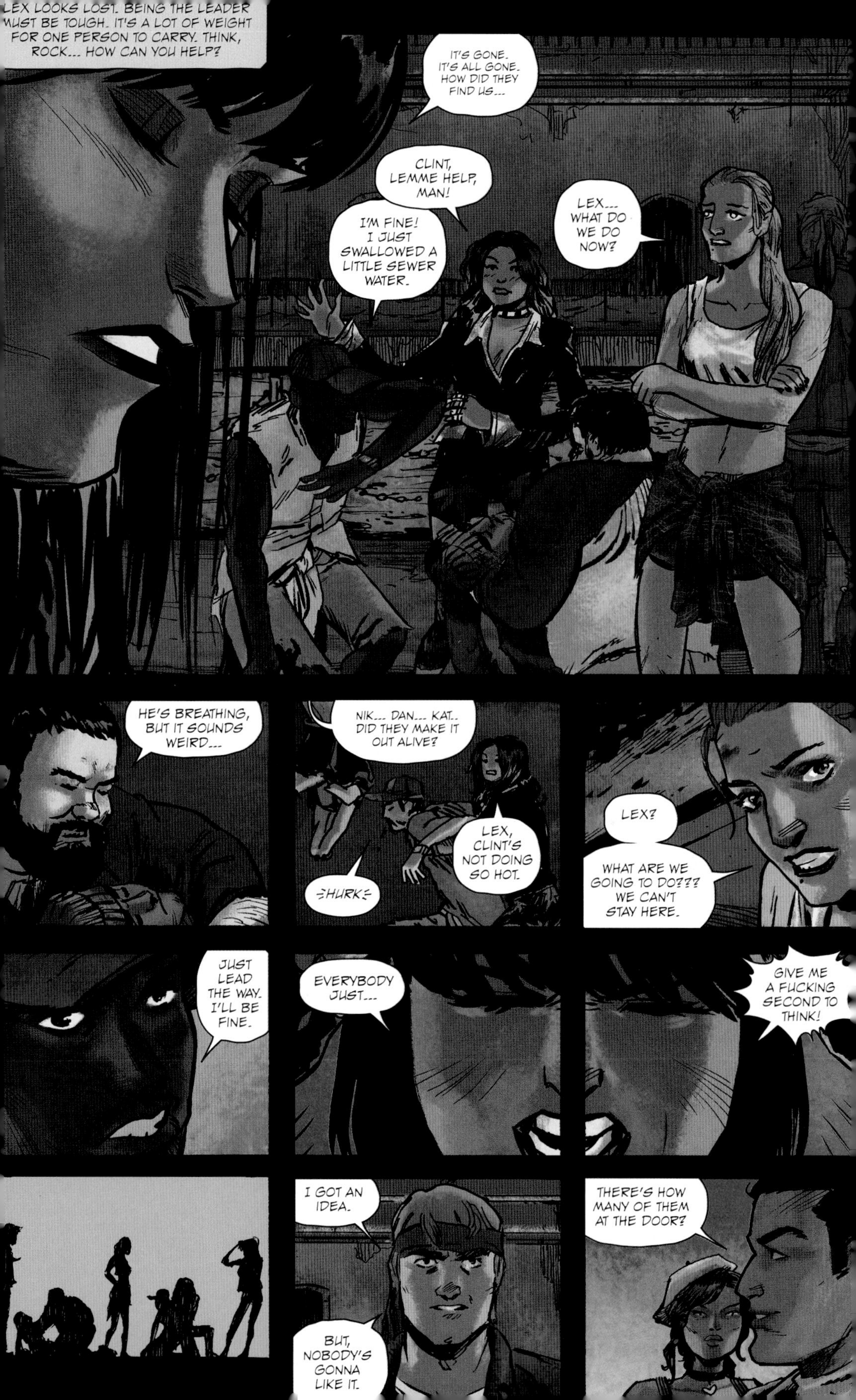
LEX LOOKS LOST. BEING THE LEADER MUST BE TOUGH. IT'S A LOT OF WEIGHT FOR ONE PERSON TO CARRY. THINK, ROCK... HOW CAN YOU HELP?
IT'S GONE. IT'S ALL GONE. HOW DID THEY FIND US...
CLINT, LEMME HELP, MAN!
I'M FINE! I JUST SWALLOWED A LITTLE SEWER WATER.
LEX... WHAT DO WE DO NOW?
HE'S BREATHING, BUT IT SOUNDS WEIRD...
NIK... DAN... KAT.. DID THEY MAKE IT OUT ALIVE?
LEX, CLINT'S NOT DOING SO HOT.
=HURK=
LEX?
WHAT ARE WE GOING TO DO??? WE CAN'T STAY HERE.
JUST LEAD THE WAY. I'LL BE FINE.
EVERYBODY JUST...
GIVE ME A FUCKING SECOND TO THINK!
I GOT AN IDEA.
BUT, NOBODY'S GONNA LIKE IT.
THERE'S HOW MANY OF THEM AT THE DOOR?

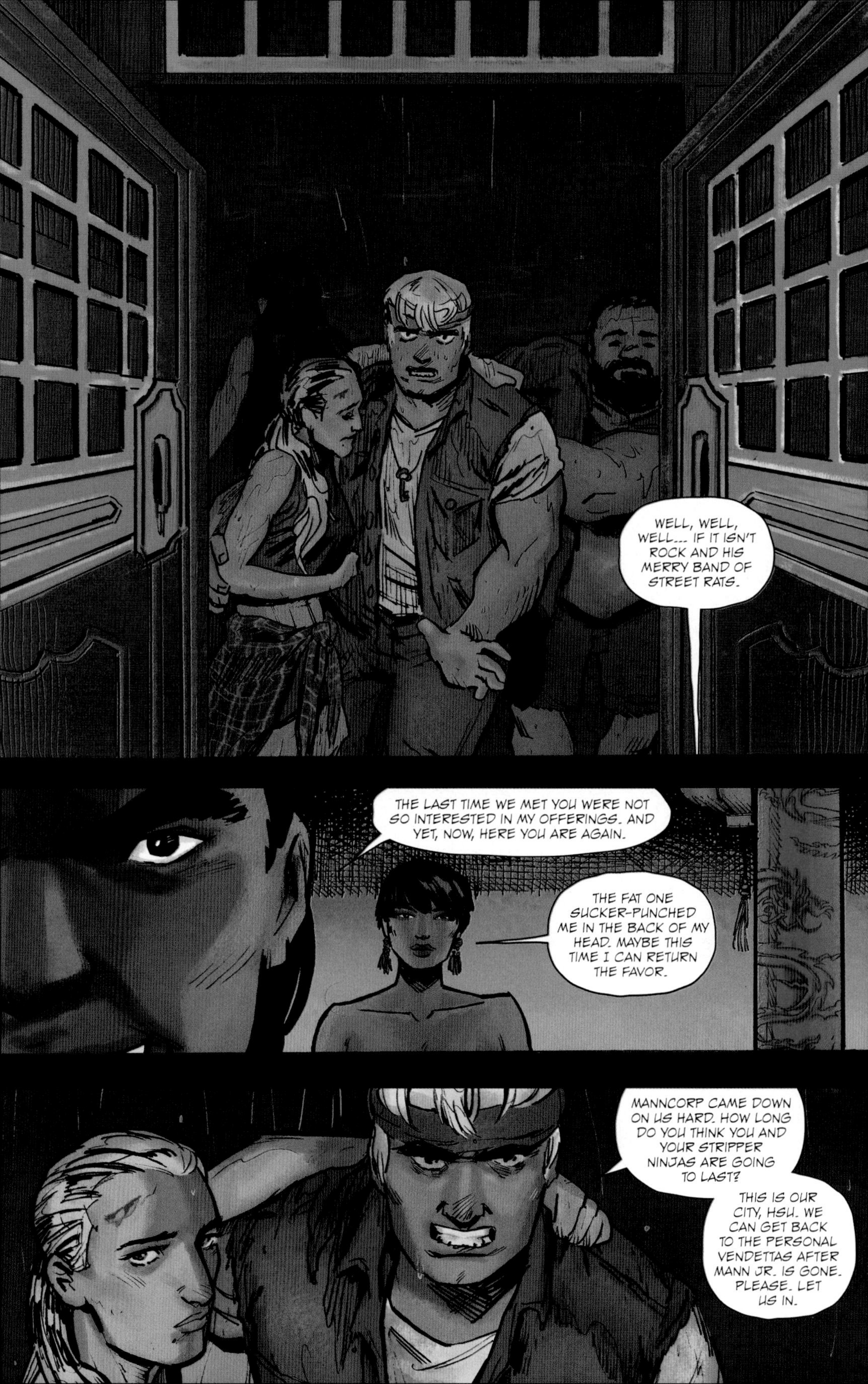
WELL, WELL, WELL... IF IT ISN'T ROCK AND HIS MERRY BAND OF STREET RATS.
THE LAST TIME WE MET YOU WERE NOT SO INTERESTED IN MY OFFERINGS. AND YET, NOW, HERE YOU ARE AGAIN.
THE FAT ONE SUCKER-PUNCHED ME IN THE BACK OF MY HEAD. MAYBE THIS TIME I CAN RETURN THE FAVOR.
MANNCORP CAME DOWN ON US HARD. HOW LONG DO YOU THINK YOU AND YOUR STRIPPER NINJAS ARE GOING TO LAST?
THIS IS OUR CITY, HSU. WE CAN GET BACK TO THE PERSONAL VENDETTAS AFTER MANN JR. IS GONE. PLEASE. LET US IN.

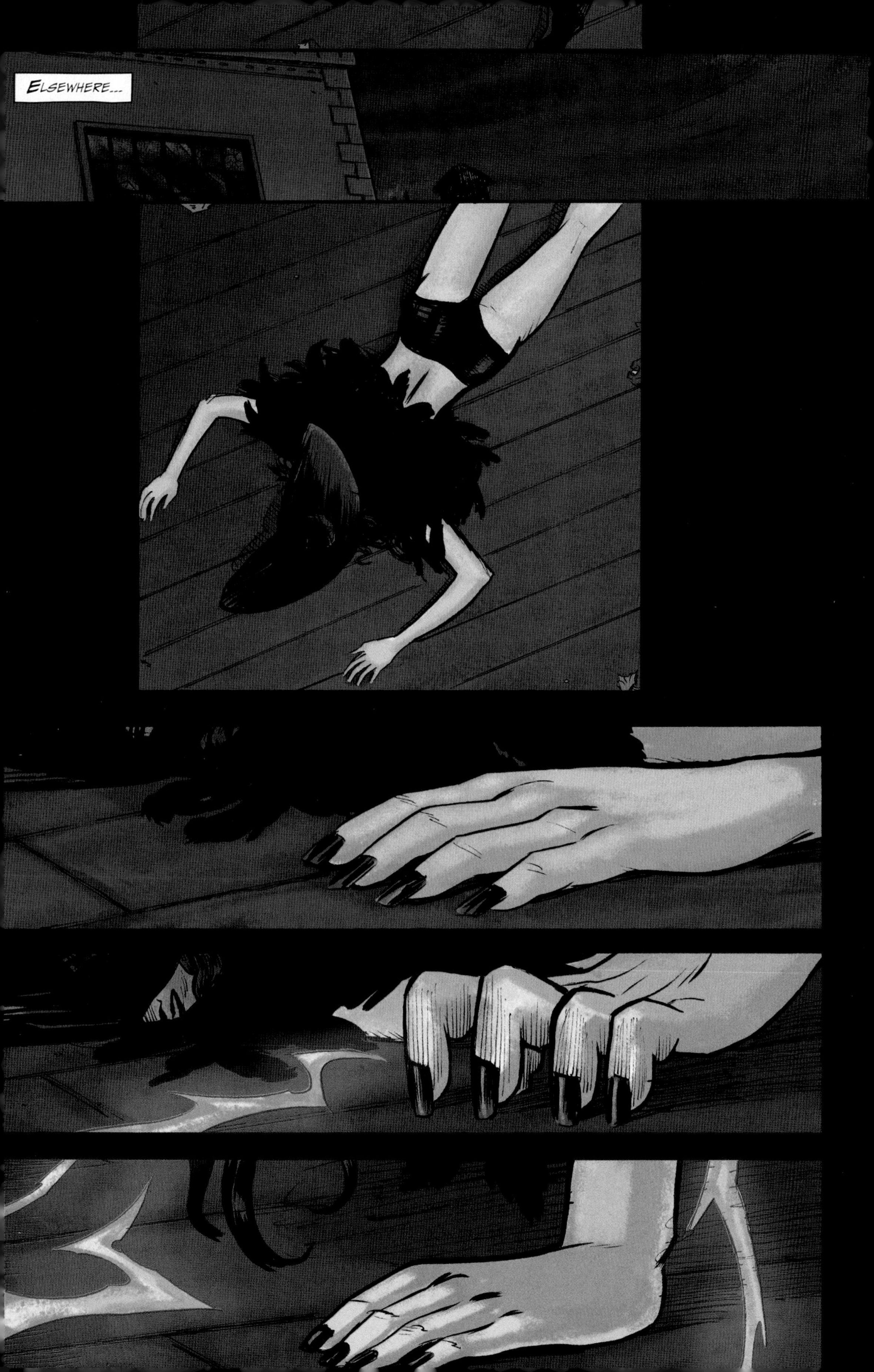
ELSEWHERE...

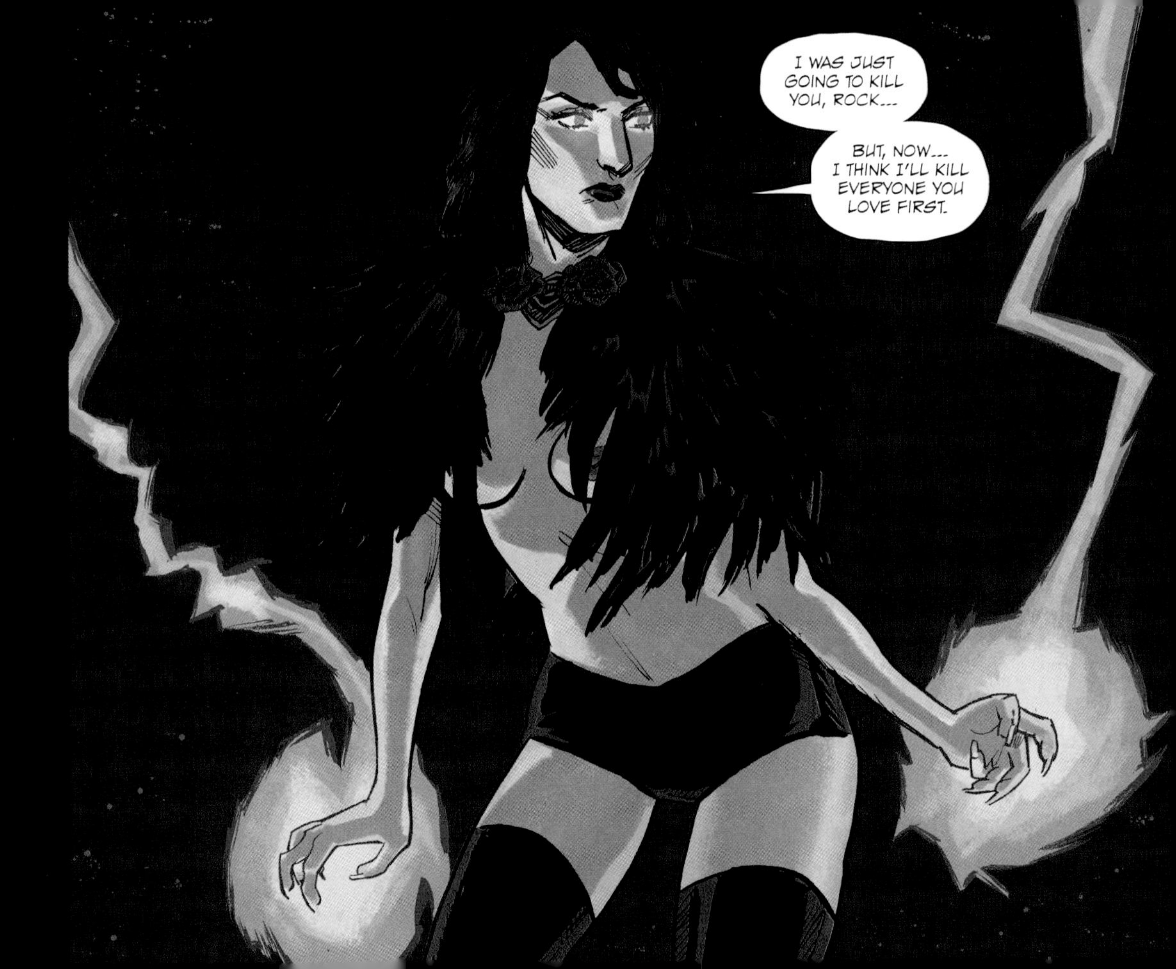
I WAS JUST GOING TO KILL YOU, ROCK...
BUT, NOW... I THINK I'LL KILL EVERYONE YOU LOVE FIRST.

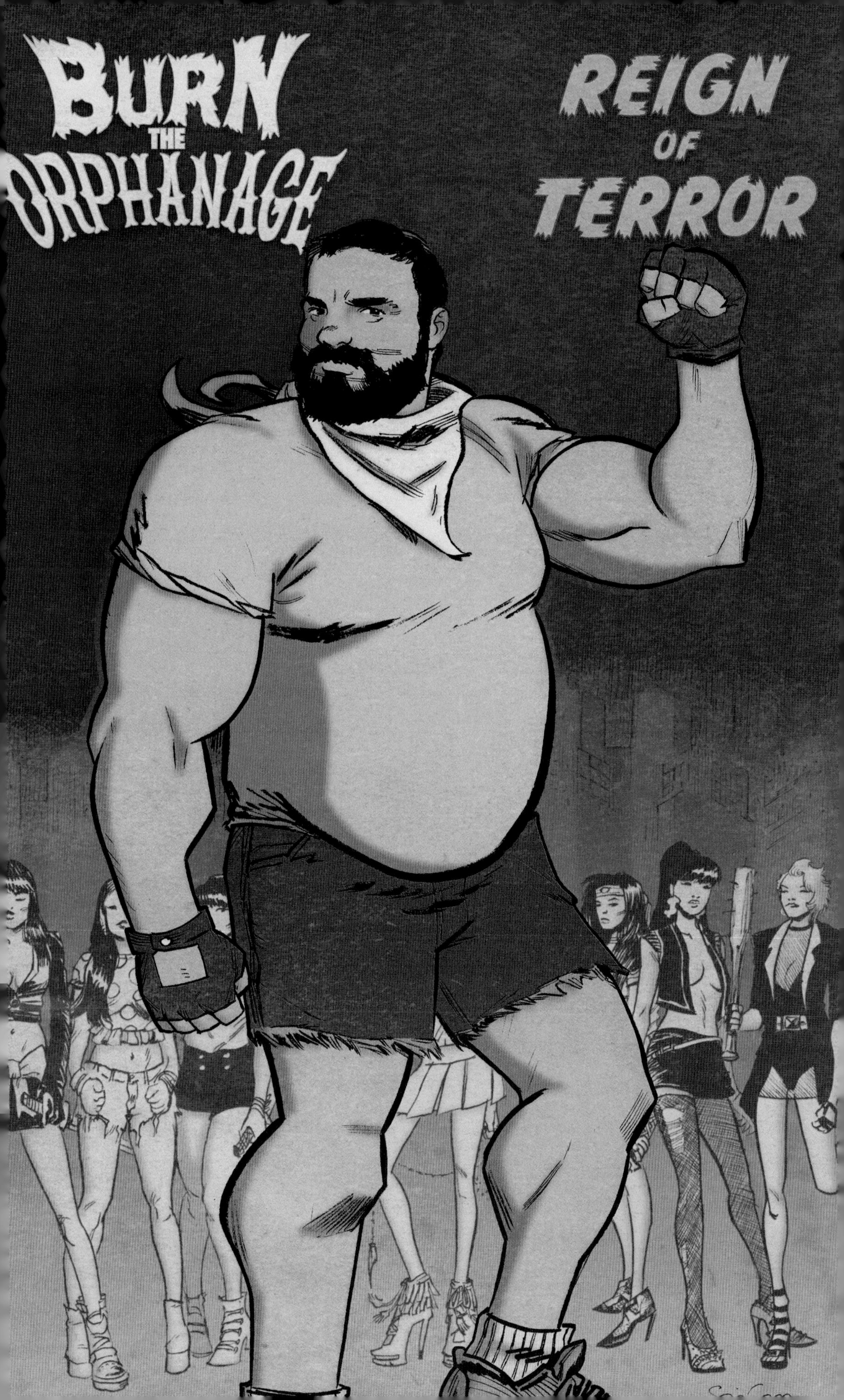
BURN THE ORPHANAGE
REIGN OF TERROR

CHAPTER THREE

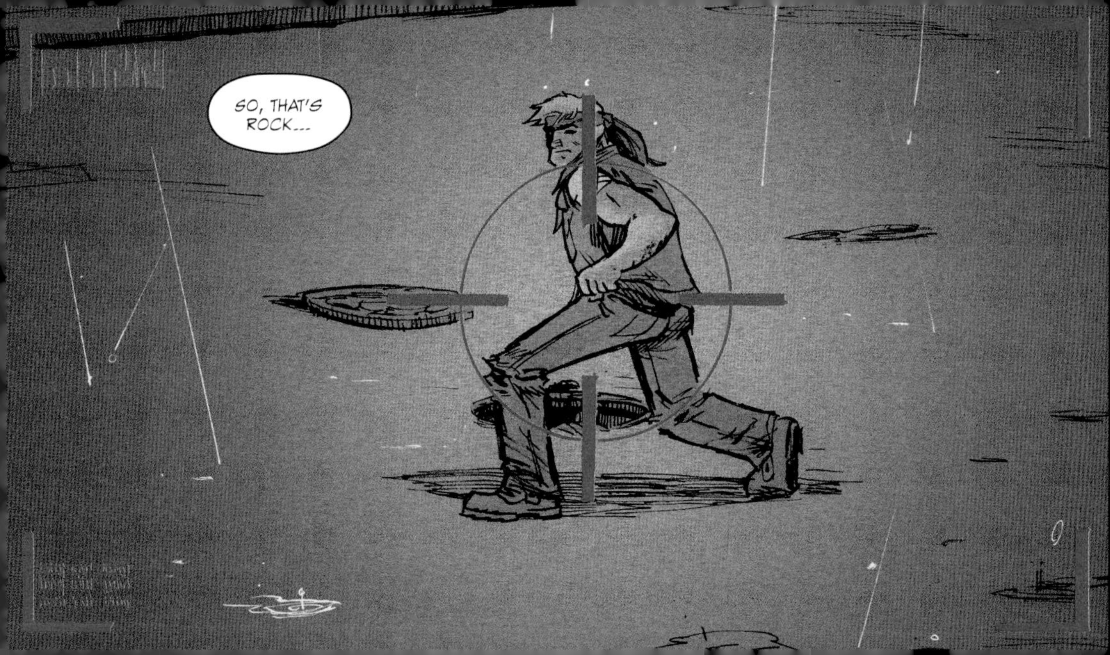
SO, THAT'S ROCK...

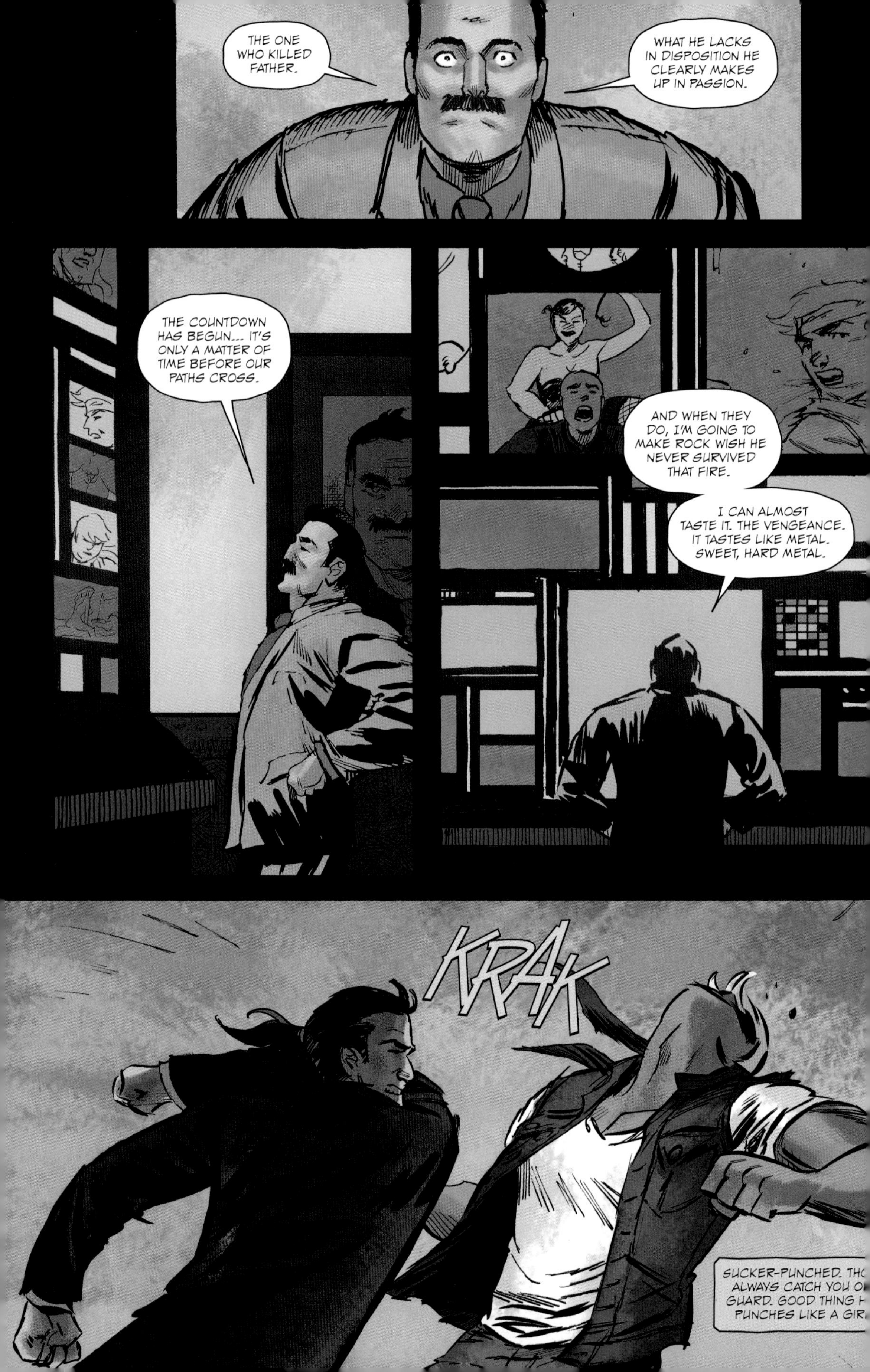
THE ONE WHO KILLED FATHER.
WHAT HE LACKS IN DISPOSITION HE CLEARLY MAKES UP IN PASSION.
THE COUNTDOWN HAS BEGUN... IT'S ONLY A MATTER OF TIME BEFORE OUR PATHS CROSS.
AND WHEN THEY DO, I'M GOING TO MAKE ROCK WISH HE NEVER SURVIVED THAT FIRE.
I CAN ALMOST TASTE IT. THE VENGEANCE. IT TASTES LIKE METAL. SWEET, HARD METAL.
KRAK
SUCKER-PUNCHED. THO ALWAYS CATCH YOU O GUARD. GOOD THING H PUNCHES LIKE A GIR

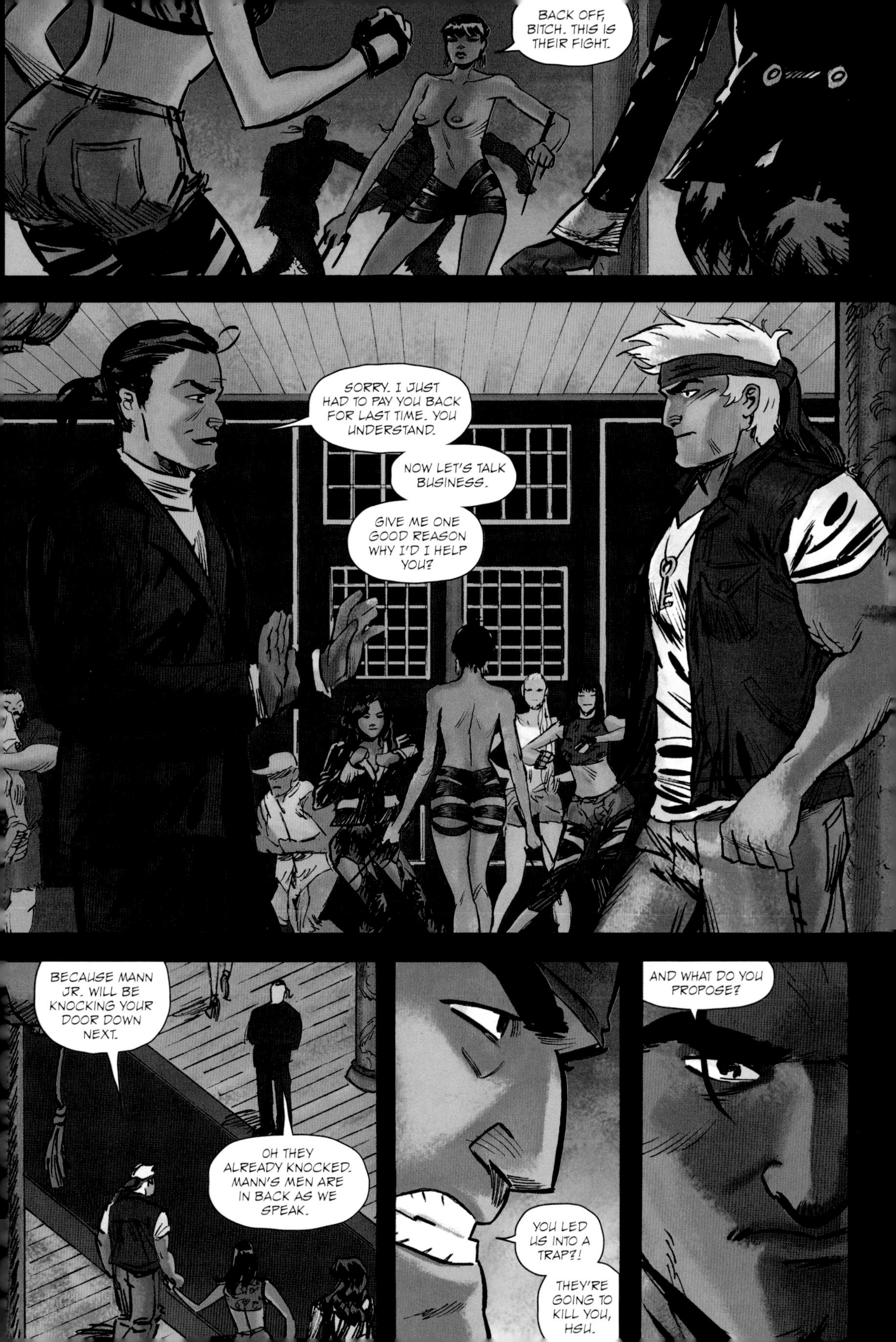
BACK OFF, BITCH. THIS IS THEIR FIGHT.
SORRY. I JUST HAD TO PAY YOU BACK FOR LAST TIME. YOU UNDERSTAND.
NOW LET'S TALK BUSINESS.
GIVE ME ONE GOOD REASON WHY I'D I HELP YOU?
BECAUSE MANN JR. WILL BE KNOCKING YOUR DOOR DOWN NEXT.
OH THEY ALREADY KNOCKED. MANN'S MEN ARE IN BACK AS WE SPEAK.
YOU LED US INTO A TRAP?!
THEY'RE GOING TO KILL YOU, HSU.
AND WHAT DO YOU PROPOSE?

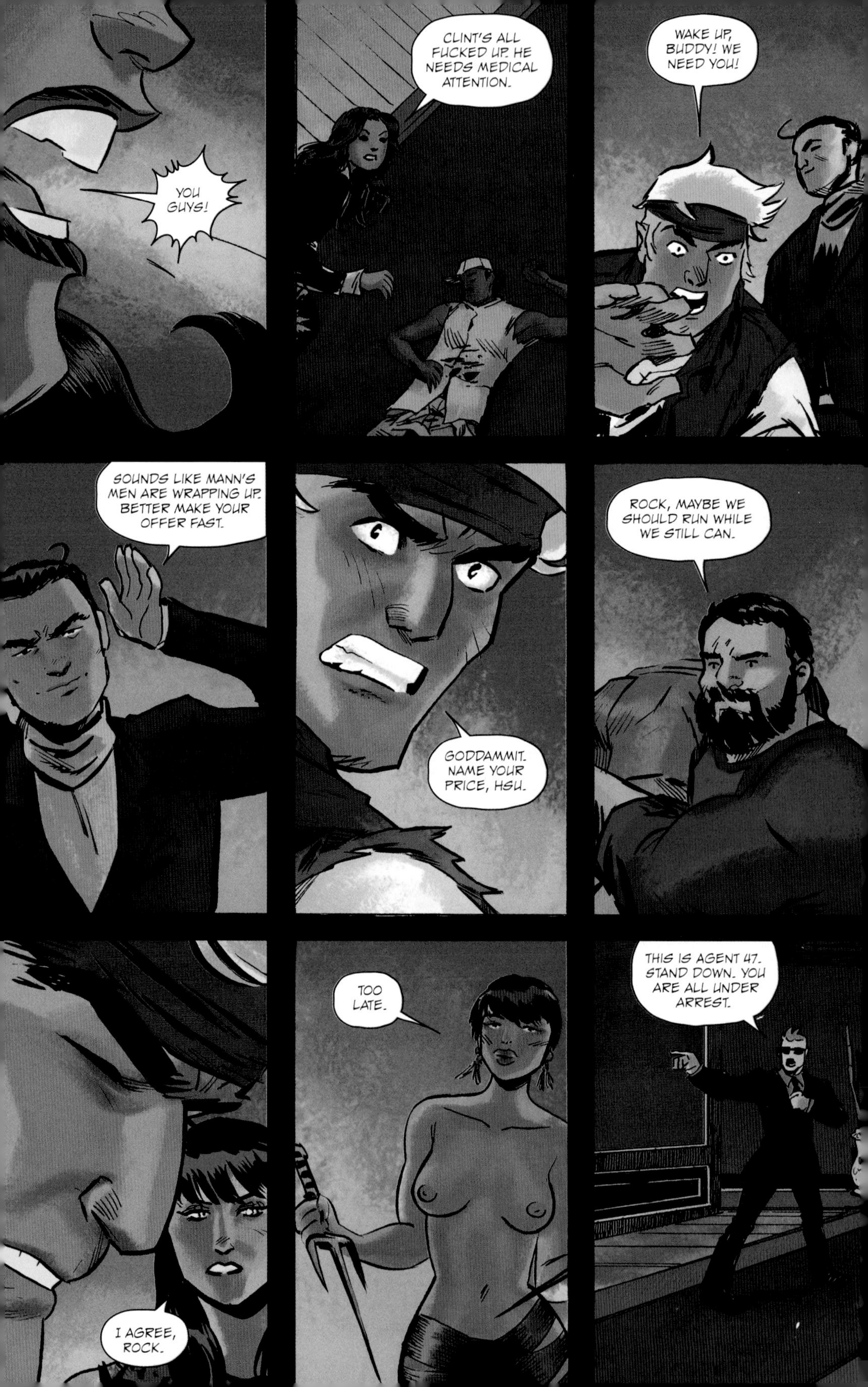
YOU GUYS!
CLINT'S ALL FUCKED UP. HE NEEDS MEDICAL ATTENTION.
WAKE UP, BUDDY! WE NEED YOU!
SOUNDS LIKE MANN'S MEN ARE WRAPPING UP. BETTER MAKE YOUR OFFER FAST.
GODDAMMIT. NAME YOUR PRICE, HSU.
ROCK, MAYBE WE SHOULD RUN WHILE WE STILL CAN.
I AGREE, ROCK.
TOO LATE.
THIS IS AGENT 47. STAND DOWN. YOU ARE ALL UNDER ARREST.

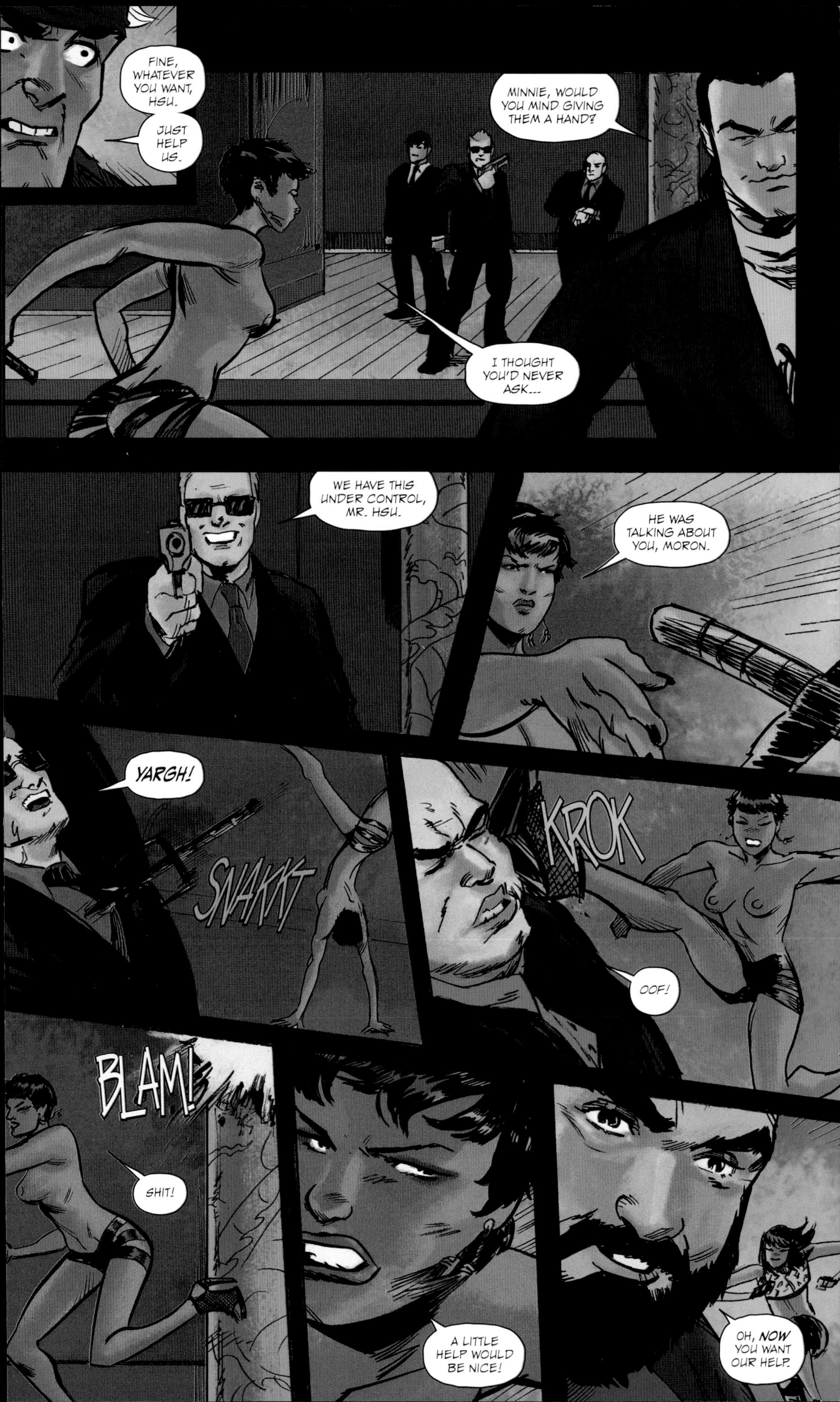
FINE, WHATEVER YOU WANT, HSU.
JUST HELP US.
MINNIE, WOULD YOU MIND GIVING THEM A HAND?
I THOUGHT YOU'D NEVER ASK...
WE HAVE THIS UNDER CONTROL, MR. HSU.
HE WAS TALKING ABOUT YOU, MORON.
YARGH!
SNAKKT
KROK
OOF!
BLAM!
SHIT!
A LITTLE HELP WOULD BE NICE!
OH, NOW YOU WANT OUR HELP.

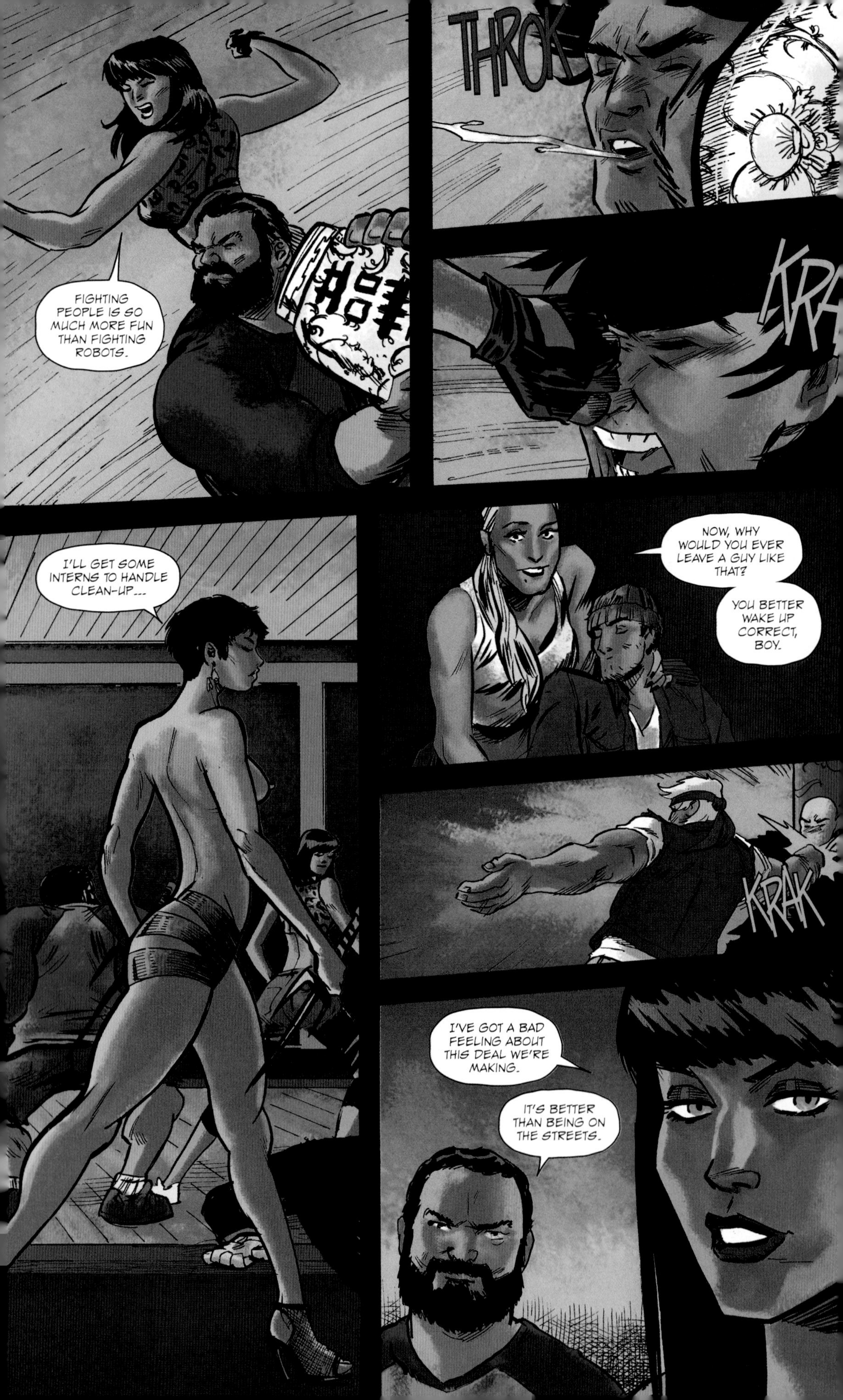
FIGHTING PEOPLE IS SO MUCH MORE FUN THAN FIGHTING ROBOTS.
THROK
KRA
I'LL GET SOME INTERNS TO HANDLE CLEAN-UP...
NOW, WHY WOULD YOU EVER LEAVE A GUY LIKE THAT?
YOU BETTER WAKE UP CORRECT, BOY.
KRAK
I'VE GOT A BAD FEELING ABOUT THIS DEAL WE'RE MAKING.
IT'S BETTER THAN BEING ON THE STREETS.

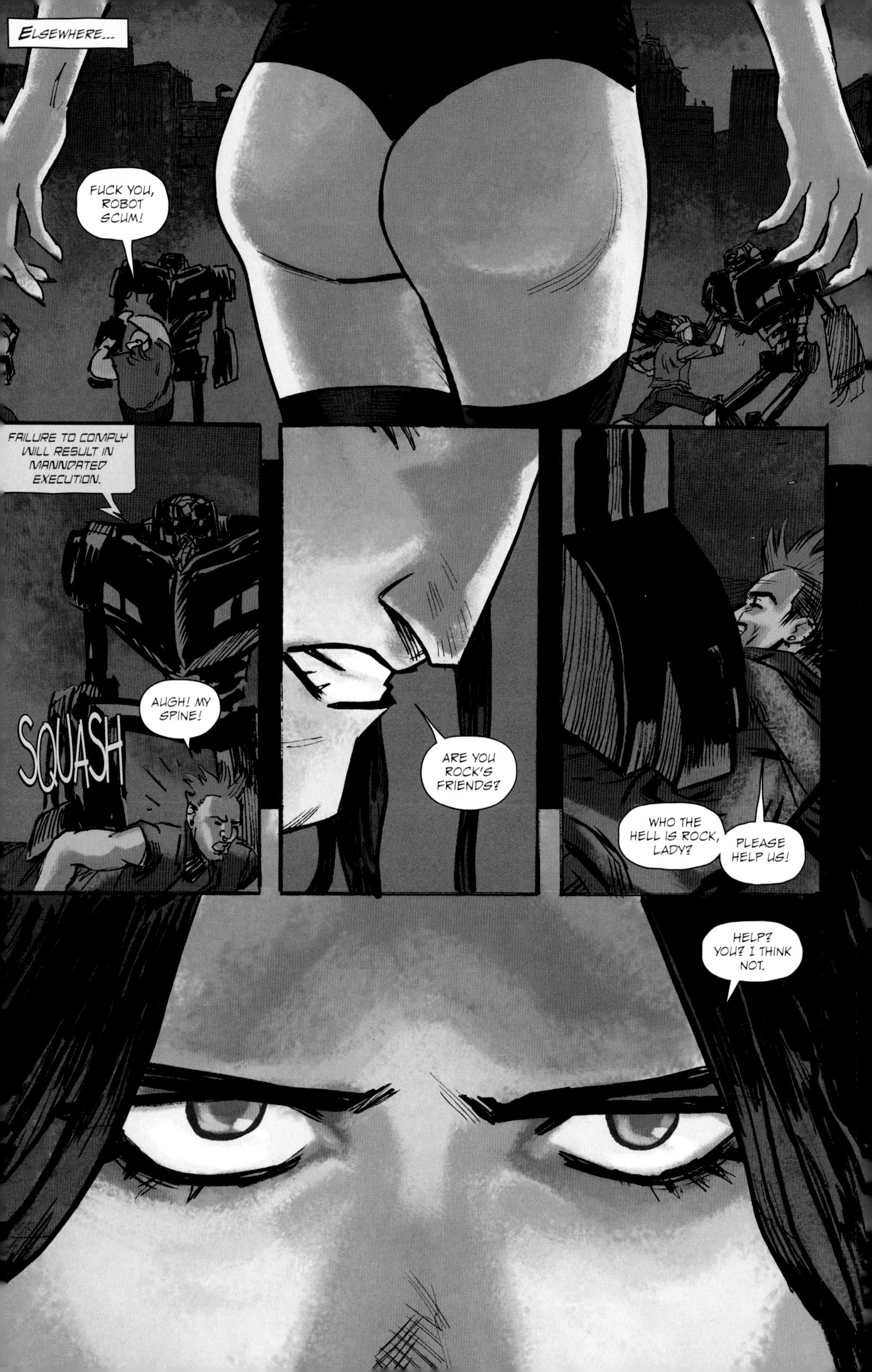

ELSEWHERE...
FUCK YOU, ROBOT SCUM!
FAILURE TO COMPLY WILL RESULT IN MANNDATED EXECUTION.
AUGH! MY SPINE!
SQUASH
ARE YOU ROCK'S FRIENDS?
WHO THE HELL IS ROCK, LADY?
PLEASE HELP US!
HELP? YOU? I THINK NOT.

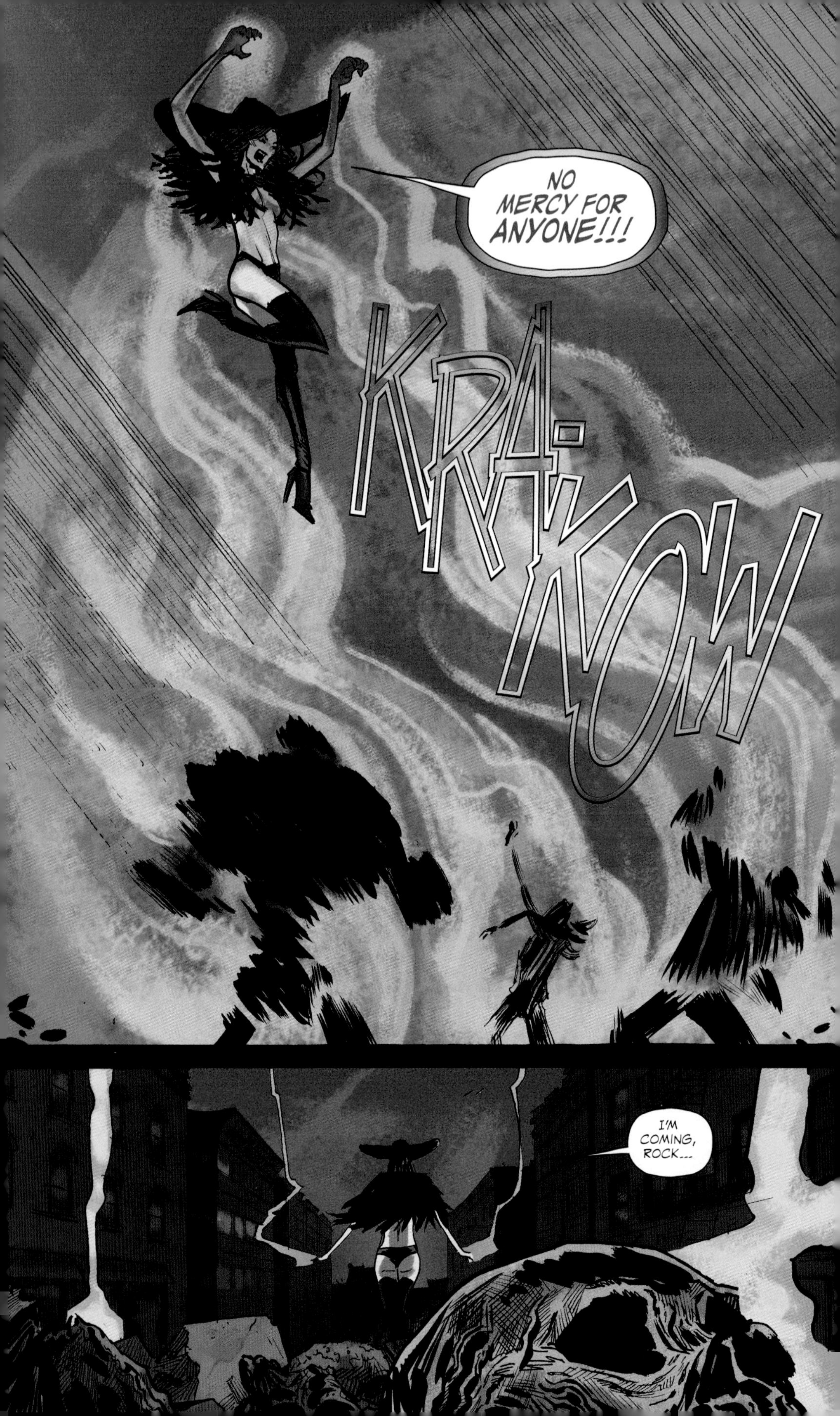
NO MERCY FOR ANYONE!!!
KRA-KOW
I'M COMING, ROCK...

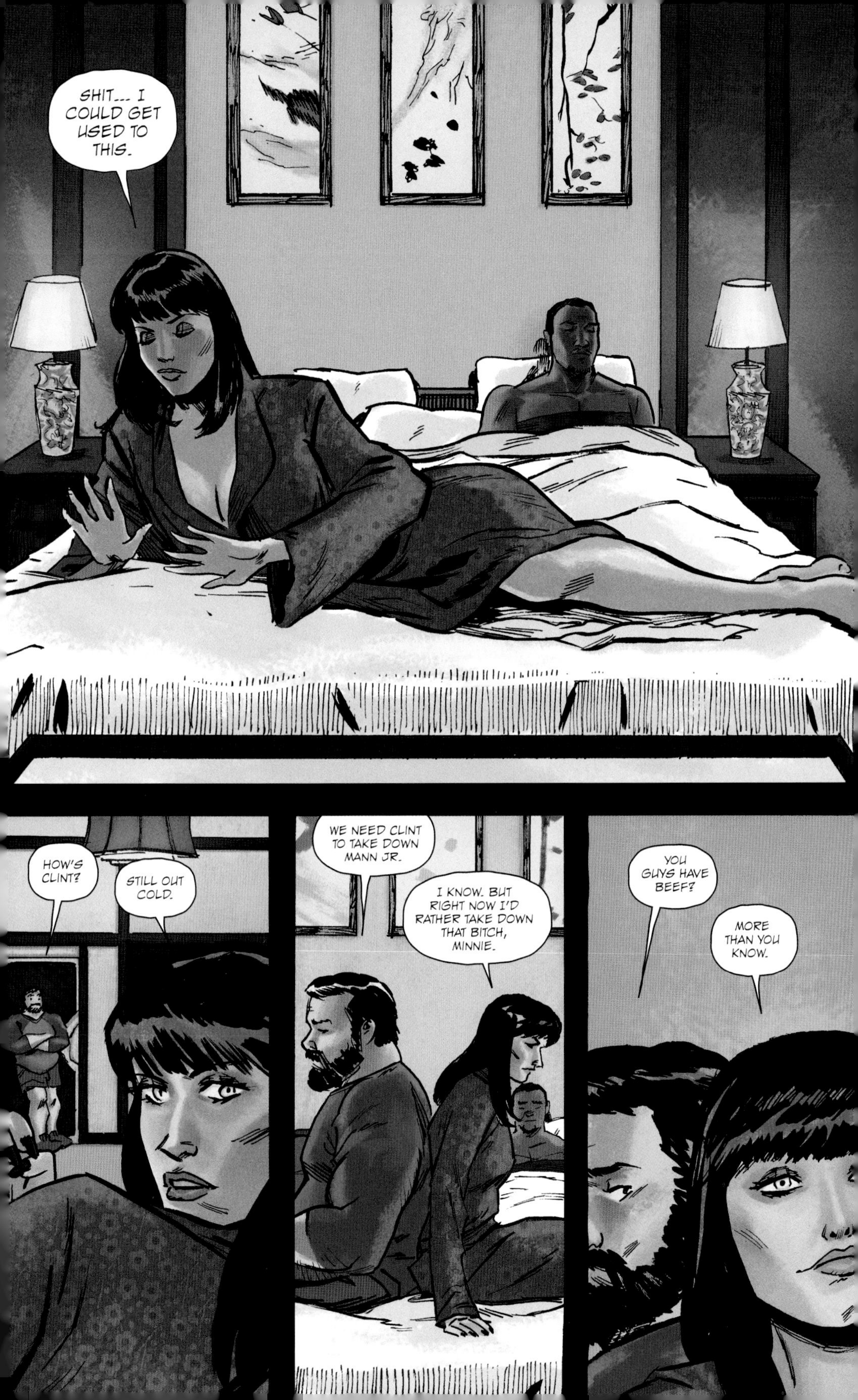
SHIT... I COULD GET USED TO THIS.
HOW'S CLINT?
STILL OUT COLD.
WE NEED CLINT TO TAKE DOWN MANN JR.
I KNOW. BUT RIGHT NOW I'D RATHER TAKE DOWN THAT BITCH, MINNIE.
YOU GUYS HAVE BEEF?
MORE THAN YOU KNOW.

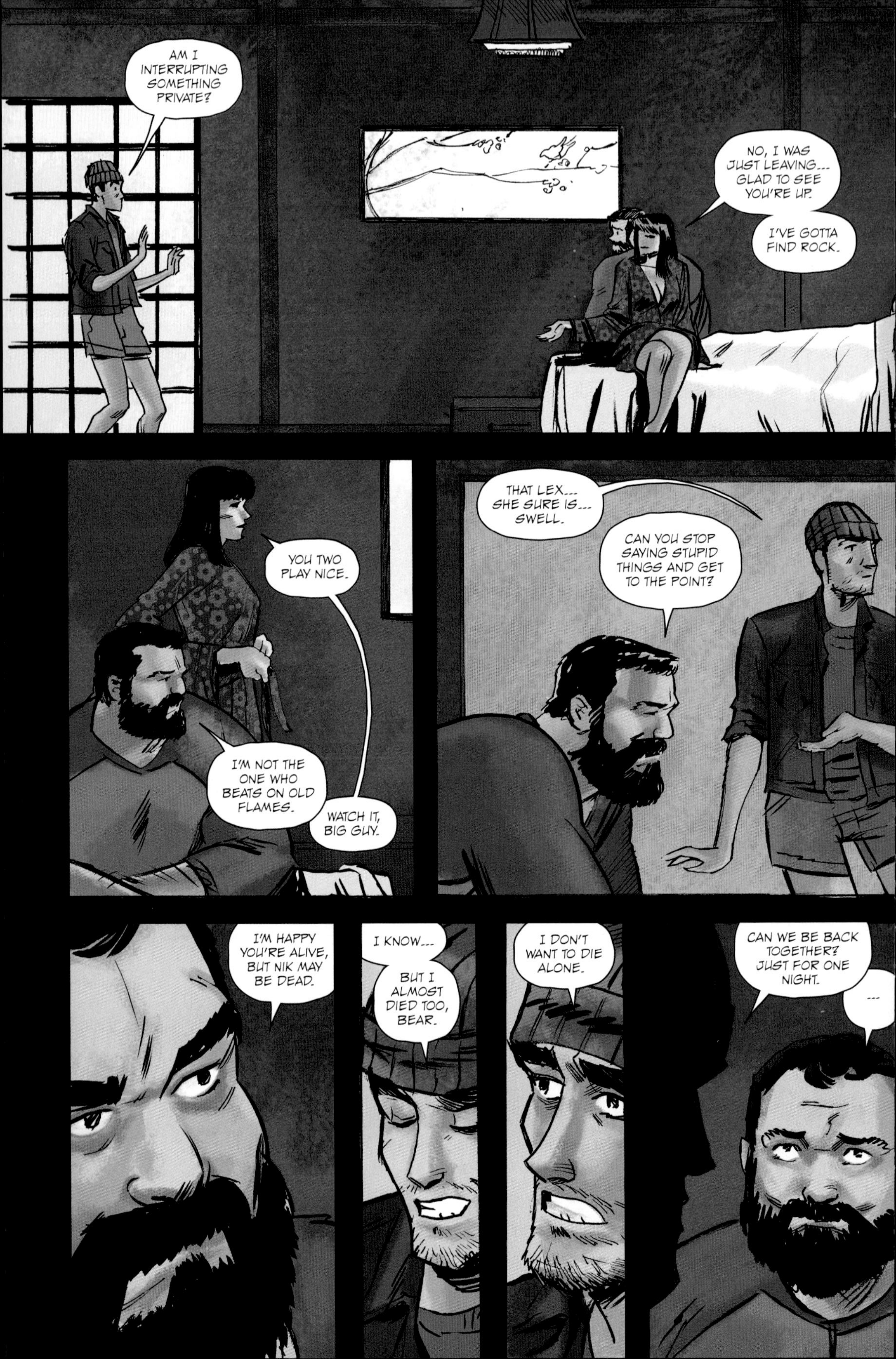
AM I INTERRUPTING SOMETHING PRIVATE?
NO, I WAS JUST LEAVING... GLAD TO SEE YOU'RE UP.
I'VE GOTTA FIND ROCK.
YOU TWO PLAY NICE.
I'M NOT THE ONE WHO BEATS ON OLD FLAMES.
WATCH IT, BIG GUY.
THAT LEX... SHE SURE IS... SWELL.
CAN YOU STOP SAYING STUPID THINGS AND GET TO THE POINT?
I'M HAPPY YOU'RE ALIVE, BUT NIK MAY BE DEAD.
I KNOW...
BUT I ALMOST DIED TOO, BEAR.
I DON'T WANT TO DIE ALONE.
CAN WE BE BACK TOGETHER? JUST FOR ONE NIGHT.
...

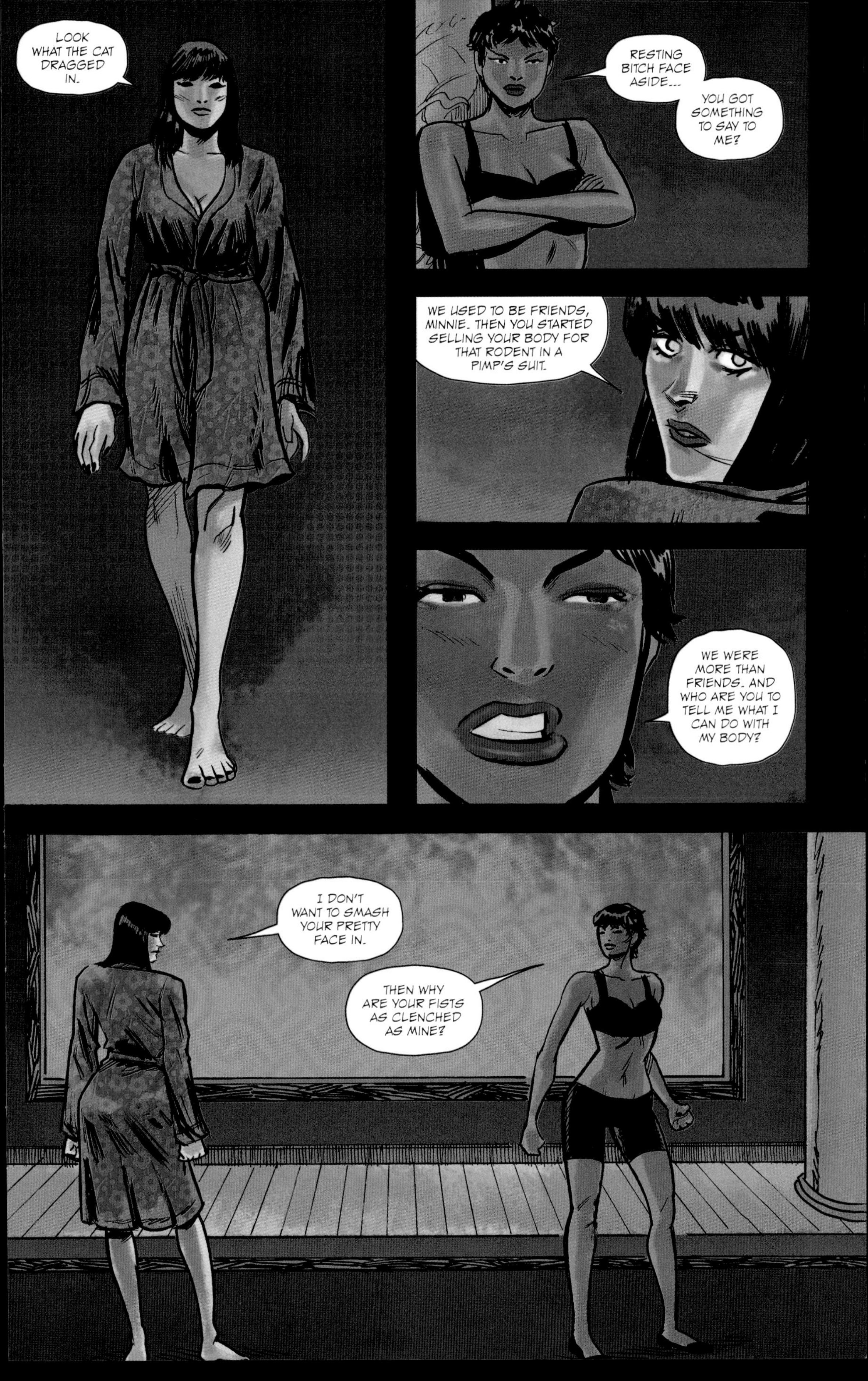
LOOK WHAT THE CAT DRAGGED IN.
RESTING BITCH FACE ASIDE...
YOU GOT SOMETHING TO SAY TO ME?
WE USED TO BE FRIENDS, MINNIE. THEN YOU STARTED SELLING YOUR BODY FOR THAT RODENT IN A PIMP'S SUIT.
WE WERE MORE THAN FRIENDS. AND WHO ARE YOU TO TELL ME WHAT I CAN DO WITH MY BODY?
I DON'T WANT TO SMASH YOUR PRETTY FACE IN.
THEN WHY ARE YOUR FISTS AS CLENCHED AS MINE?

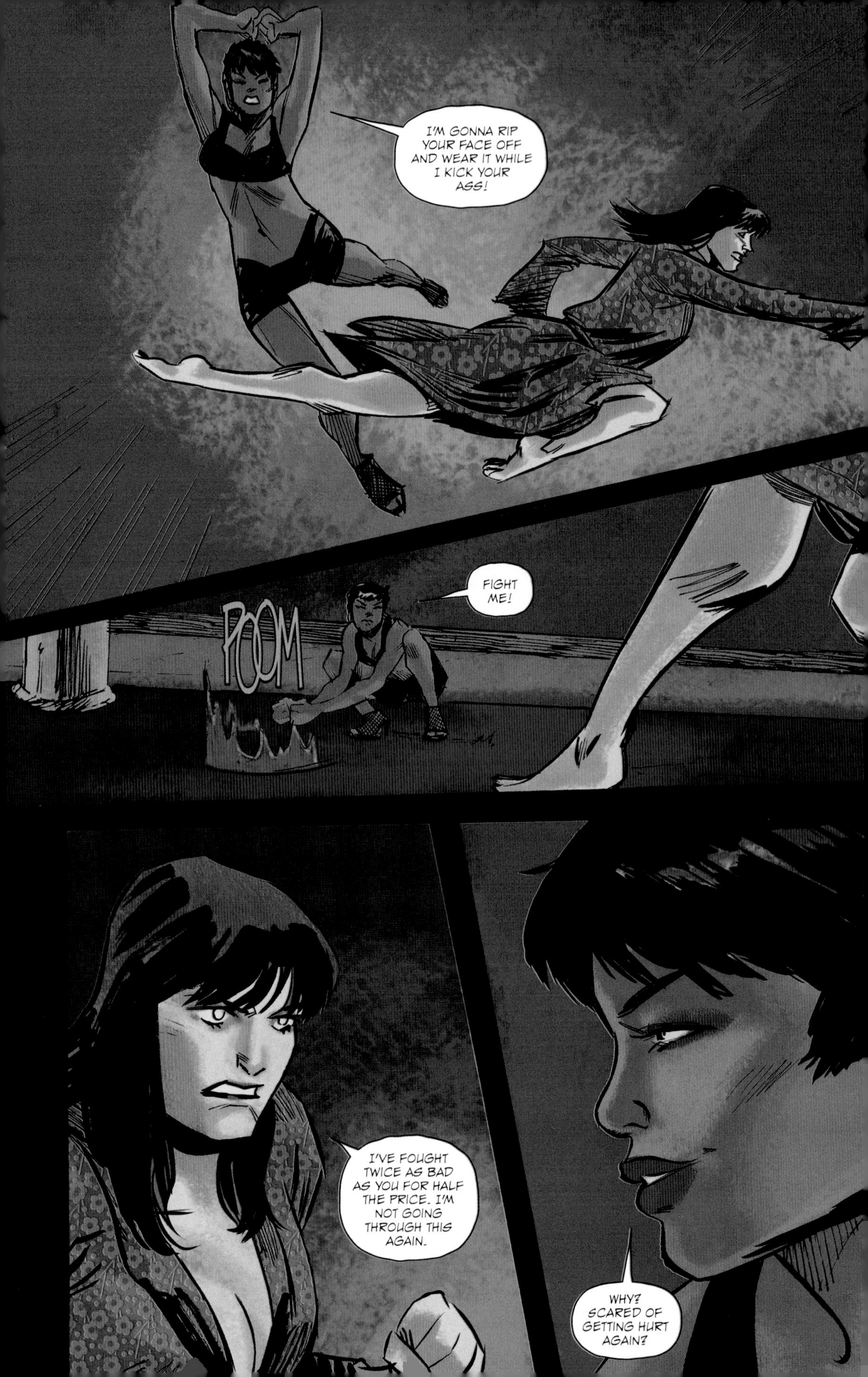
I'M GONNA RIP YOUR FACE OFF AND WEAR IT WHILE I KICK YOUR ASS!
POOM
FIGHT ME!
I'VE FOUGHT TWICE AS BAD AS YOU FOR HALF THE PRICE. I'M NOT GOING THROUGH THIS AGAIN.
WHY? SCARED OF GETTING HURT AGAIN?

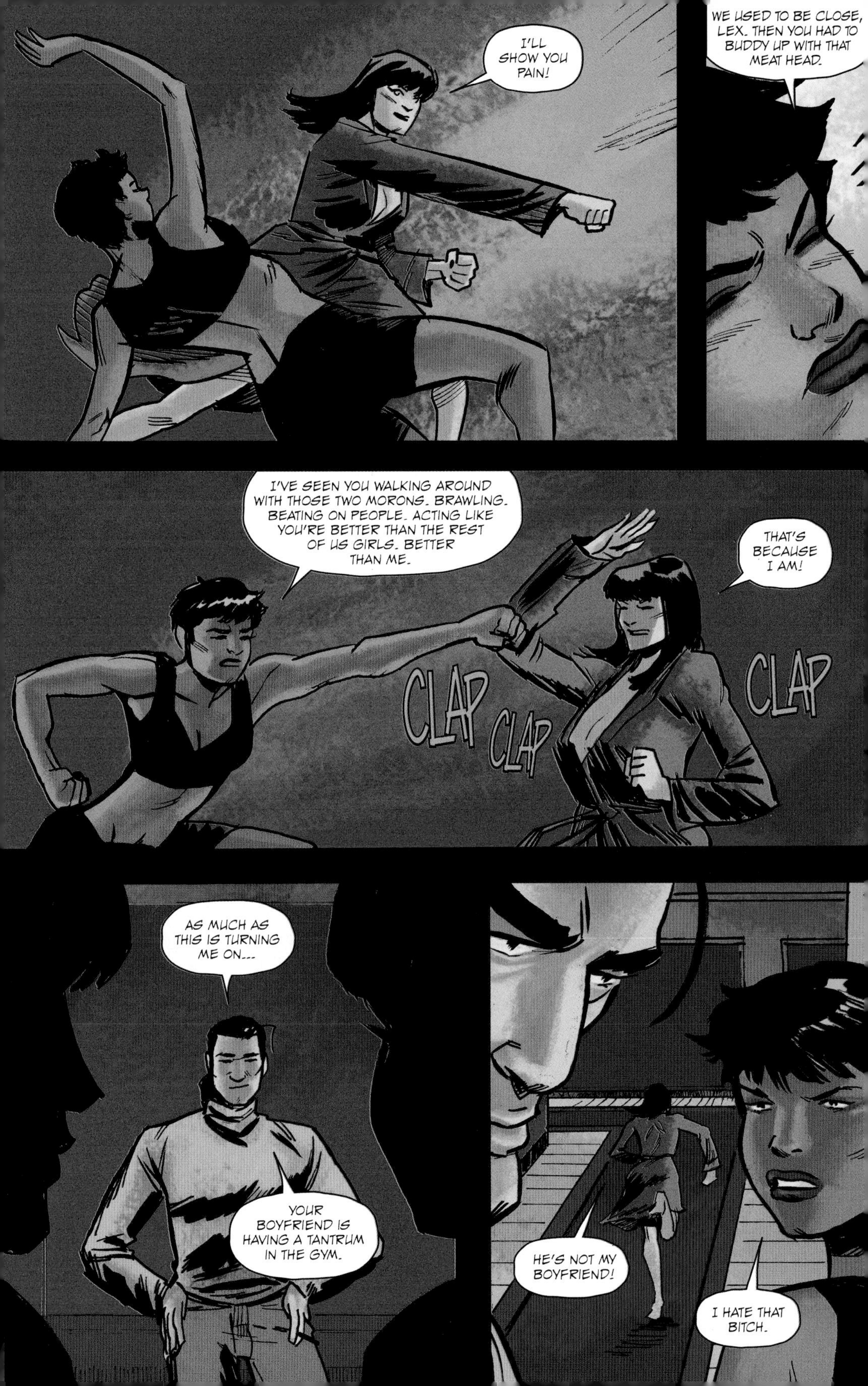
I'LL SHOW YOU PAIN!
WE USED TO BE CLOSE, LEX. THEN YOU HAD TO BUDDY UP WITH THAT MEAT HEAD.
I'VE SEEN YOU WALKING AROUND WITH THOSE TWO MORONS. BRAWLING. BEATING ON PEOPLE. ACTING LIKE YOU'RE BETTER THAN THE REST OF US GIRLS. BETTER THAN ME.
THAT'S BECAUSE I AM!
CLAP
CLAP
CLAP
AS MUCH AS THIS IS TURNING ME ON...
YOUR BOYFRIEND IS HAVING A TANTRUM IN THE GYM.
HE'S NOT MY BOYFRIEND!
I HATE THAT BITCH.

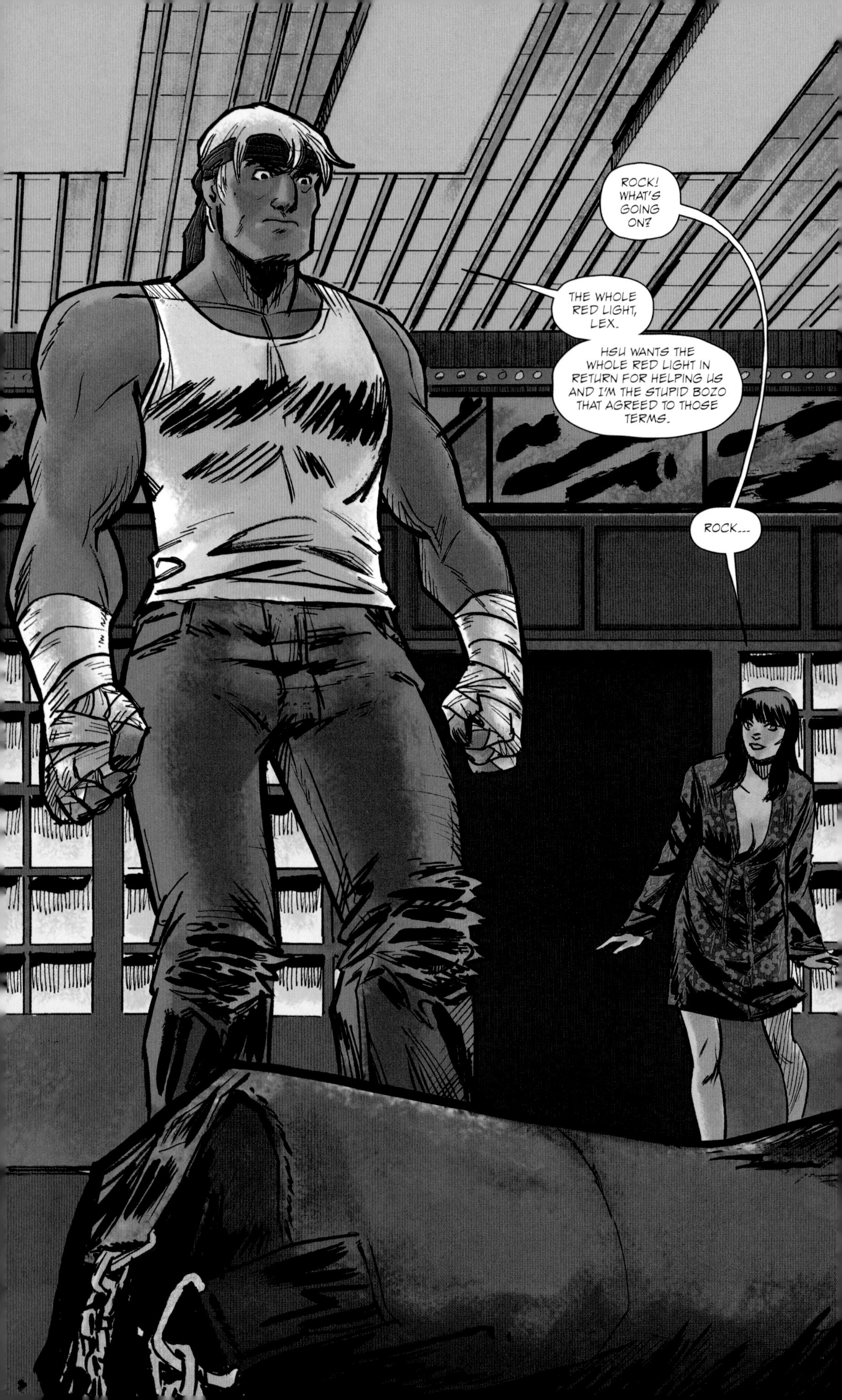
ROCK! WHAT'S GOING ON?
THE WHOLE RED LIGHT, LEX.
HSU WANTS THE WHOLE RED LIGHT IN RETURN FOR HELPING US AND I'M THE STUPID BOZO THAT AGREED TO THOSE TERMS.
ROCK...

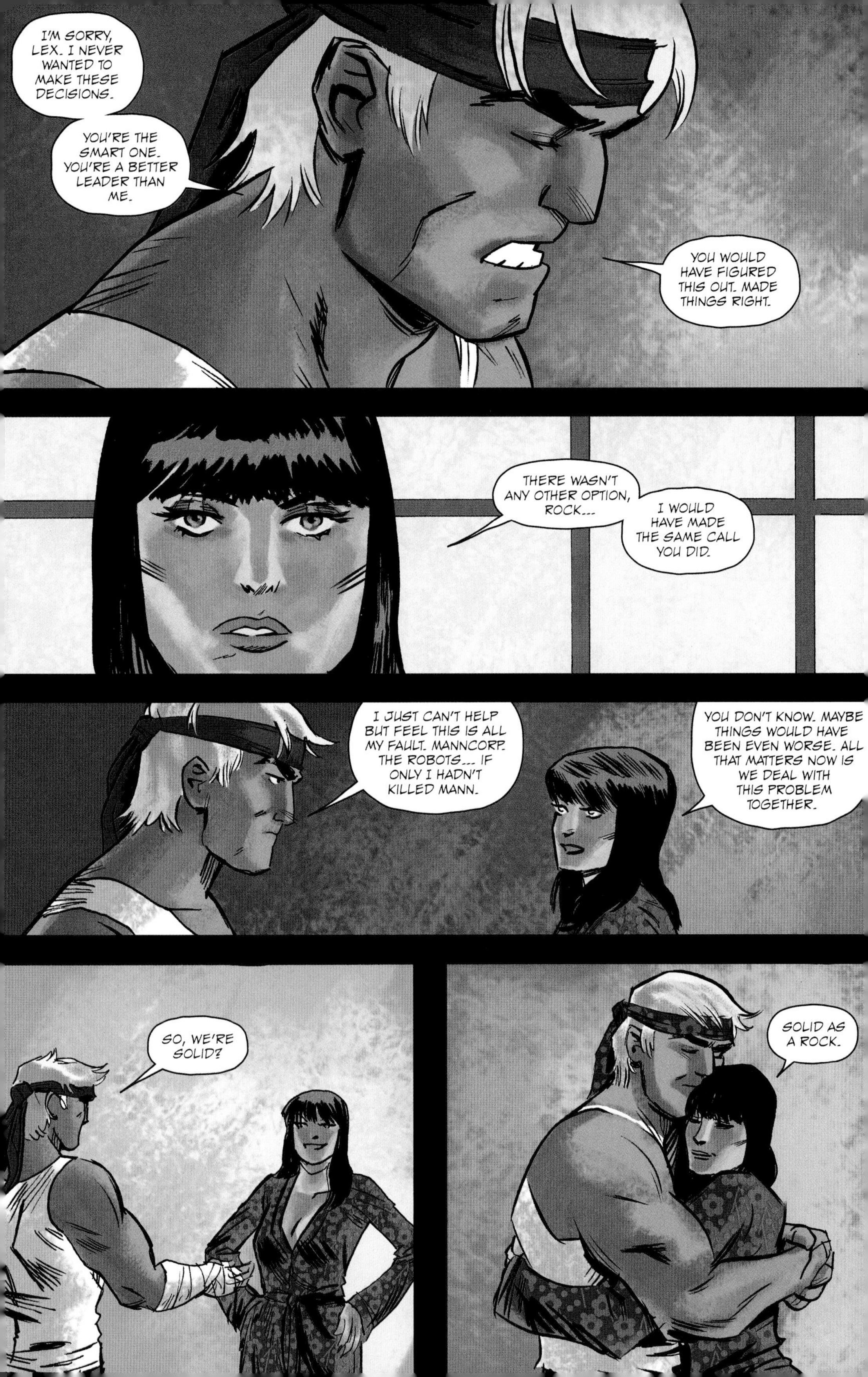
I'M SORRY, LEX. I NEVER WANTED TO MAKE THESE DECISIONS.
YOU'RE THE SMART ONE. YOU'RE A BETTER LEADER THAN ME.
YOU WOULD HAVE FIGURED THIS OUT. MADE THINGS RIGHT.
THERE WASN'T ANY OTHER OPTION, ROCK...
I WOULD HAVE MADE THE SAME CALL YOU DID.
I JUST CAN'T HELP BUT FEEL THIS IS ALL MY FAULT. MANNCORP. THE ROBOTS... IF ONLY I HADN'T KILLED MANN.
YOU DON'T KNOW. MAYBE THINGS WOULD HAVE BEEN EVEN WORSE. ALL THAT MATTERS NOW IS WE DEAL WITH THIS PROBLEM TOGETHER.
SO, WE'RE SOLID?
SOLID AS A ROCK.

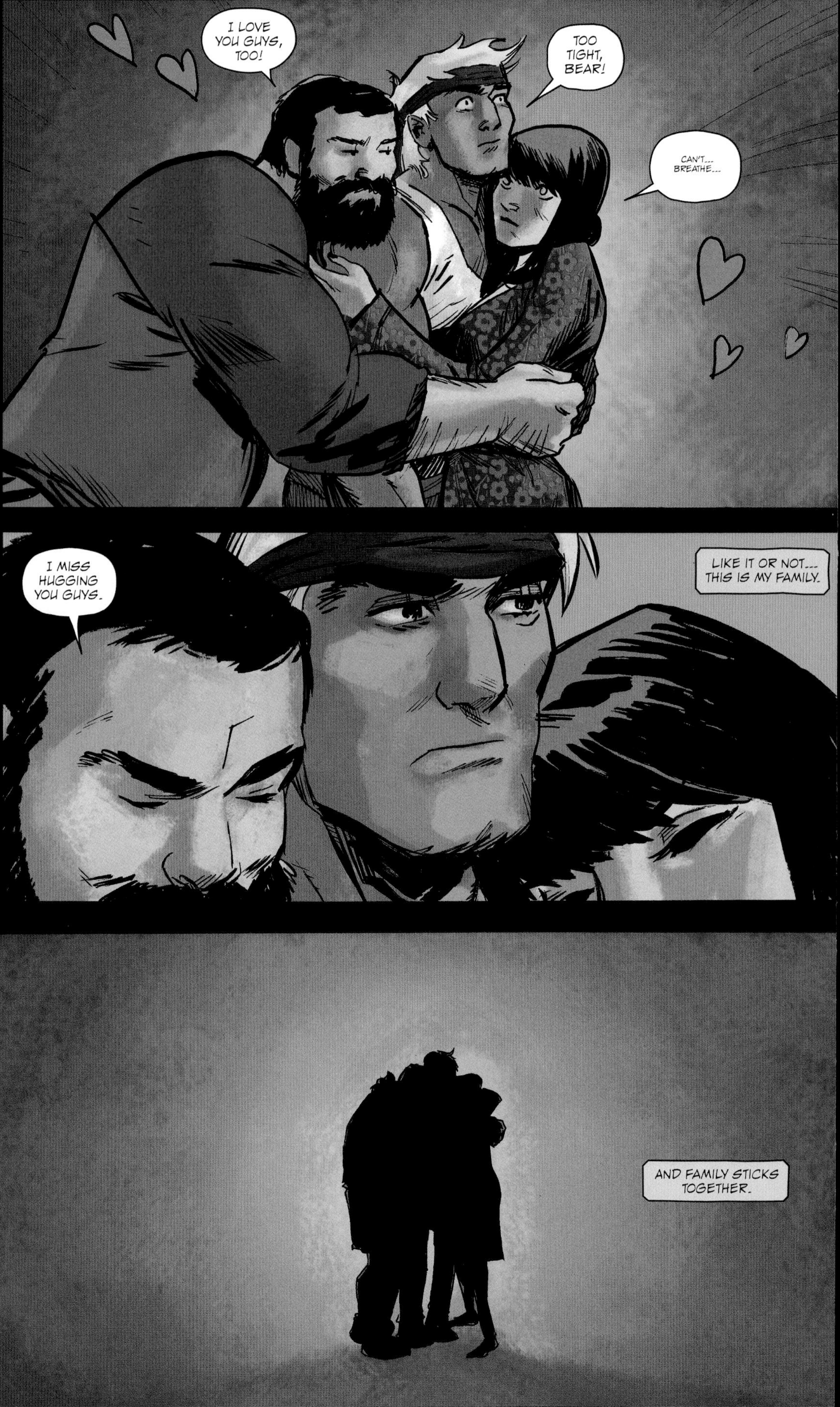
I LOVE YOU GUYS, TOO!
TOO TIGHT, BEAR!
CAN'T... BREATHE...
I MISS HUGGING YOU GUYS.
LIKE IT OR NOT... THIS IS MY FAMILY.
AND FAMILY STICKS TOGETHER.

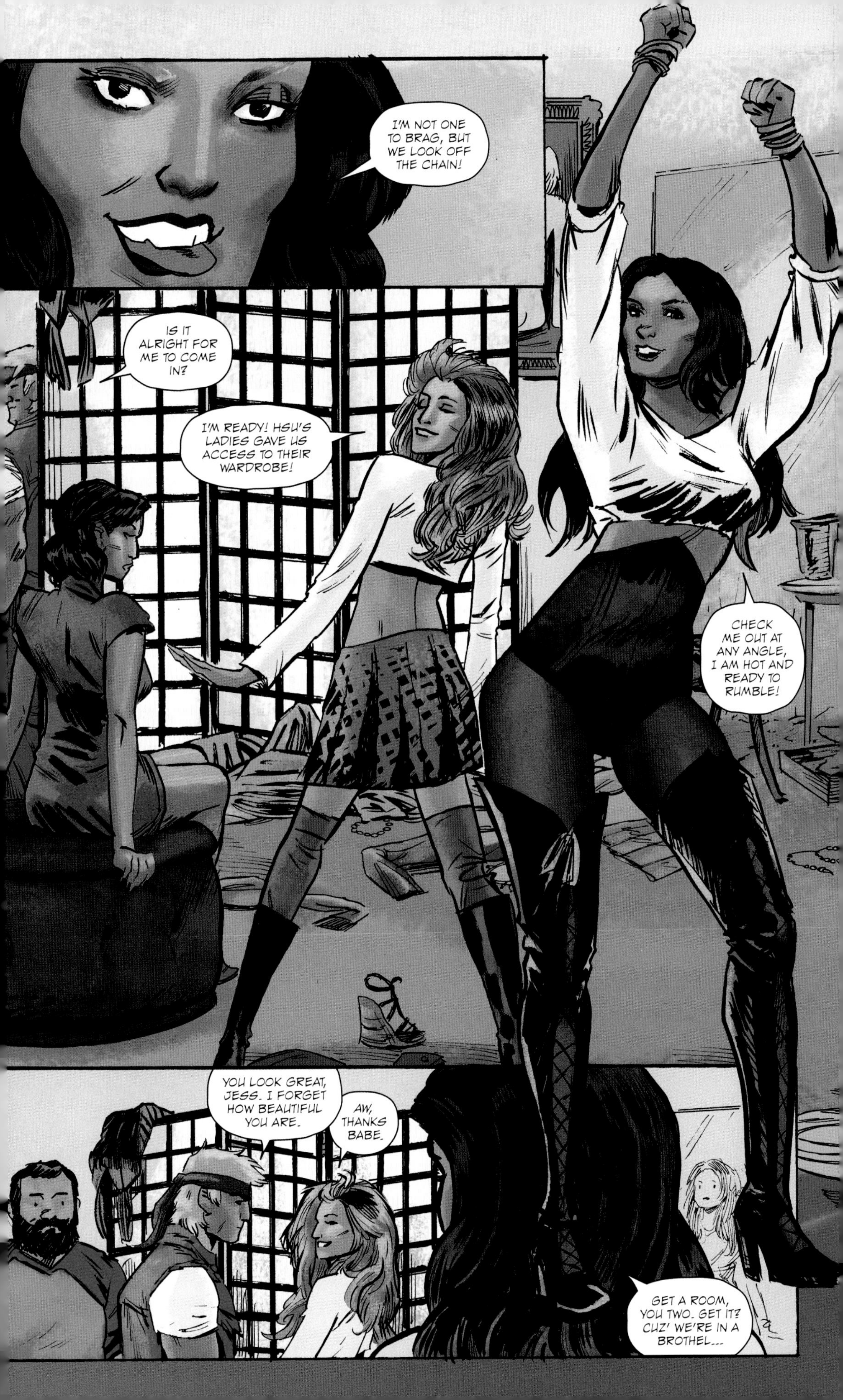
I'M NOT ONE TO BRAG, BUT WE LOOK OFF THE CHAIN!
IS IT ALRIGHT FOR ME TO COME IN?
I'M READY! HSU'S LADIES GAVE US ACCESS TO THEIR WARDROBE!
CHECK ME OUT AT ANY ANGLE, I AM HOT AND READY TO RUMBLE!
YOU LOOK GREAT, JESS. I FORGET HOW BEAUTIFUL YOU ARE.
AW, THANKS BABE.
GET A ROOM, YOU TWO. GET IT? CUZ' WE'RE IN A BROTHEL...

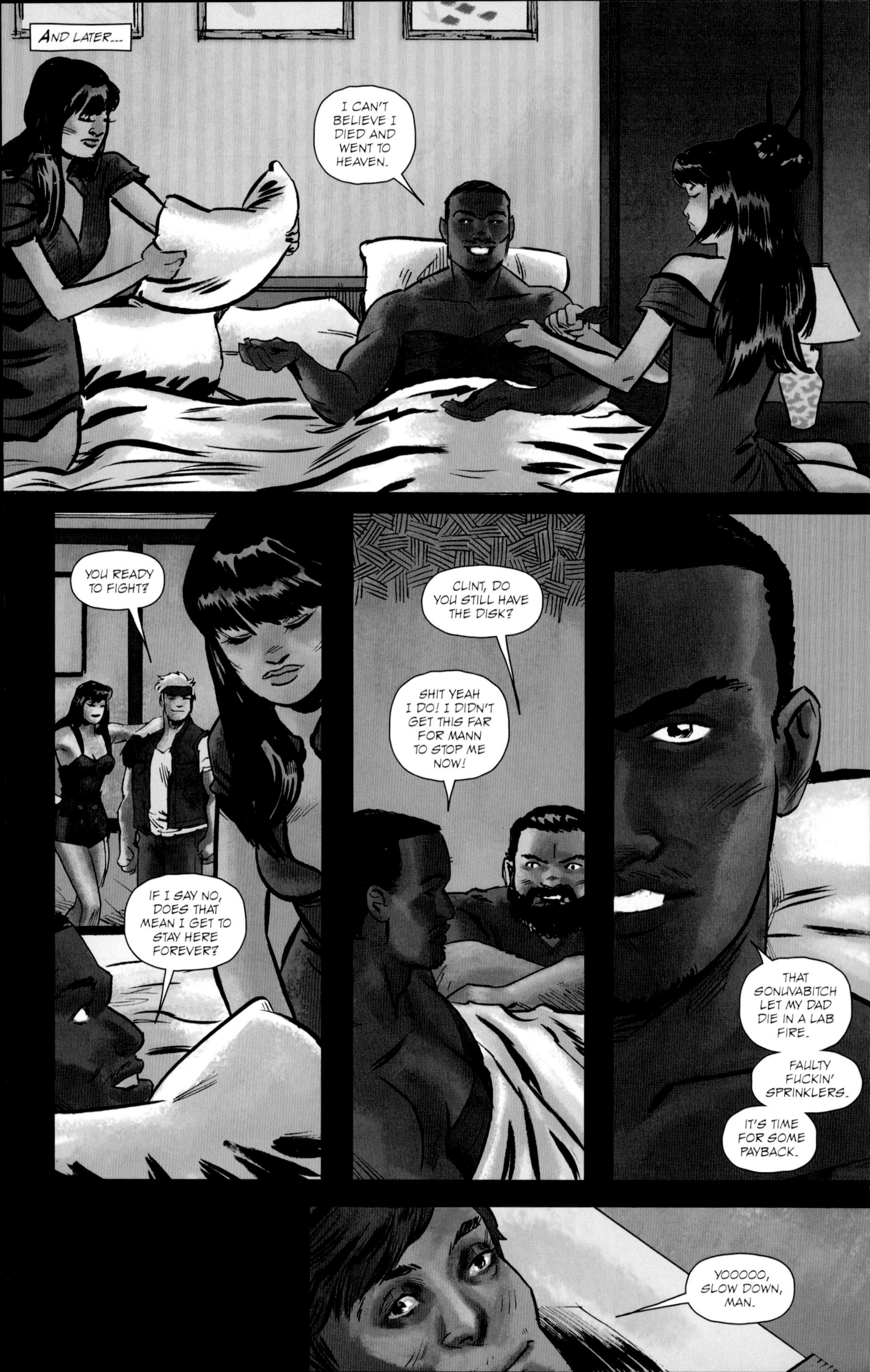
AND LATER...
I CAN'T BELIEVE I DIED AND WENT TO HEAVEN.
YOU READY TO FIGHT?
IF I SAY NO, DOES THAT MEAN I GET TO STAY HERE FOREVER?
CLINT, DO YOU STILL HAVE THE DISK?
SHIT YEAH I DO! I DIDN'T GET THIS FAR FOR MANN TO STOP ME NOW!
THAT SONUVABITCH LET MY DAD DIE IN A LAB FIRE.
FAULTY FUCKIN' SPRINKLERS.
IT'S TIME FOR SOME PAYBACK.
YOOOOO, SLOW DOWN, MAN.

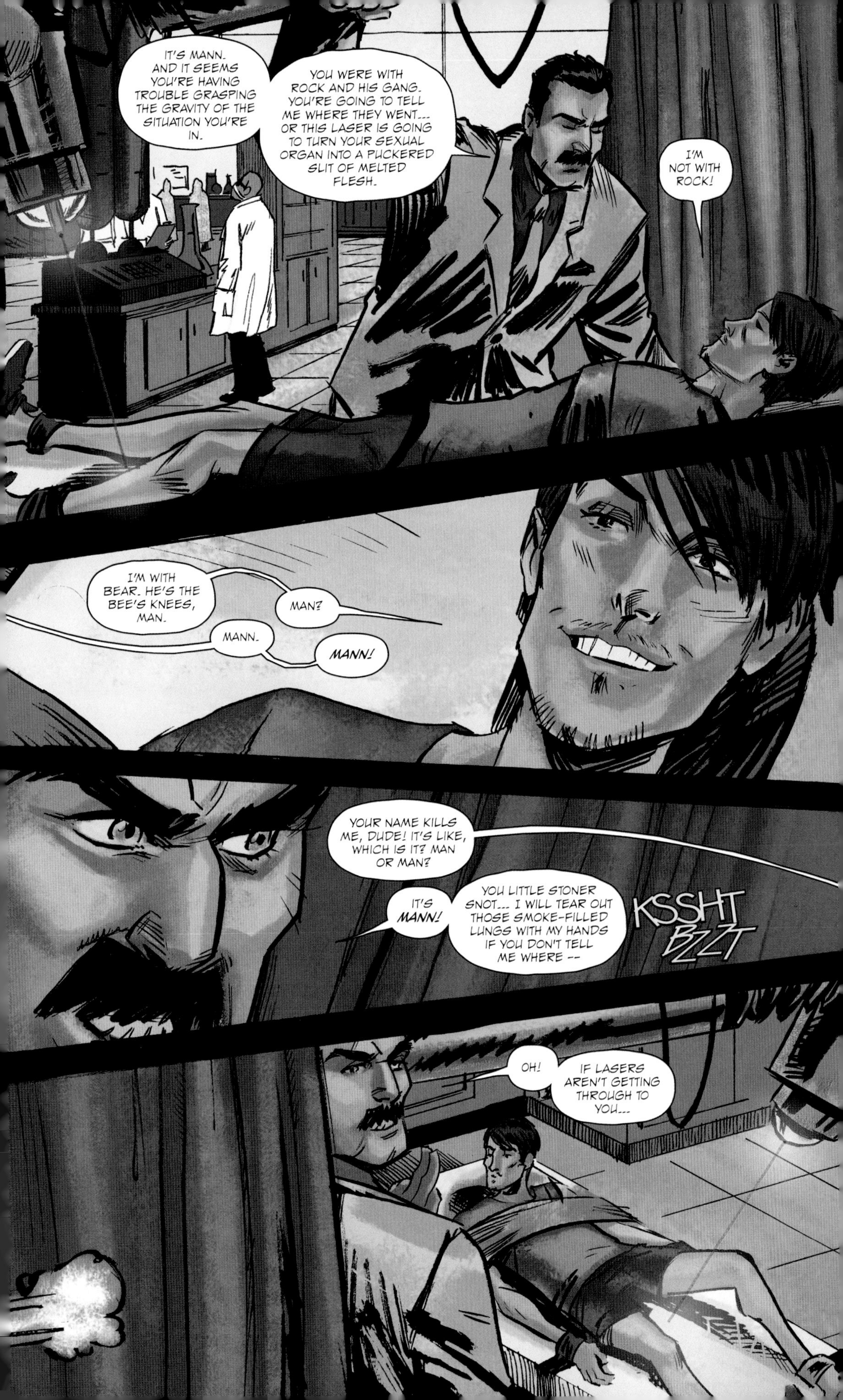
IT'S MANN. AND IT SEEMS YOU'RE HAVING TROUBLE GRASPING THE GRAVITY OF THE SITUATION YOU'RE IN.
YOU WERE WITH ROCK AND HIS GANG. YOU'RE GOING TO TELL ME WHERE THEY WENT... OR THIS LASER IS GOING TO TURN YOUR SEXUAL ORGAN INTO A PUCKERED SLIT OF MELTED FLESH.
I'M NOT WITH ROCK!
I'M WITH BEAR. HE'S THE BEE'S KNEES, MAN.
MAN?
MANN.
MANN!
YOUR NAME KILLS ME, DUDE! IT'S LIKE, WHICH IS IT? MAN OR MAN?
IT'S MANN!
YOU LITTLE STONER SNOT... I WILL TEAR OUT THOSE SMOKE-FILLED LUNGS WITH MY HANDS IF YOU DON'T TELL ME WHERE --
KSSHT
BZZT
OH!
IF LASERS AREN'T GETTING THROUGH TO YOU...

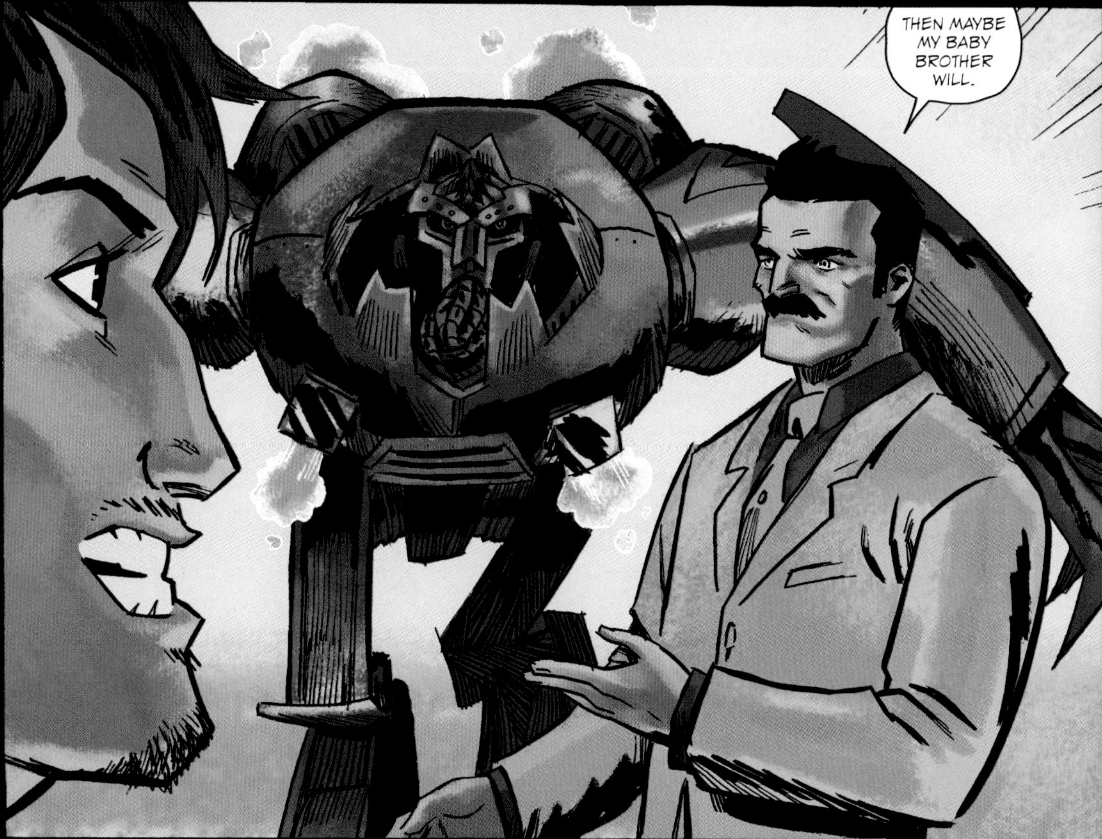
THEN MAYBE MY BABY BROTHER WILL.

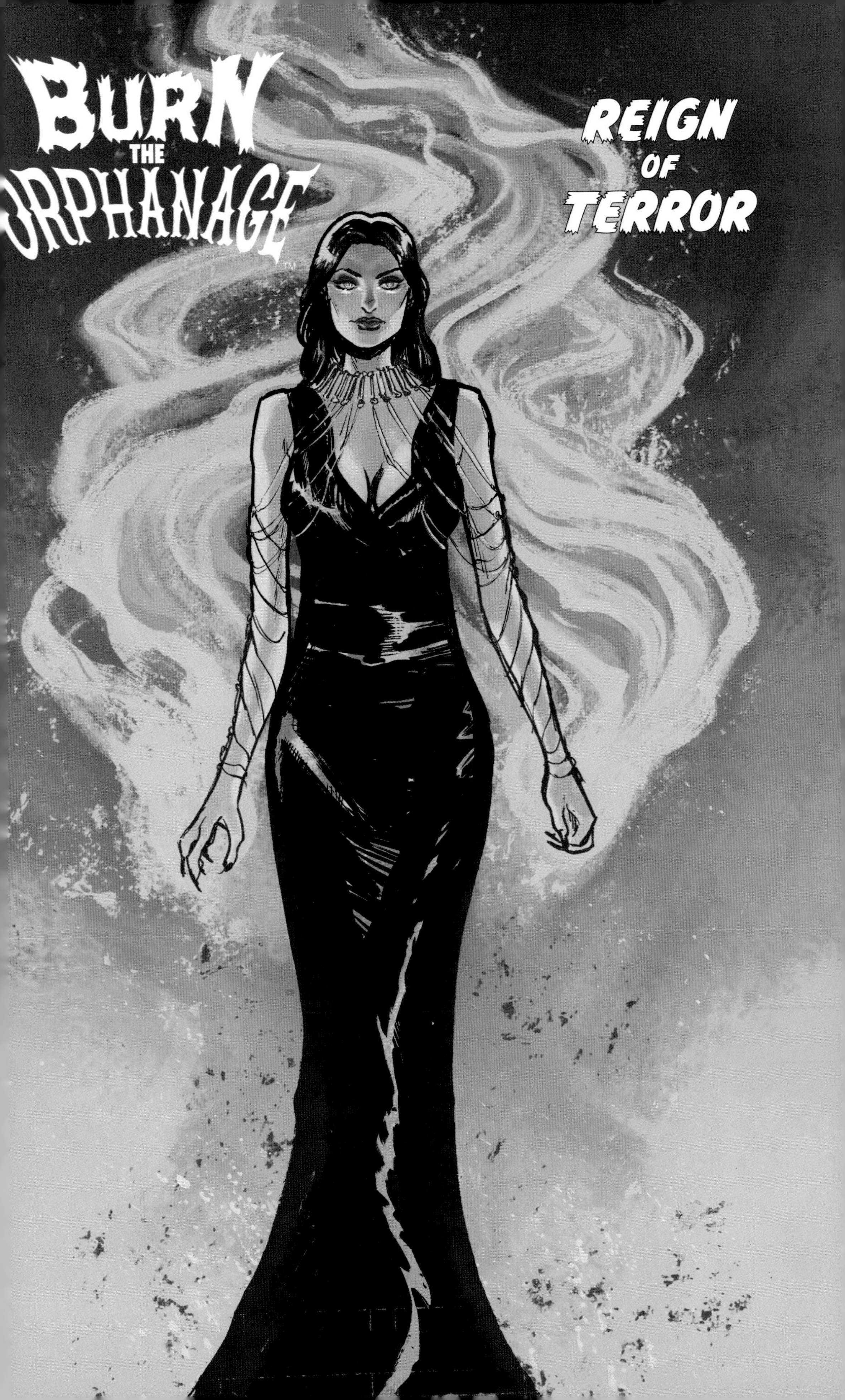

BURN THE ORPHANAGE™
REIGN OF TERROR

CHAPTER FOUR

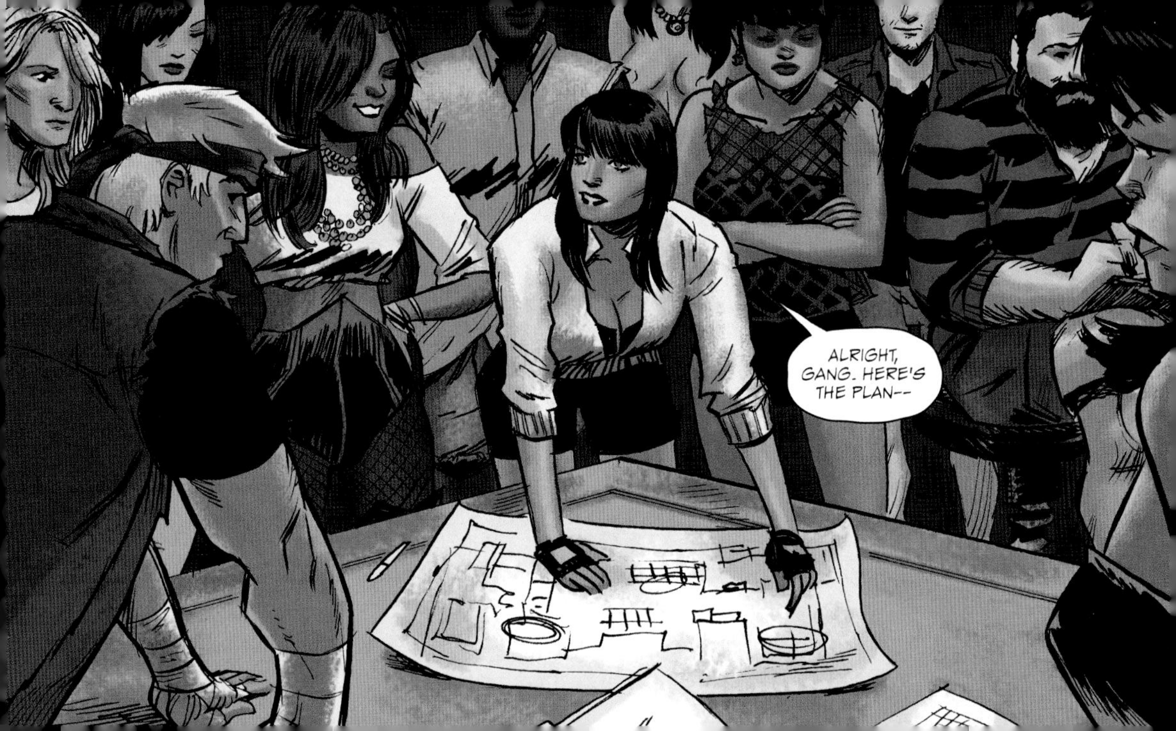
ALRIGHT, GANG. HERE'S THE PLAN--

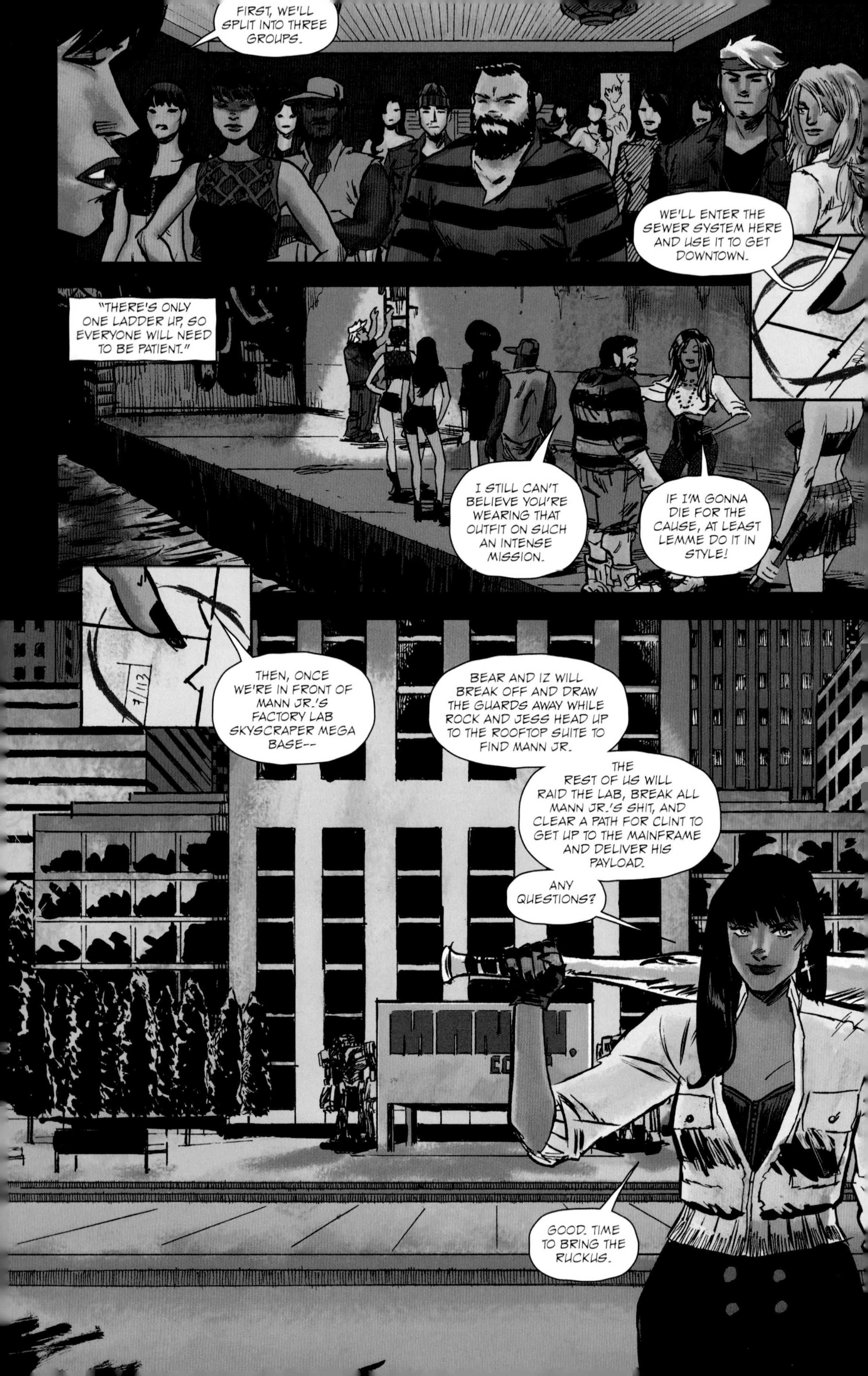
FIRST, WE'LL SPLIT INTO THREE GROUPS.
WE'LL ENTER THE SEWER SYSTEM HERE AND USE IT TO GET DOWNTOWN.
"THERE'S ONLY ONE LADDER UP, SO EVERYONE WILL NEED TO BE PATIENT."
I STILL CAN'T BELIEVE YOU'RE WEARING THAT OUTFIT ON SUCH AN INTENSE MISSION.
IF I'M GONNA DIE FOR THE CAUSE, AT LEAST LEMME DO IT IN STYLE!
THEN, ONCE WE'RE IN FRONT OF MANN JR.'S FACTORY LAB SKYSCRAPER MEGA BASE--
BEAR AND IZ WILL BREAK OFF AND DRAW THE GUARDS AWAY WHILE ROCK AND JESS HEAD UP TO THE ROOFTOP SUITE TO FIND MANN JR.
THE REST OF US WILL RAID THE LAB, BREAK ALL MANN JR.'S SHIT, AND CLEAR A PATH FOR CLINT TO GET UP TO THE MAINFRAME AND DELIVER HIS PAYLOAD.
ANY QUESTIONS?
GOOD. TIME TO BRING THE RUCKUS.

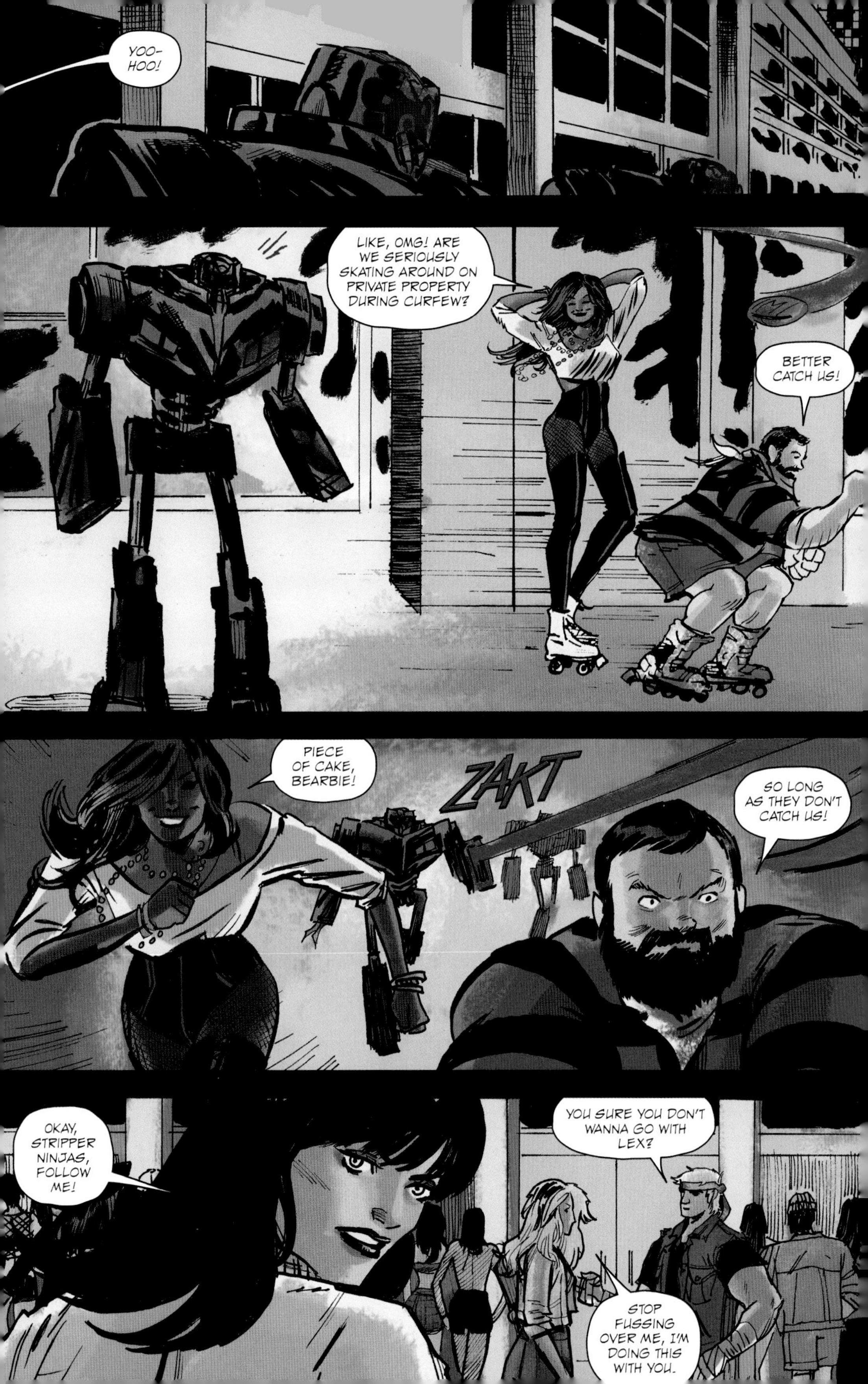
YOO-HOO!
LIKE, OMG! ARE WE SERIOUSLY SKATING AROUND ON PRIVATE PROPERTY DURING CURFEW?
BETTER CATCH US!
PIECE OF CAKE, BEARBIE!
ZAKT
SO LONG AS THEY DON'T CATCH US!
OKAY, STRIPPER NINJAS, FOLLOW ME!
YOU SURE YOU DON'T WANNA GO WITH LEX?
STOP FUSSING OVER ME, I'M DOING THIS WITH YOU.

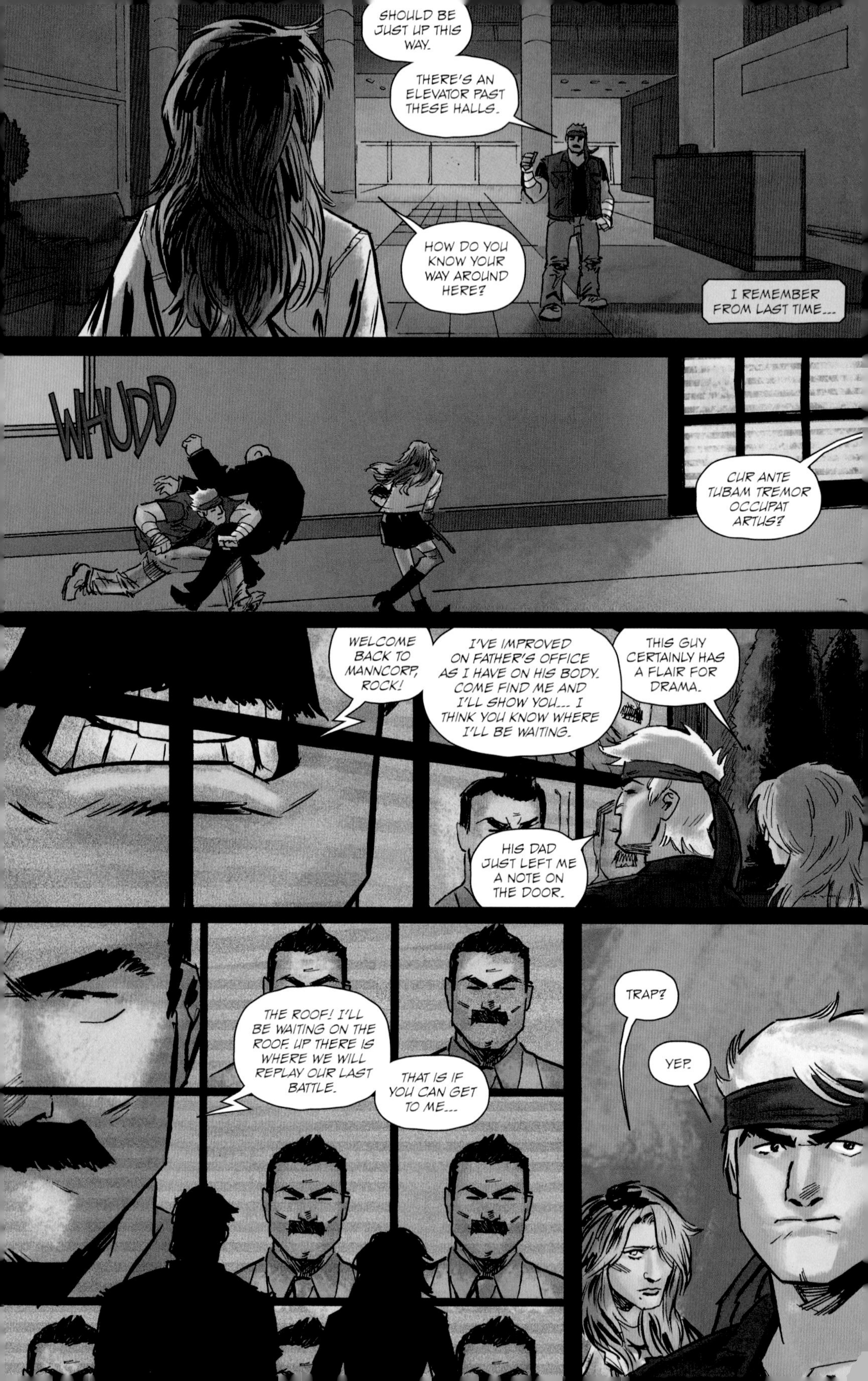

SHOULD BE JUST UP THIS WAY.
THERE'S AN ELEVATOR PAST THESE HALLS.
HOW DO YOU KNOW YOUR WAY AROUND HERE?
I REMEMBER FROM LAST TIME...
WHUDD
CUR ANTE TUBAM TREMOR OCCUPAT ARTUS?
WELCOME BACK TO MANNCORP, ROCK!
I'VE IMPROVED ON FATHER'S OFFICE AS I HAVE ON HIS BODY. COME FIND ME AND I'LL SHOW YOU... I THINK YOU KNOW WHERE I'LL BE WAITING.
THIS GUY CERTAINLY HAS A FLAIR FOR DRAMA.
HIS DAD JUST LEFT ME A NOTE ON THE DOOR.
THE ROOF! I'LL BE WAITING ON THE ROOF. UP THERE IS WHERE WE WILL REPLAY OUR LAST BATTLE.
THAT IS IF YOU CAN GET TO ME...
TRAP?
YEP.

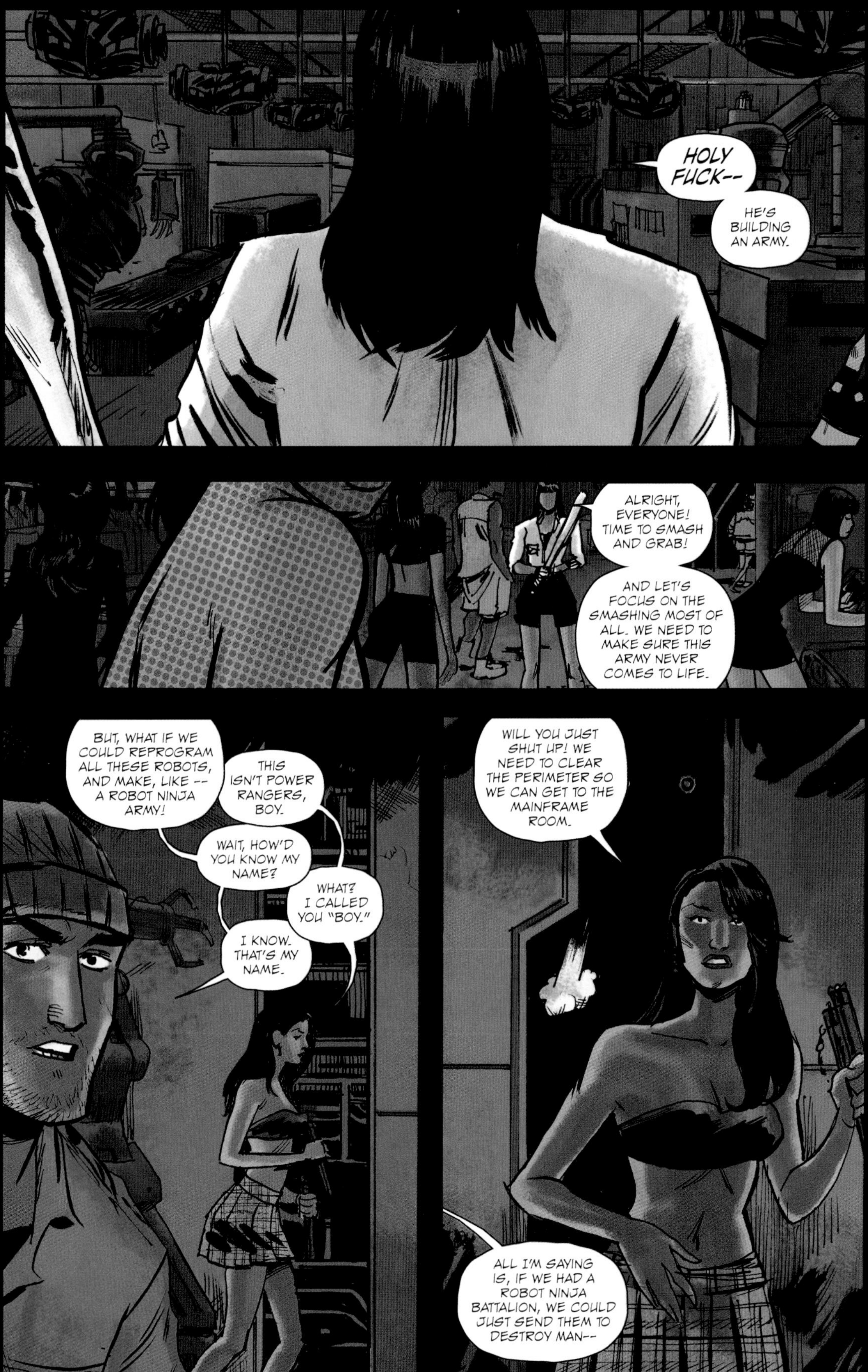
HOLY FUCK--
HE'S BUILDING AN ARMY.
ALRIGHT, EVERYONE! TIME TO SMASH AND GRAB!
AND LET'S FOCUS ON THE SMASHING MOST OF ALL. WE NEED TO MAKE SURE THIS ARMY NEVER COMES TO LIFE.
BUT, WHAT IF WE COULD REPROGRAM ALL THESE ROBOTS, AND MAKE, LIKE -- A ROBOT NINJA ARMY!
THIS ISN'T POWER RANGERS, BOY.
WAIT, HOW'D YOU KNOW MY NAME?
WHAT? I CALLED YOU "BOY."
I KNOW. THAT'S MY NAME.
WILL YOU JUST SHUT UP! WE NEED TO CLEAR THE PERIMETER SO WE CAN GET TO THE MAINFRAME ROOM.
ALL I'M SAYING IS, IF WE HAD A ROBOT NINJA BATTALION, WE COULD JUST SEND THEM TO DESTROY MAN--

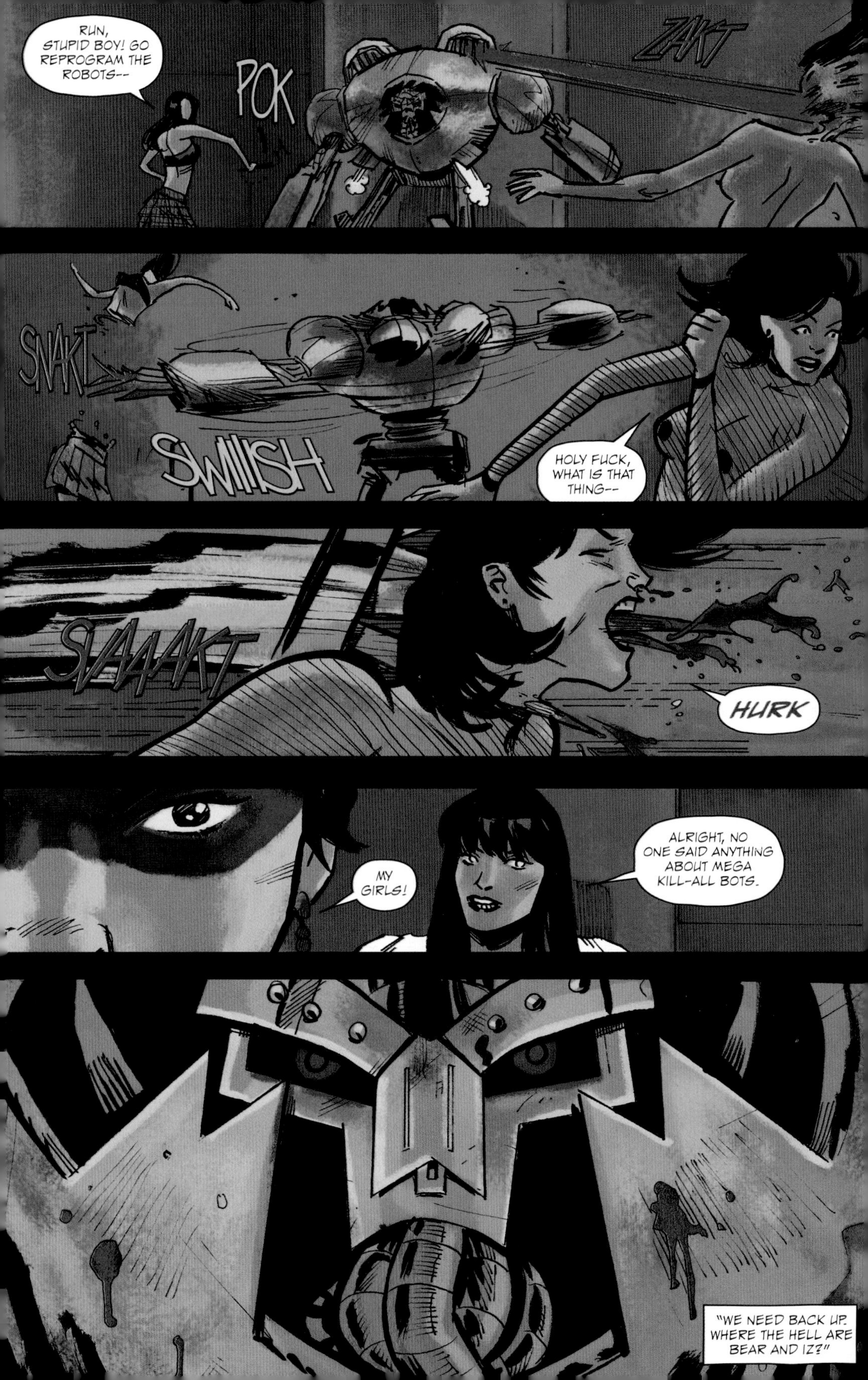
RUN, STUPID BOY! GO REPROGRAM THE ROBOTS--
POK
ZAKT
SNAKT
SWIIISH
HOLY FUCK, WHAT IS THAT THING--
SNAAKT
HURK
MY GIRLS!
ALRIGHT, NO ONE SAID ANYTHING ABOUT MEGA KILL-ALL BOTS.
"WE NEED BACK UP. WHERE THE HELL ARE BEAR AND IZ?"

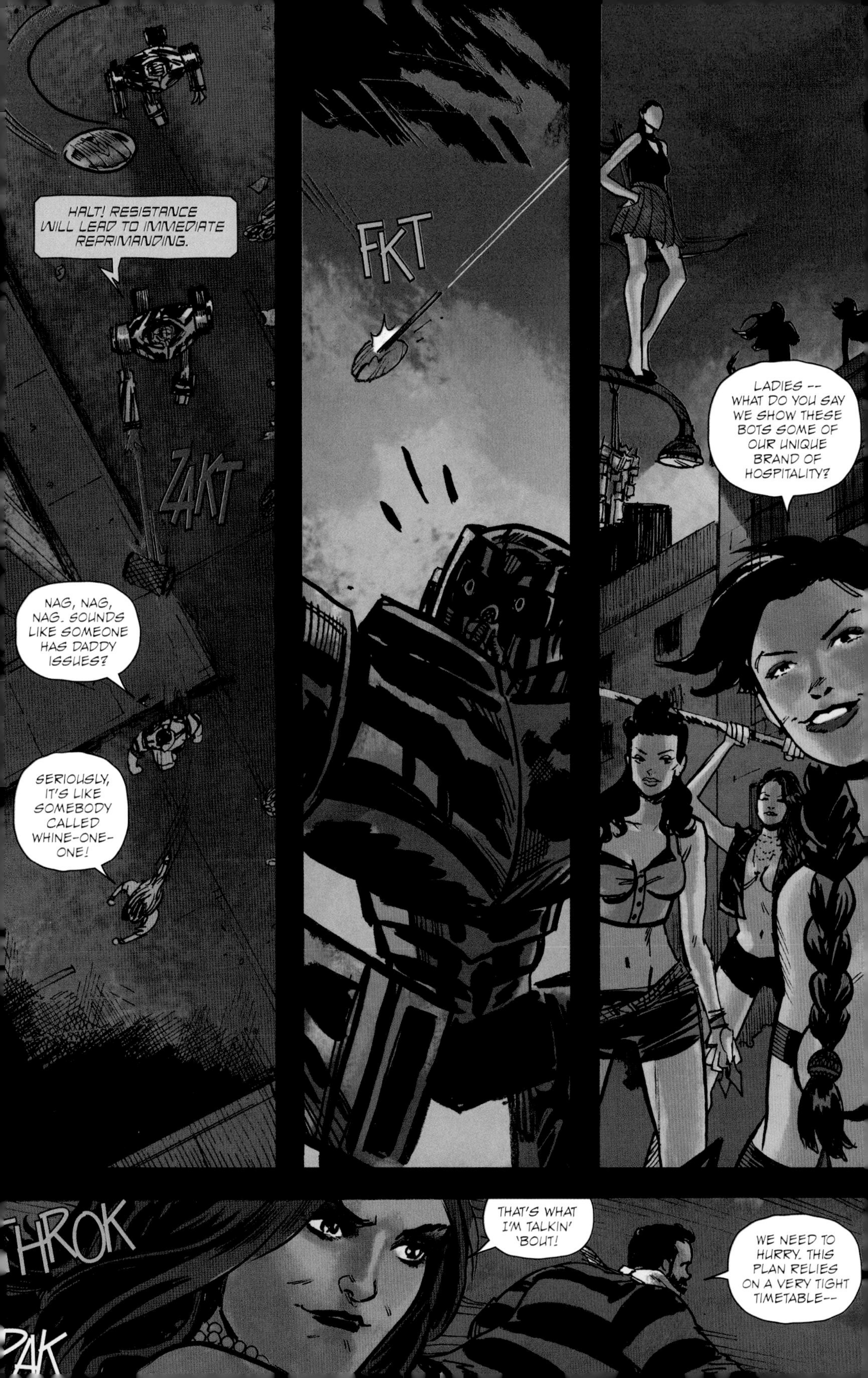
HALT! RESISTANCE WILL LEAD TO IMMEDIATE REPRIMANDING.
ZAKT
NAG, NAG, NAG. SOUNDS LIKE SOMEONE HAS DADDY ISSUES?
SERIOUSLY, IT'S LIKE SOMEBODY CALLED WHINE-ONE-ONE!
FKT
LADIES -- WHAT DO YOU SAY WE SHOW THESE BOTS SOME OF OUR UNIQUE BRAND OF HOSPITALITY?
THROK
PAK
THAT'S WHAT I'M TALKIN' 'BOUT!
WE NEED TO HURRY. THIS PLAN RELIES ON A VERY TIGHT TIMETABLE--

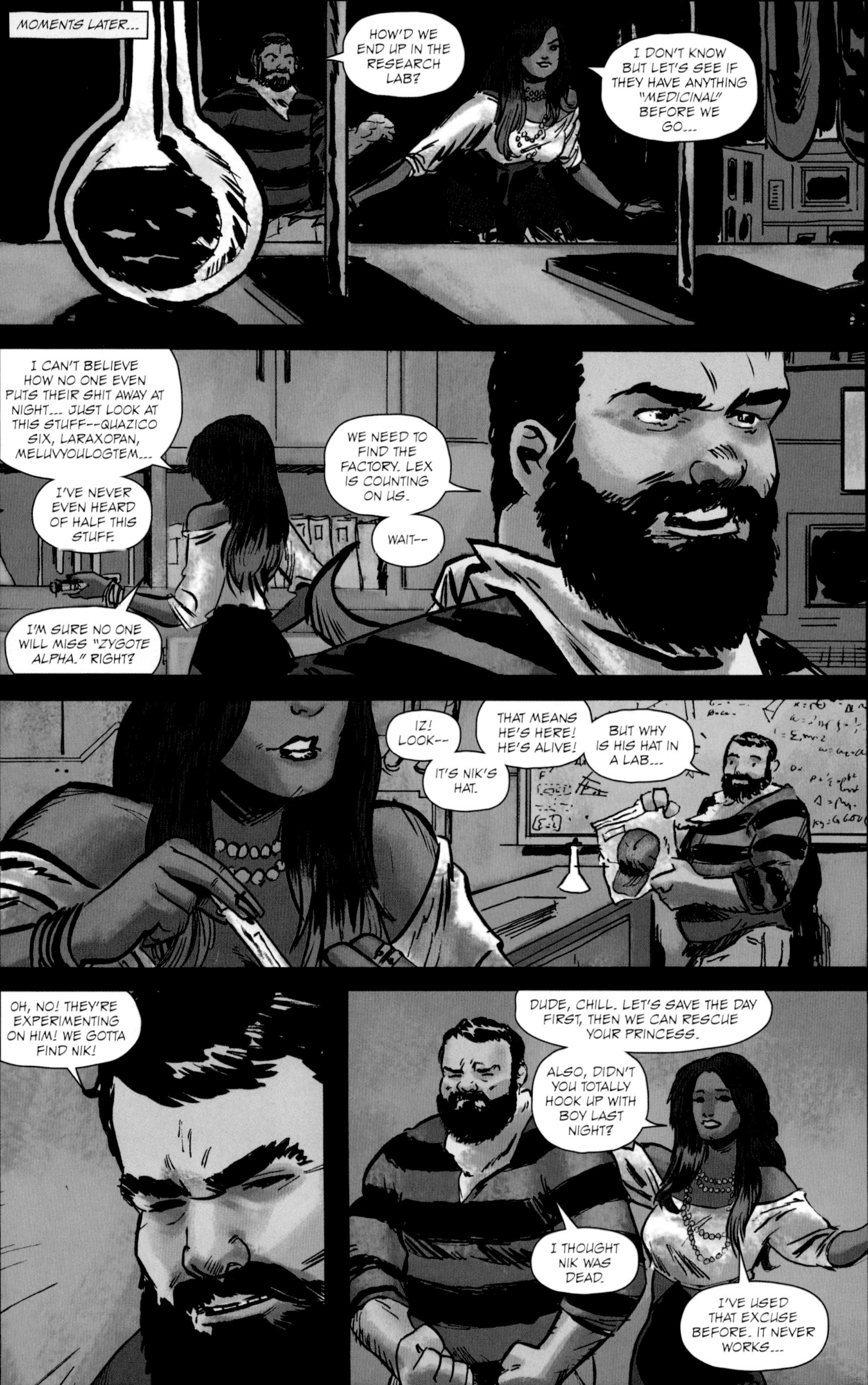
MOMENTS LATER...
HOW'D WE END UP IN THE RESEARCH LAB?
I DON'T KNOW BUT LET'S SEE IF THEY HAVE ANYTHING "MEDICINAL" BEFORE WE GO...
I CAN'T BELIEVE HOW NO ONE EVEN PUTS THEIR SHIT AWAY AT NIGHT... JUST LOOK AT THIS STUFF--QUAZICO SIX, LARAXOPAN, MELUVYOULOGTEM...
I'VE NEVER EVEN HEARD OF HALF THIS STUFF.
WE NEED TO FIND THE FACTORY. LEX IS COUNTING ON US.
WAIT--
I'M SURE NO ONE WILL MISS "ZYGOTE ALPHA." RIGHT?
IZ! LOOK--
IT'S NIK'S HAT.
THAT MEANS HE'S HERE! HE'S ALIVE!
BUT WHY IS HIS HAT IN A LAB...
OH, NO! THEY'RE EXPERIMENTING ON HIM! WE GOTTA FIND NIK!
DUDE, CHILL. LET'S SAVE THE DAY FIRST, THEN WE CAN RESCUE YOUR PRINCESS.
ALSO, DIDN'T YOU TOTALLY HOOK UP WITH BOY LAST NIGHT?
I THOUGHT NIK WAS DEAD.
I'VE USED THAT EXCUSE BEFORE. IT NEVER WORKS...

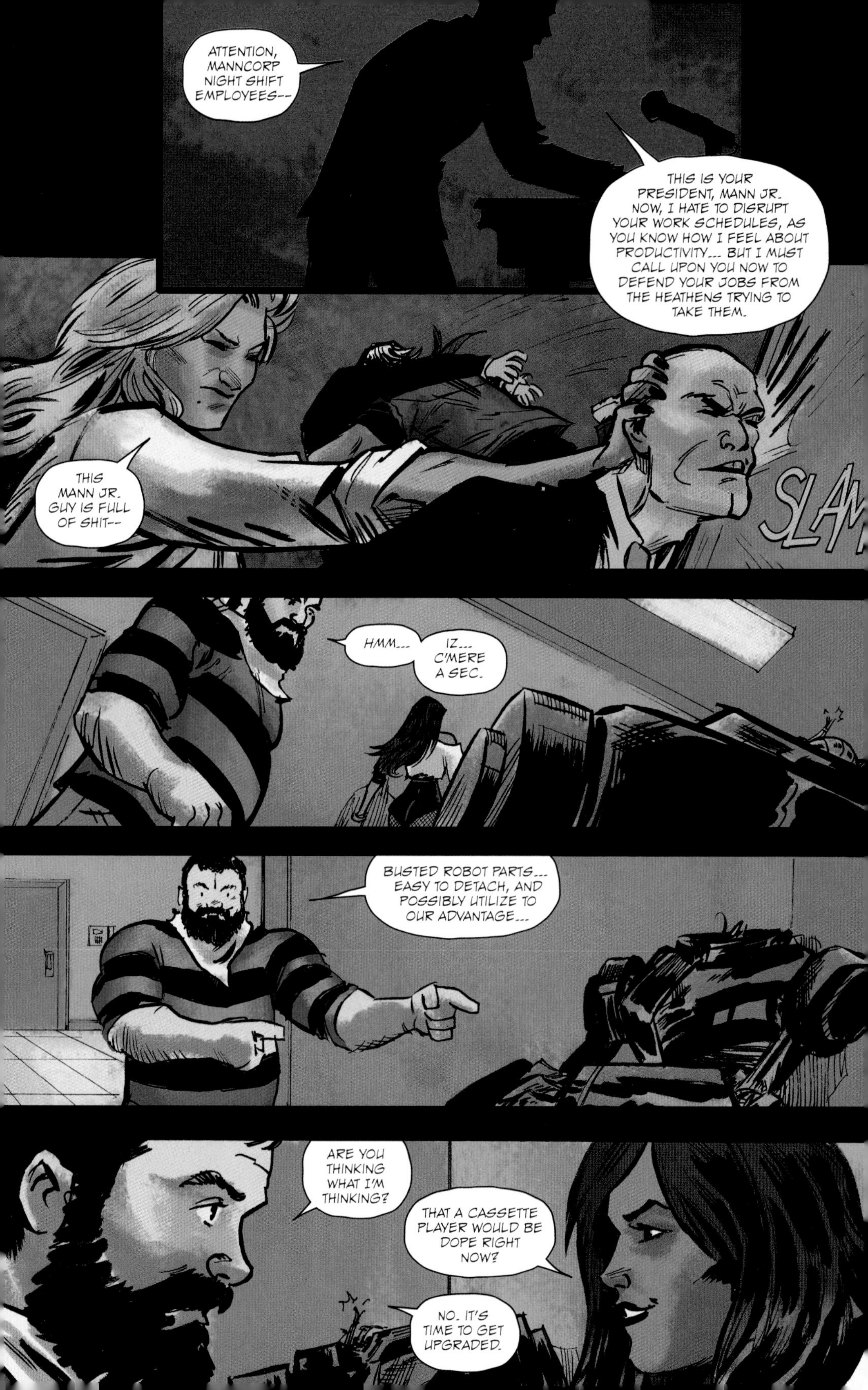
ATTENTION, MANNCORP NIGHT SHIFT EMPLOYEES--
THIS IS YOUR PRESIDENT, MANN JR. NOW, I HATE TO DISRUPT YOUR WORK SCHEDULES, AS YOU KNOW HOW I FEEL ABOUT PRODUCTIVITY... BUT I MUST CALL UPON YOU NOW TO DEFEND YOUR JOBS FROM THE HEATHENS TRYING TO TAKE THEM.
THIS MANN JR. GUY IS FULL OF SHIT--
SLAM
HMM...
IZ... C'MERE A SEC.
BUSTED ROBOT PARTS... EASY TO DETACH, AND POSSIBLY UTILIZE TO OUR ADVANTAGE...
ARE YOU THINKING WHAT I'M THINKING?
THAT A CASSETTE PLAYER WOULD BE DOPE RIGHT NOW?
NO. IT'S TIME TO GET UPGRADED.

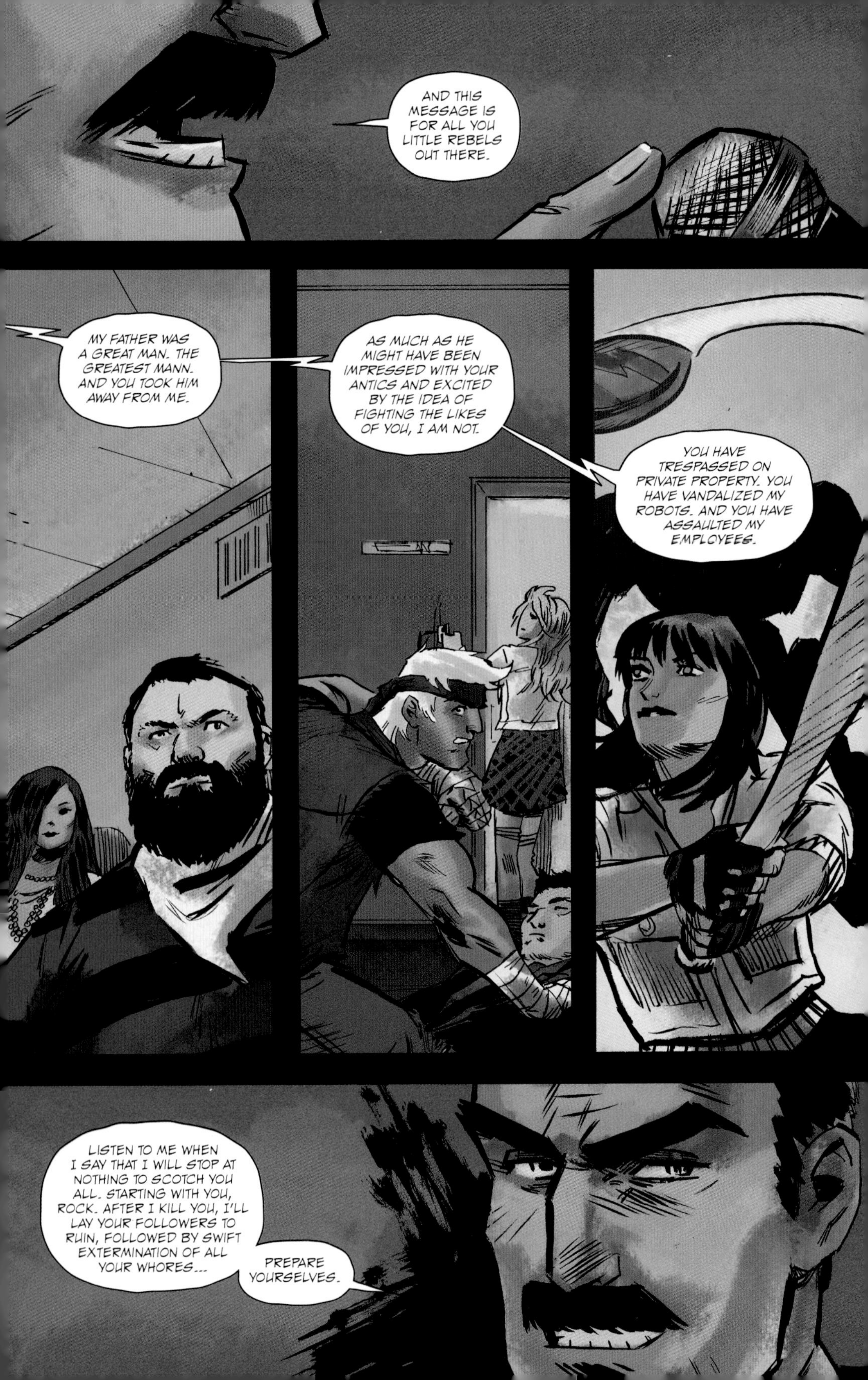
AND THIS MESSAGE IS FOR ALL YOU LITTLE REBELS OUT THERE.
MY FATHER WAS A GREAT MAN. THE GREATEST MANN. AND YOU TOOK HIM AWAY FROM ME.
AS MUCH AS HE MIGHT HAVE BEEN IMPRESSED WITH YOUR ANTICS AND EXCITED BY THE IDEA OF FIGHTING THE LIKES OF YOU, I AM NOT.
YOU HAVE TRESPASSED ON PRIVATE PROPERTY. YOU HAVE VANDALIZED MY ROBOTS. AND YOU HAVE ASSAULTED MY EMPLOYEES.
LISTEN TO ME WHEN I SAY THAT I WILL STOP AT NOTHING TO SCOTCH YOU ALL. STARTING WITH YOU, ROCK. AFTER I KILL YOU, I'LL LAY YOUR FOLLOWERS TO RUIN, FOLLOWED BY SWIFT EXTERMINATION OF ALL YOUR WHORES...
PREPARE YOURSELVES.

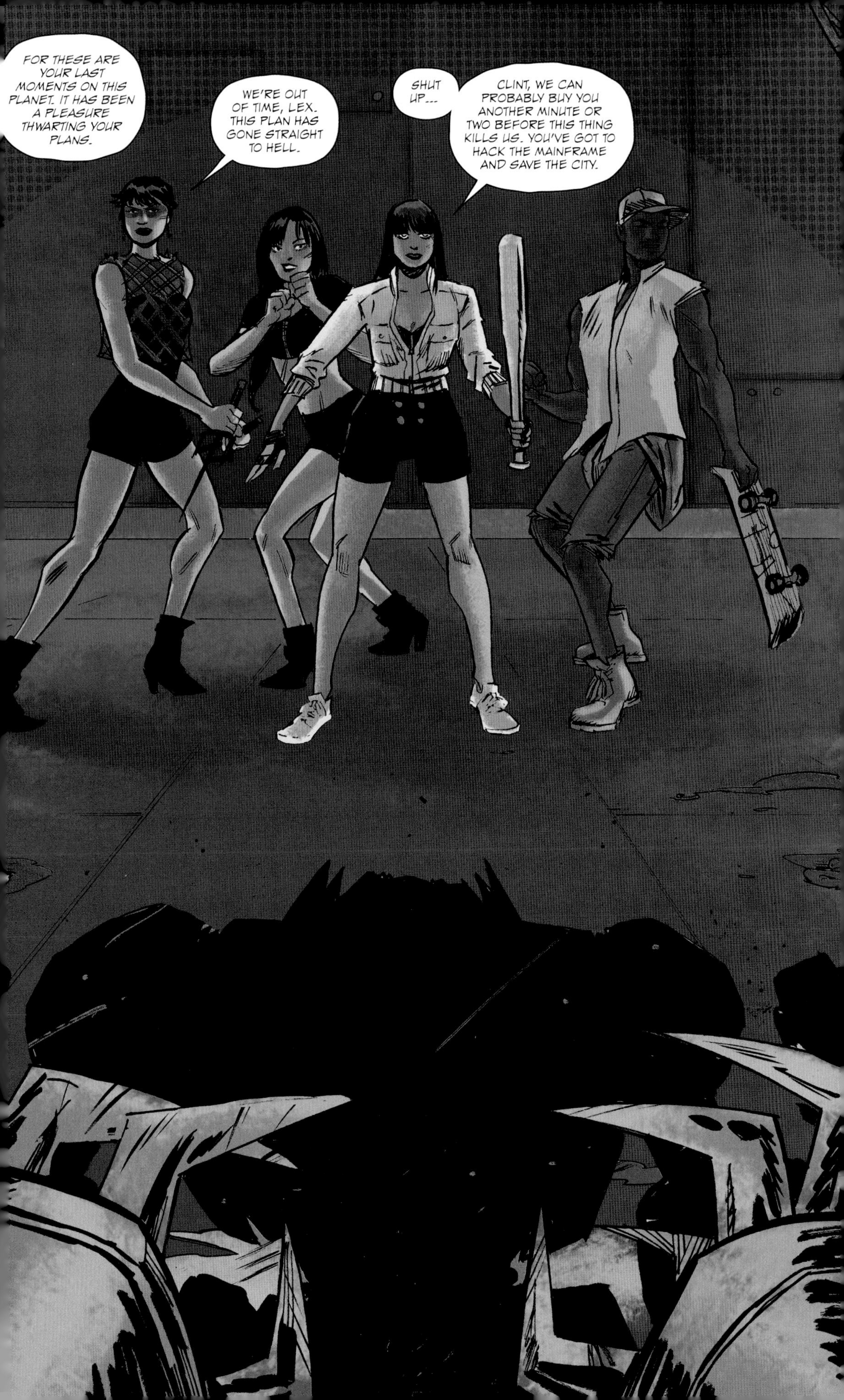
FOR THESE ARE YOUR LAST MOMENTS ON THIS PLANET. IT HAS BEEN A PLEASURE THWARTING YOUR PLANS.
WE'RE OUT OF TIME, LEX. THIS PLAN HAS GONE STRAIGHT TO HELL.
SHUT UP...
CLINT, WE CAN PROBABLY BUY YOU ANOTHER MINUTE OR TWO BEFORE THIS THING KILLS US. YOU'VE GOT TO HACK THE MAINFRAME AND SAVE THE CITY.

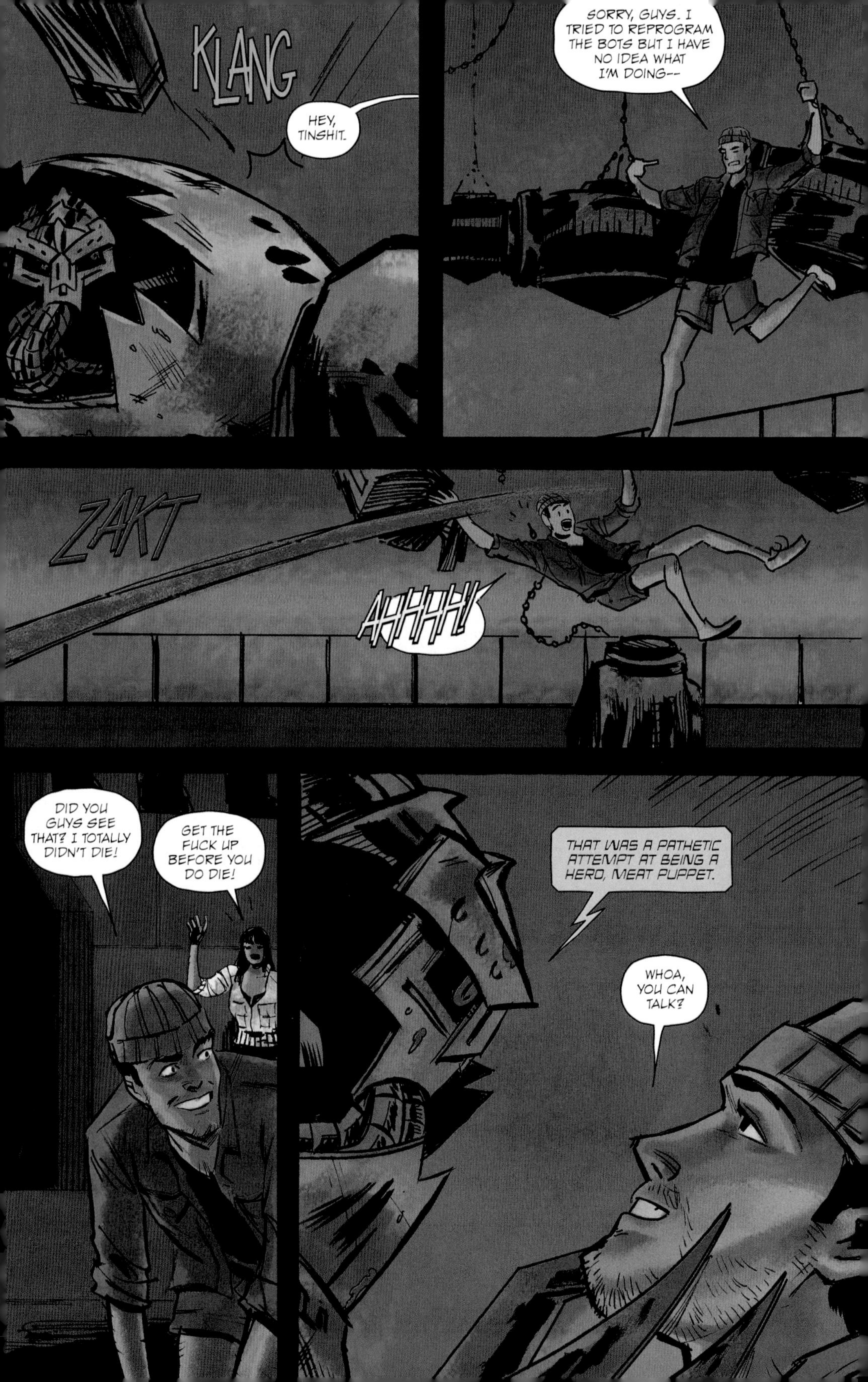
KLANG
HEY, TINSHIT.
SORRY, GUYS. I TRIED TO REPROGRAM THE BOTS BUT I HAVE NO IDEA WHAT I'M DOING--
ZAKT
AHHHH!
DID YOU GUYS SEE THAT? I TOTALLY DIDN'T DIE!
GET THE FUCK UP BEFORE YOU DO DIE!
THAT WAS A PATHETIC ATTEMPT AT BEING A HERO, MEAT PUPPET.
WHOA, YOU CAN TALK?

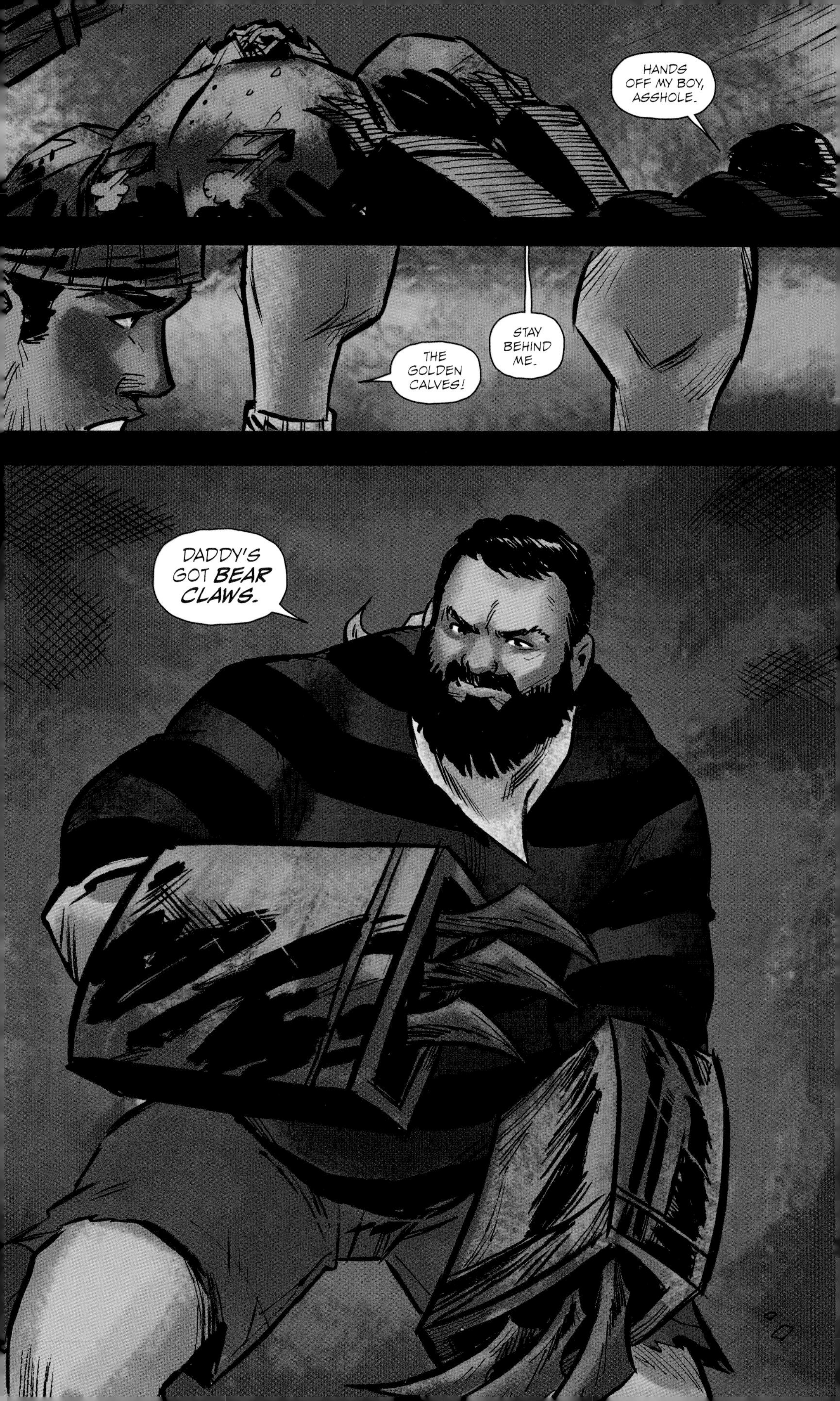
HANDS OFF MY BOY, ASSHOLE.
STAY BEHIND ME.
THE GOLDEN CALVES!
DADDY'S GOT **BEAR CLAWS.**

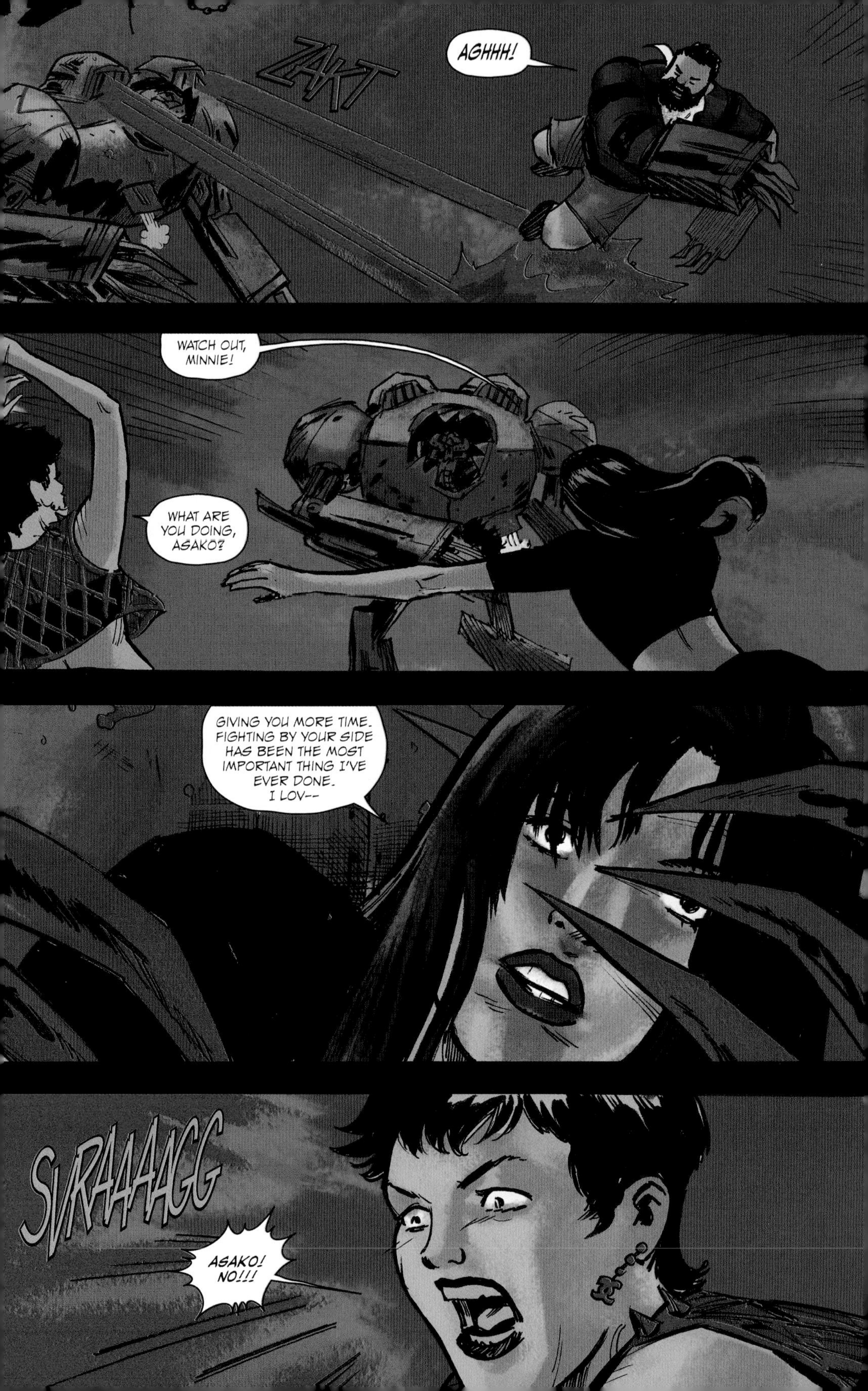
ZAKT
AGHHH!
WATCH OUT, MINNIE!
WHAT ARE YOU DOING, ASAKO?
GIVING YOU MORE TIME. FIGHTING BY YOUR SIDE HAS BEEN THE MOST IMPORTANT THING I'VE EVER DONE. I LOV--
SVRAAAAGG
ASAKO! NO!!!

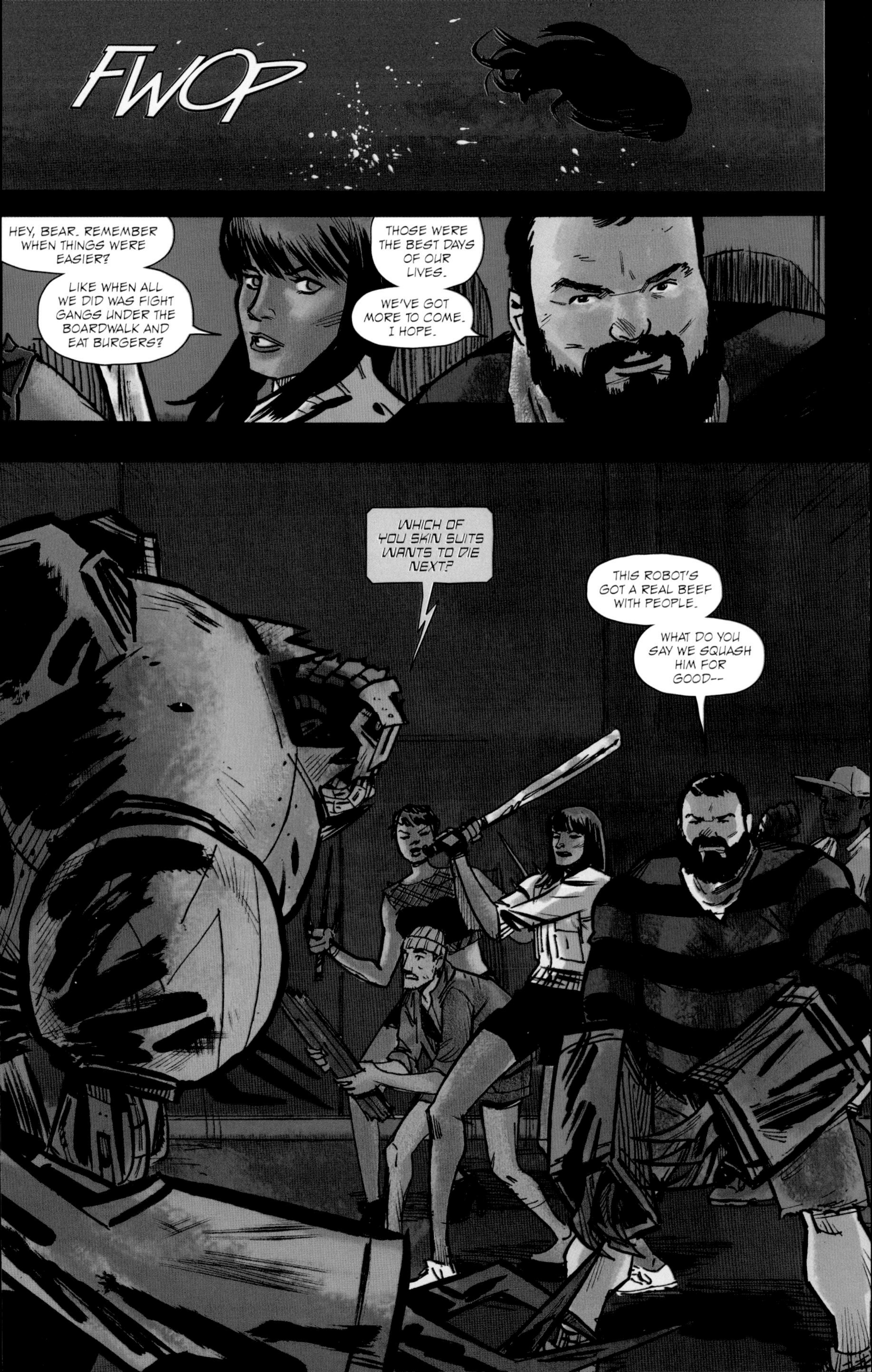
FWOP
HEY, BEAR. REMEMBER WHEN THINGS WERE EASIER?
LIKE WHEN ALL WE DID WAS FIGHT GANGS UNDER THE BOARDWALK AND EAT BURGERS?
THOSE WERE THE BEST DAYS OF OUR LIVES.
WE'VE GOT MORE TO COME. I HOPE.
WHICH OF YOU SKIN SUITS WANTS TO DIE NEXT?
THIS ROBOT'S GOT A REAL BEEF WITH PEOPLE.
WHAT DO YOU SAY WE SQUASH HIM FOR GOOD--

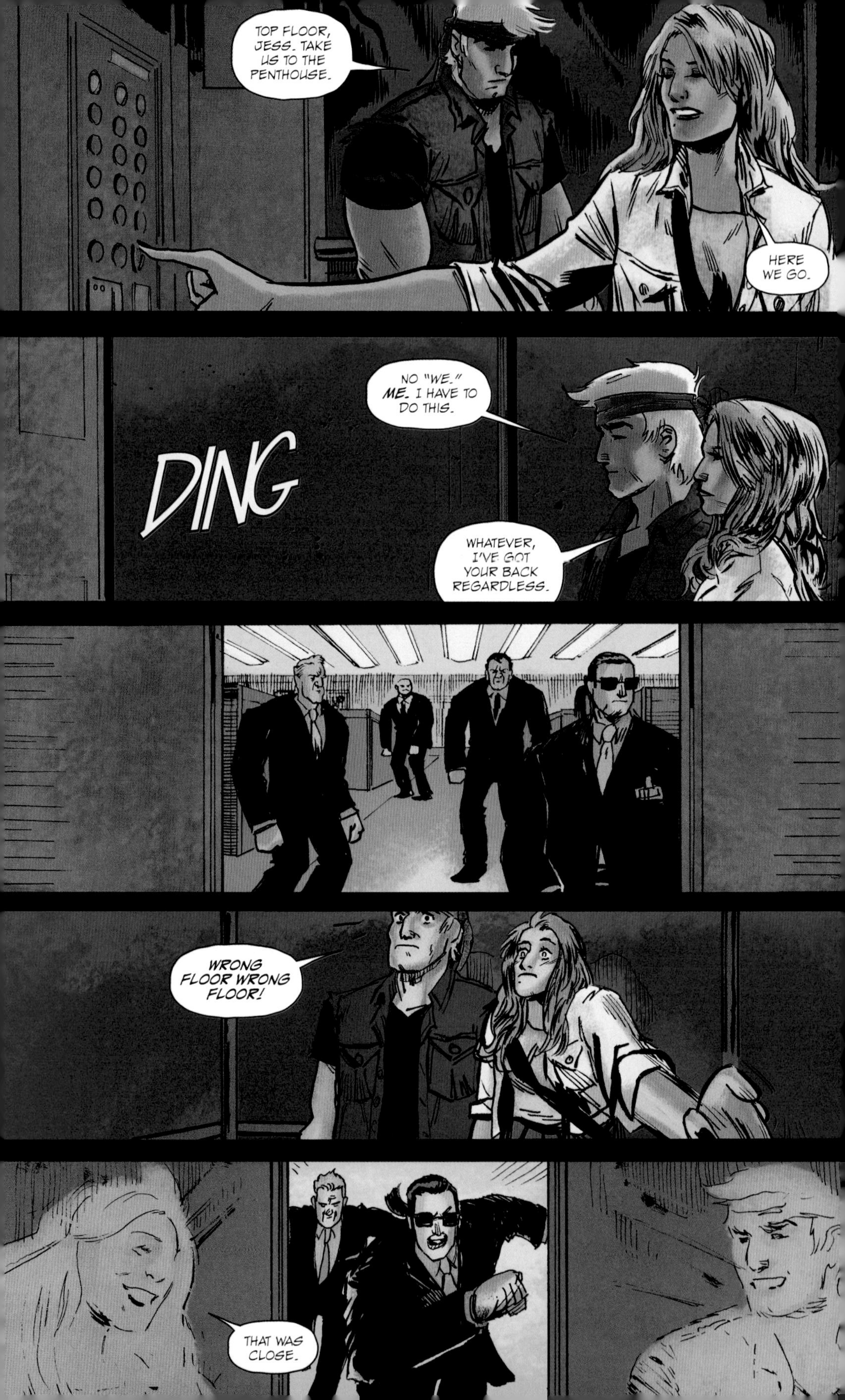
TOP FLOOR, JESS. TAKE US TO THE PENTHOUSE.
HERE WE GO.
DING
NO "WE." ME. I HAVE TO DO THIS.
WHATEVER, I'VE GOT YOUR BACK REGARDLESS.
WRONG FLOOR WRONG FLOOR!
THAT WAS CLOSE.

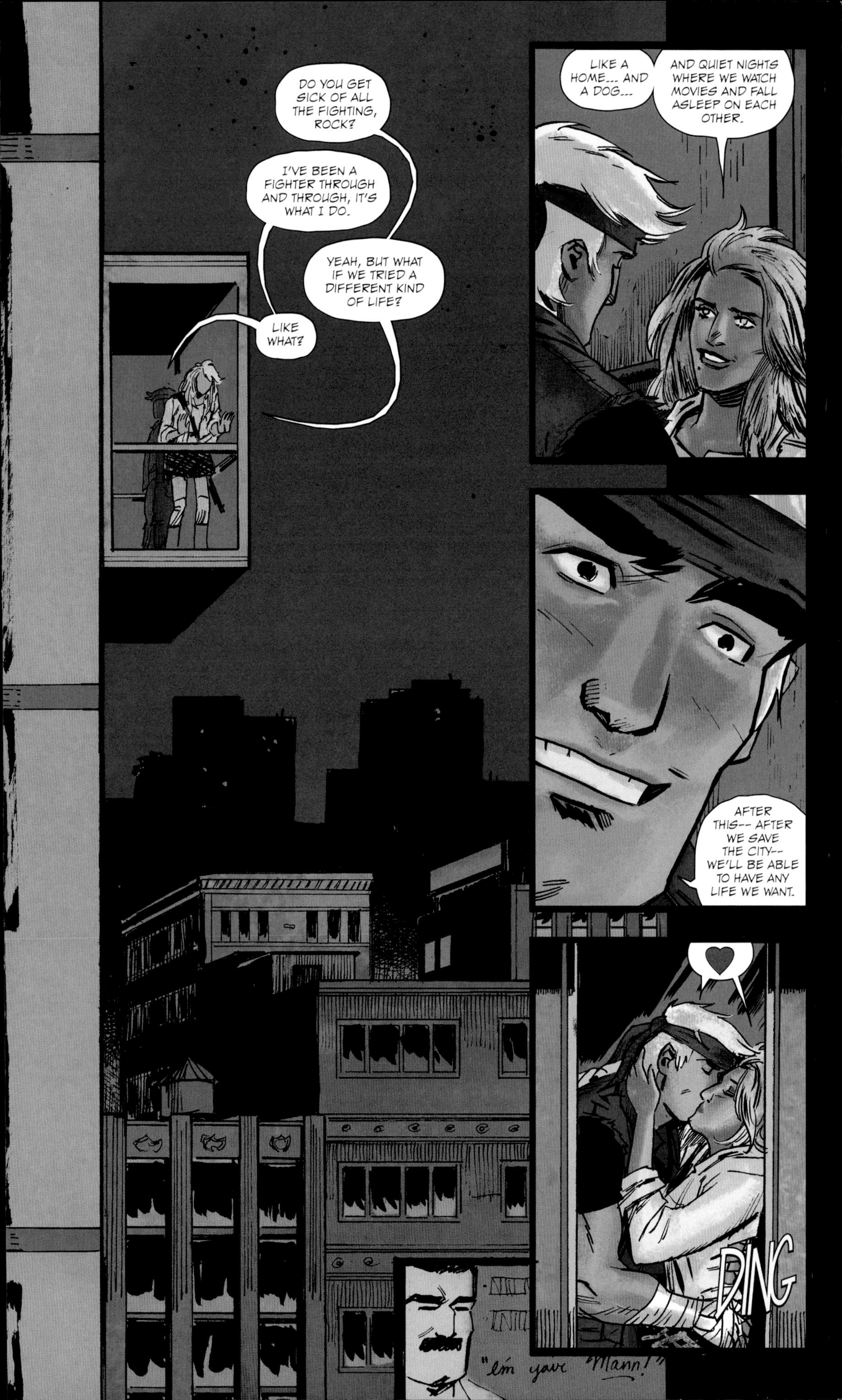

DO YOU GET SICK OF ALL THE FIGHTING, ROCK?
I'VE BEEN A FIGHTER THROUGH AND THROUGH, IT'S WHAT I DO.
YEAH, BUT WHAT IF WE TRIED A DIFFERENT KIND OF LIFE?
LIKE WHAT?
LIKE A HOME... AND A DOG...
AND QUIET NIGHTS WHERE WE WATCH MOVIES AND FALL ASLEEP ON EACH OTHER.
AFTER THIS-- AFTER WE SAVE THE CITY-- WE'LL BE ABLE TO HAVE ANY LIFE WE WANT.
DING
"I'm your Mann!"

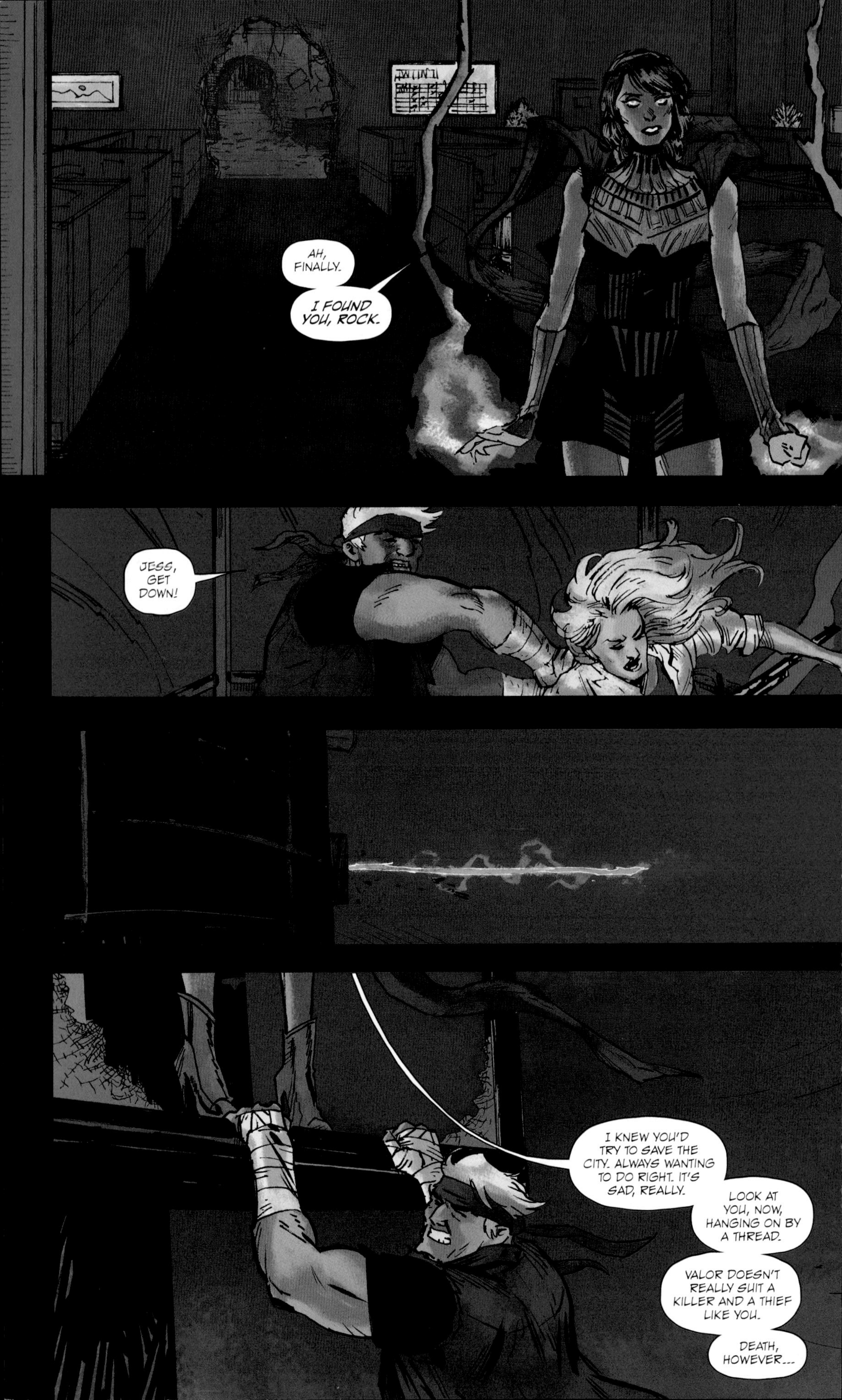
AH, FINALLY.
I FOUND YOU, ROCK.
JESS, GET DOWN!
I KNEW YOU'D TRY TO SAVE THE CITY. ALWAYS WANTING TO DO RIGHT. IT'S SAD, REALLY.
LOOK AT YOU, NOW, HANGING ON BY A THREAD.
VALOR DOESN'T REALLY SUIT A KILLER AND A THIEF LIKE YOU.
DEATH, HOWEVER...

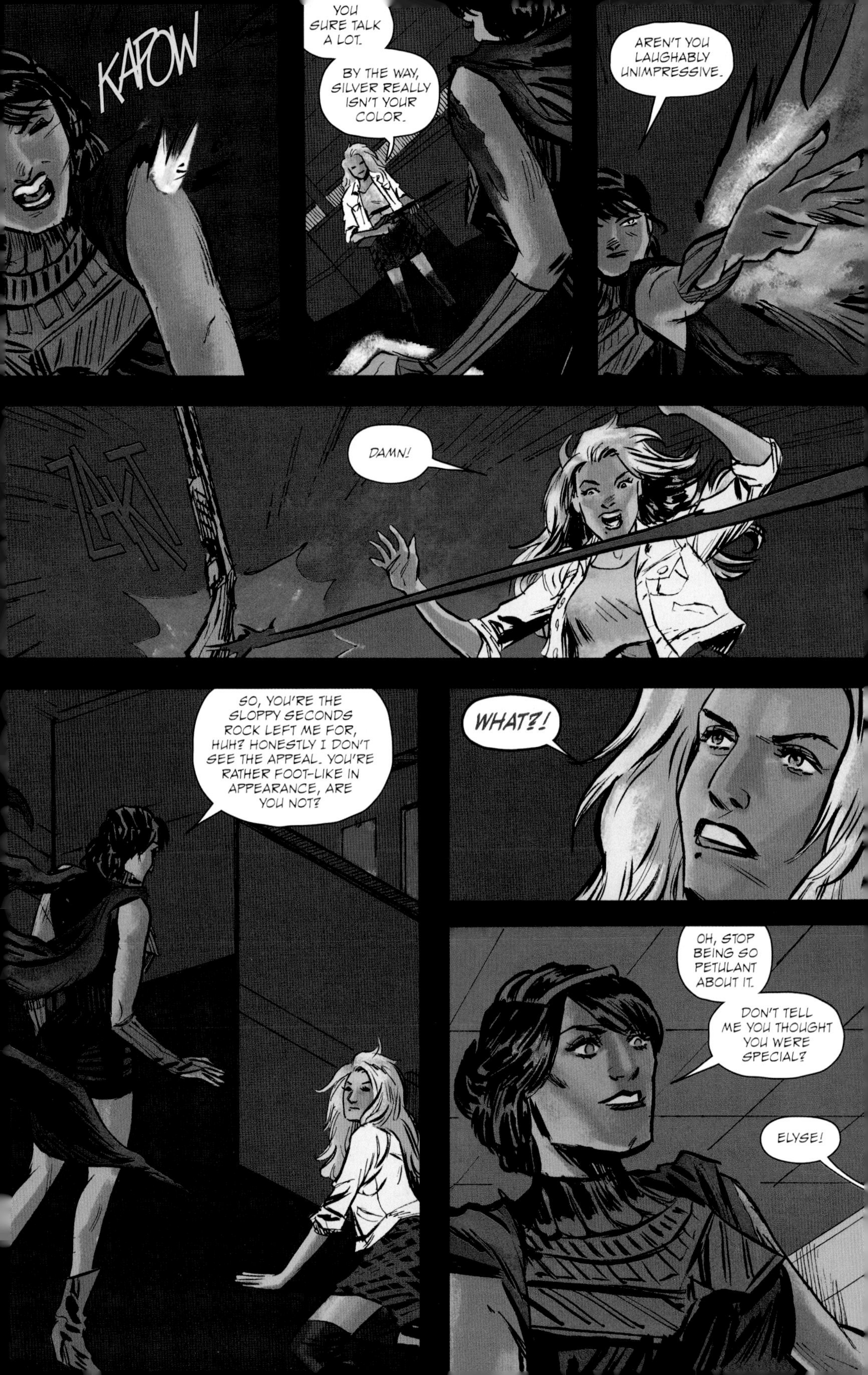

KAPOW
YOU SURE TALK A LOT.
BY THE WAY, SILVER REALLY ISN'T YOUR COLOR.
AREN'T YOU LAUGHABLY UNIMPRESSIVE.
ZAKT
DAMN!
SO, YOU'RE THE SLOPPY SECONDS ROCK LEFT ME FOR, HUH? HONESTLY I DON'T SEE THE APPEAL. YOU'RE RATHER FOOT-LIKE IN APPEARANCE, ARE YOU NOT?
WHAT?!
OH, STOP BEING SO PETULANT ABOUT IT.
DON'T TELL ME YOU THOUGHT YOU WERE SPECIAL?
ELYSE!

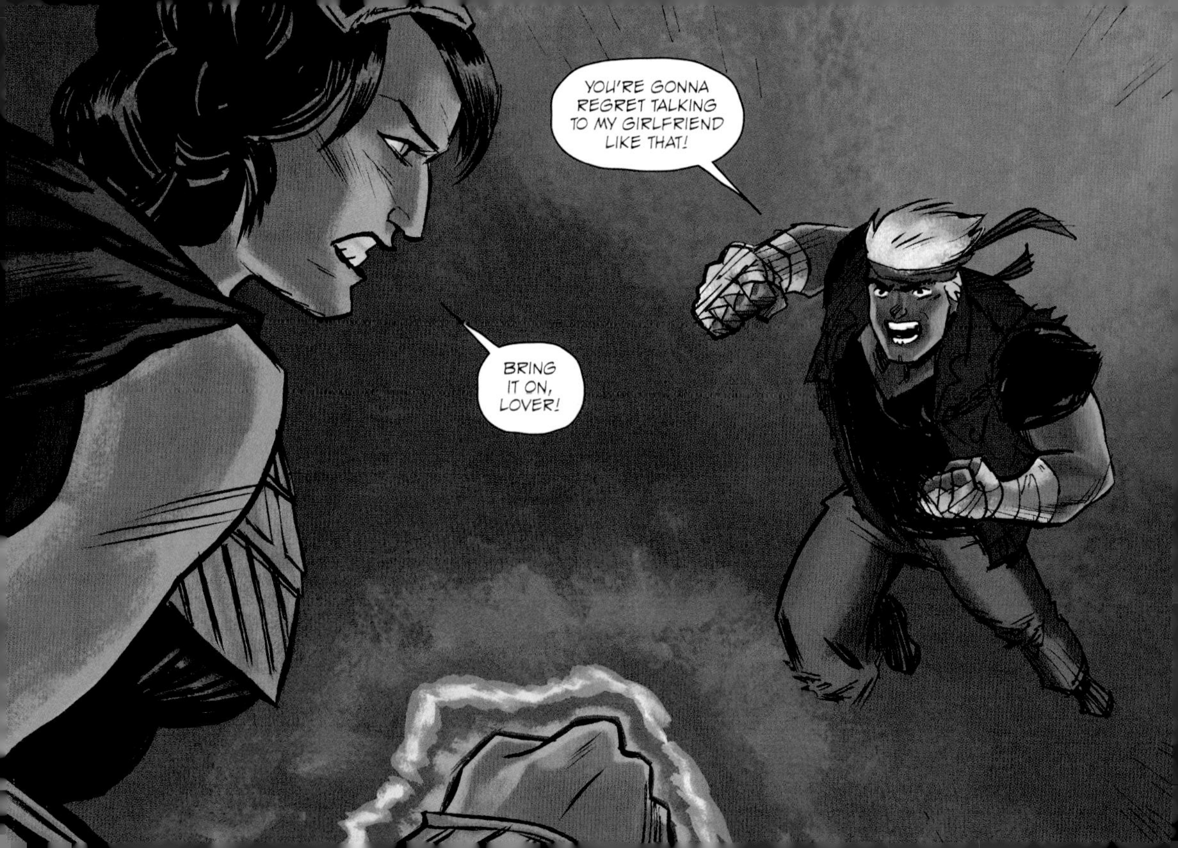
YOU'RE GONNA REGRET TALKING TO MY GIRLFRIEND LIKE THAT!
BRING IT ON, LOVER!

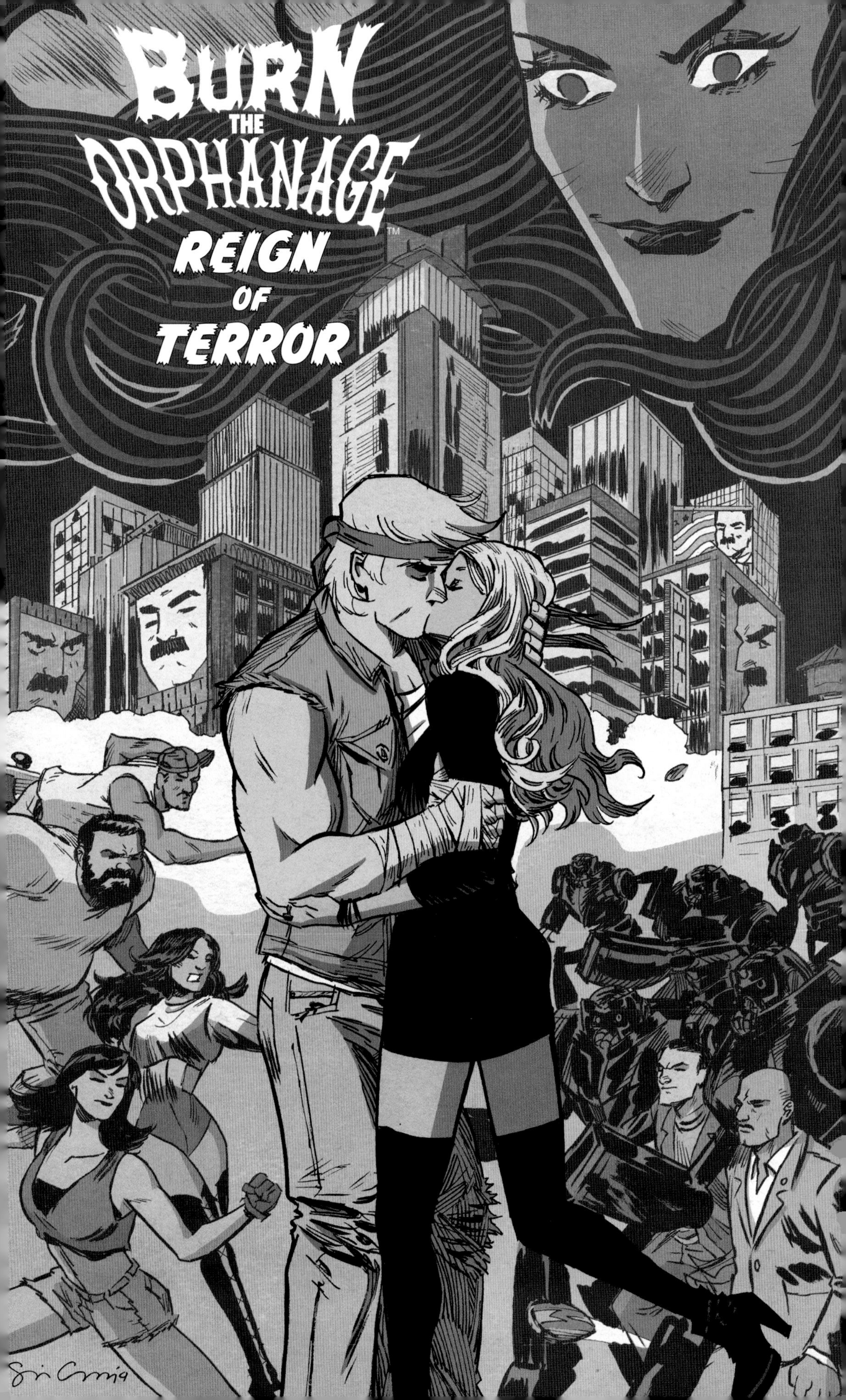
BURN THE ORPHANAGE™
REIGN OF TERROR

CHAPTER FIVE

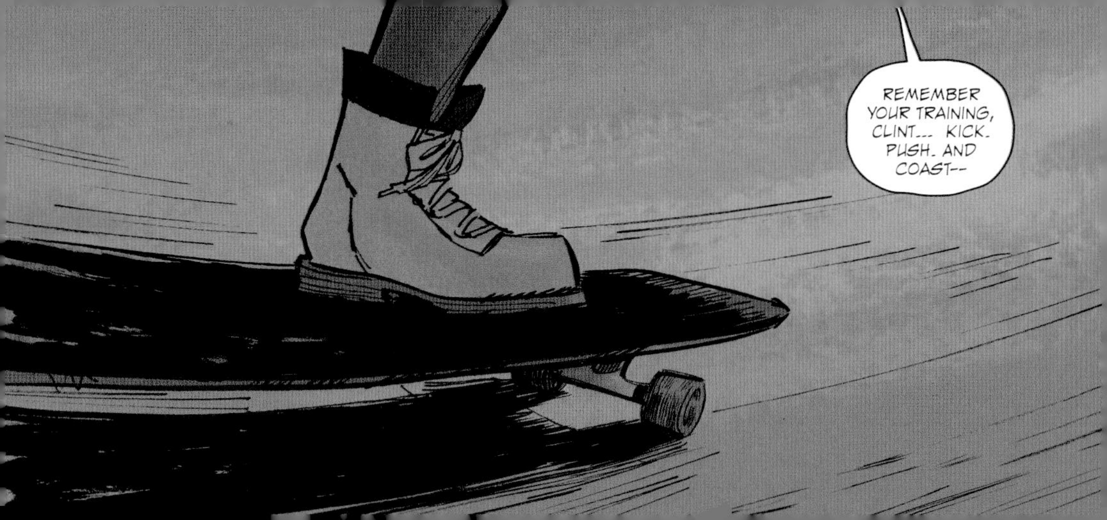
REMEMBER YOUR TRAINING, CLINT... KICK. PUSH. AND COAST--

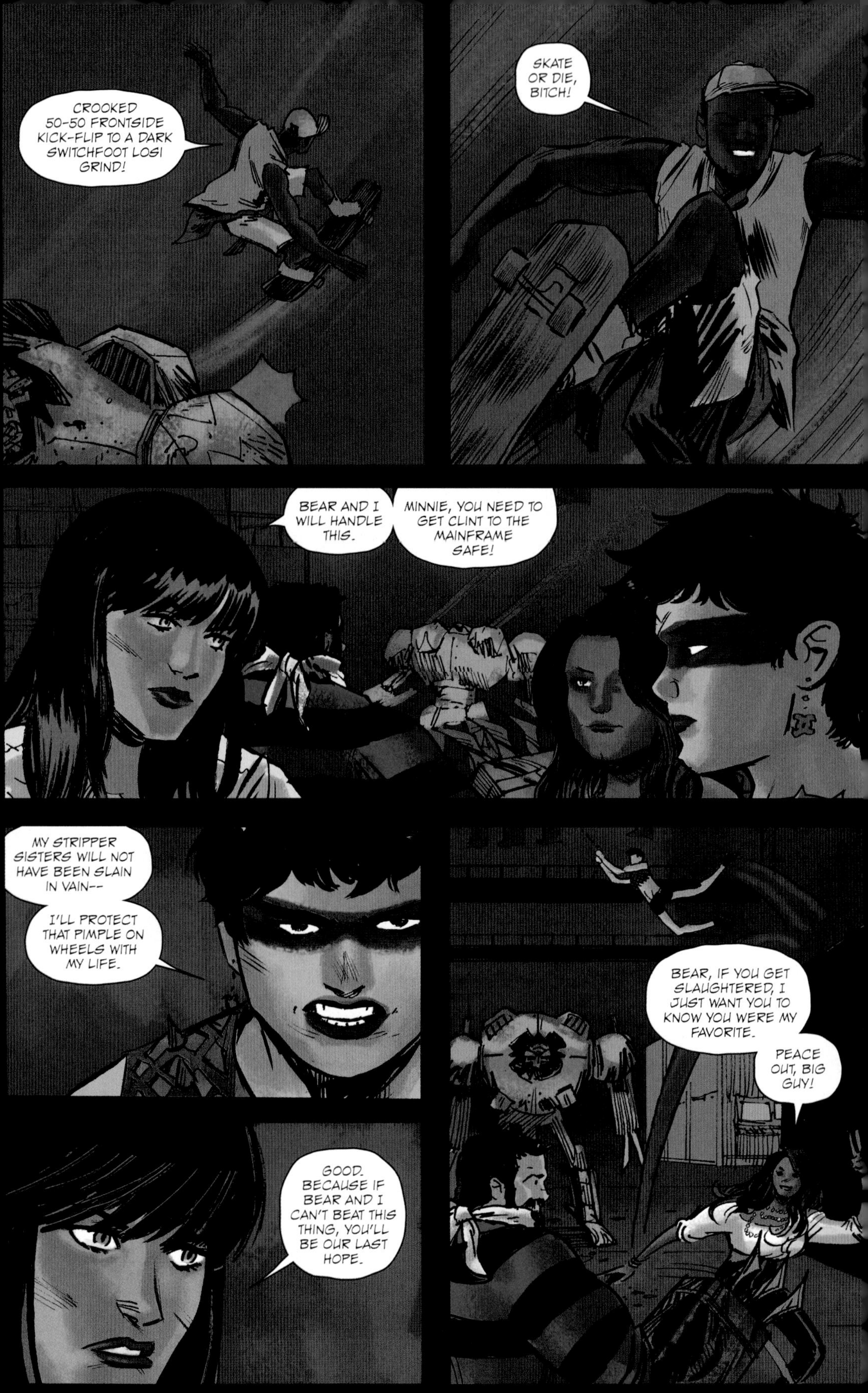
CROOKED 50-50 FRONTSIDE KICK-FLIP TO A DARK SWITCHFOOT LOSI GRIND!
SKATE OR DIE, BITCH!
BEAR AND I WILL HANDLE THIS.
MINNIE, YOU NEED TO GET CLINT TO THE MAINFRAME SAFE!
MY STRIPPER SISTERS WILL NOT HAVE BEEN SLAIN IN VAIN--
I'LL PROTECT THAT PIMPLE ON WHEELS WITH MY LIFE.
GOOD. BECAUSE IF BEAR AND I CAN'T BEAT THIS THING, YOU'LL BE OUR LAST HOPE.
BEAR, IF YOU GET SLAUGHTERED, I JUST WANT YOU TO KNOW YOU WERE MY FAVORITE.
PEACE OUT, BIG GUY!

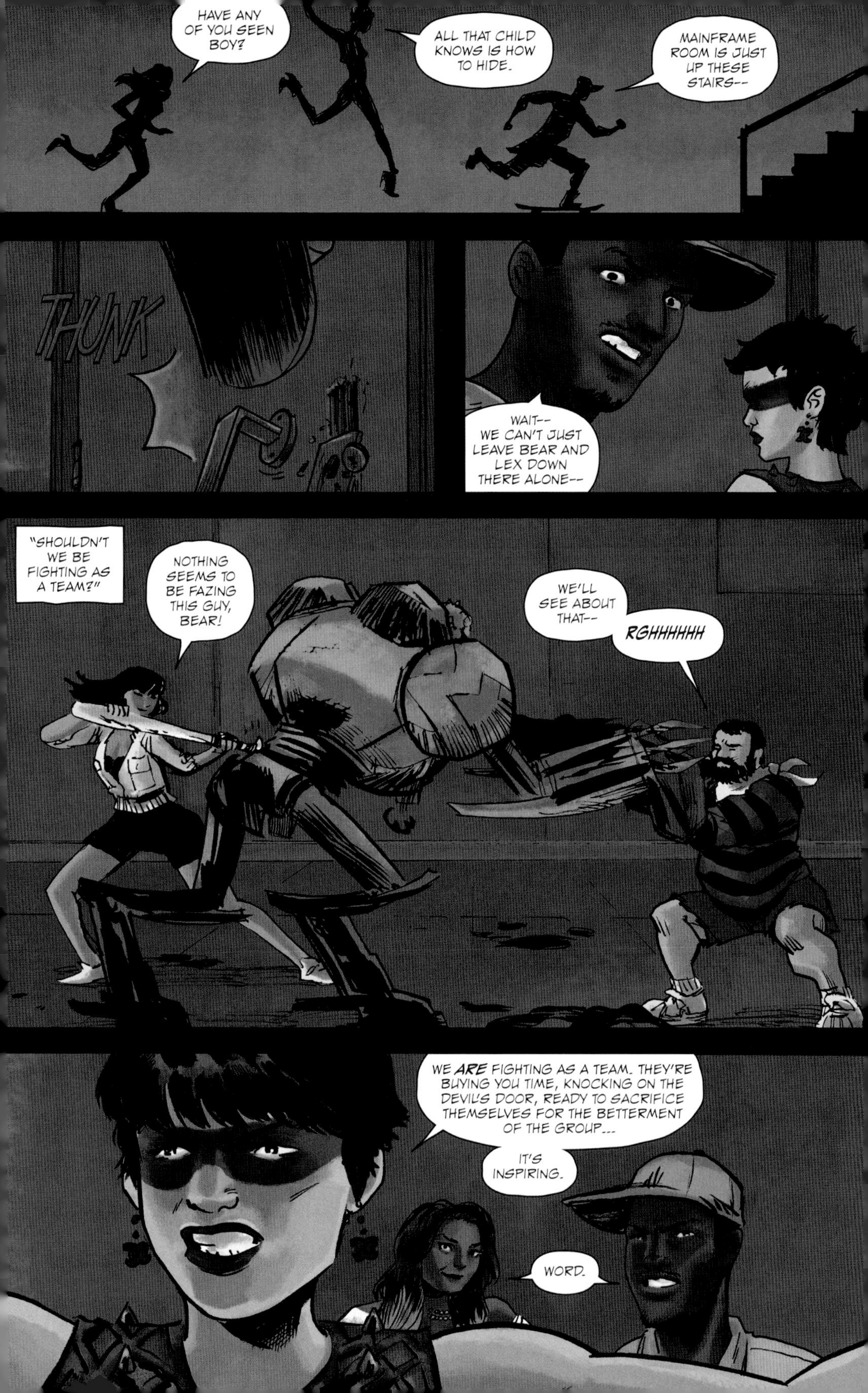
HAVE ANY OF YOU SEEN BOY?
ALL THAT CHILD KNOWS IS HOW TO HIDE.
MAINFRAME ROOM IS JUST UP THESE STAIRS--
THUNK
WAIT-- WE CAN'T JUST LEAVE BEAR AND LEX DOWN THERE ALONE--
"SHOULDN'T WE BE FIGHTING AS A TEAM?"
NOTHING SEEMS TO BE FAZING THIS GUY, BEAR!
WE'LL SEE ABOUT THAT--
RGHHHHHH
WE *ARE* FIGHTING AS A TEAM. THEY'RE BUYING YOU TIME, KNOCKING ON THE DEVIL'S DOOR, READY TO SACRIFICE THEMSELVES FOR THE BETTERMENT OF THE GROUP...
IT'S INSPIRING.
WORD.

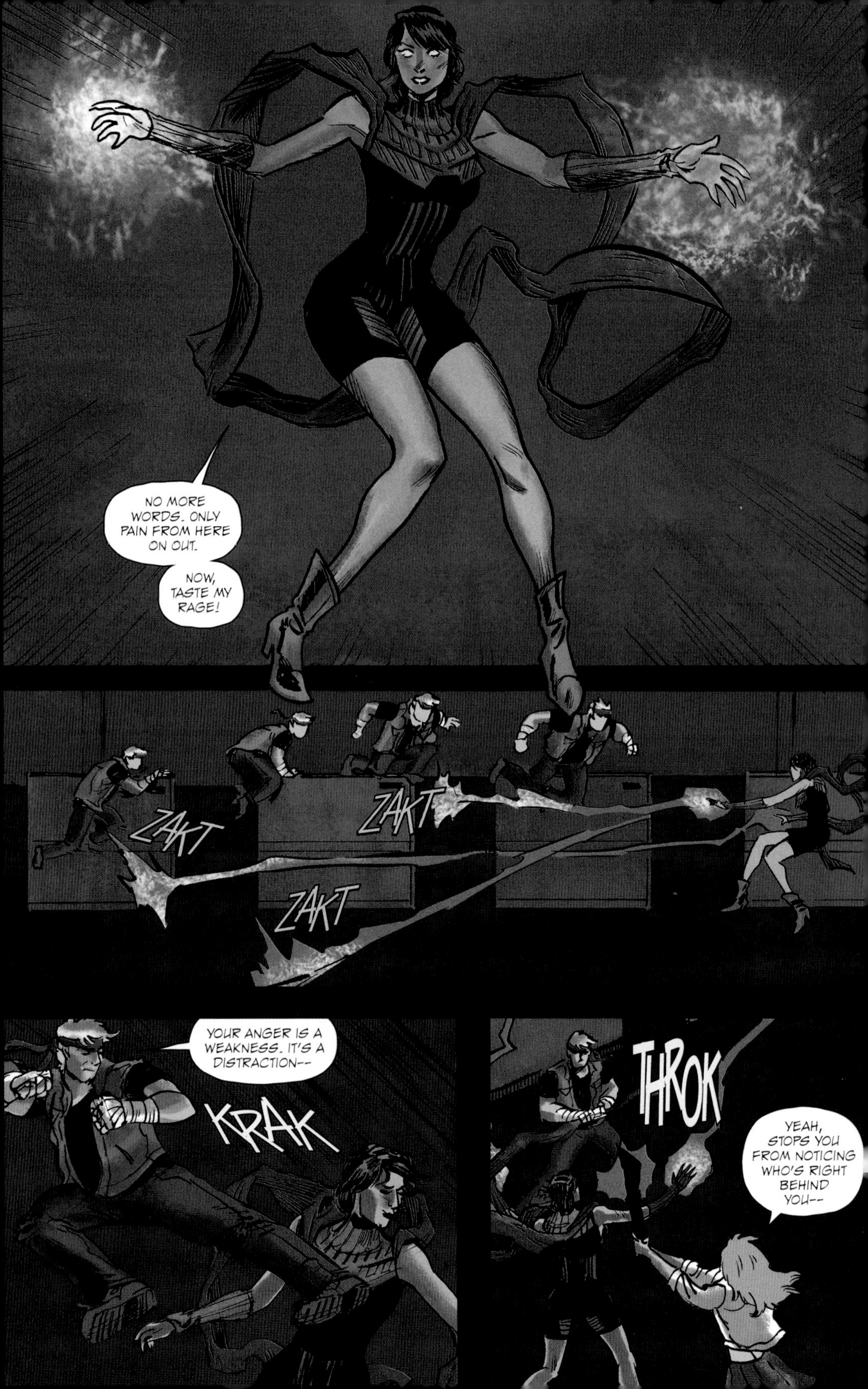
NO MORE WORDS. ONLY PAIN FROM HERE ON OUT.
NOW, TASTE MY RAGE!
ZAKT
ZAKT
ZAKT
YOUR ANGER IS A WEAKNESS. IT'S A DISTRACTION--
KRAK
THROK
YEAH, STOPS YOU FROM NOTICING WHO'S RIGHT BEHIND YOU--

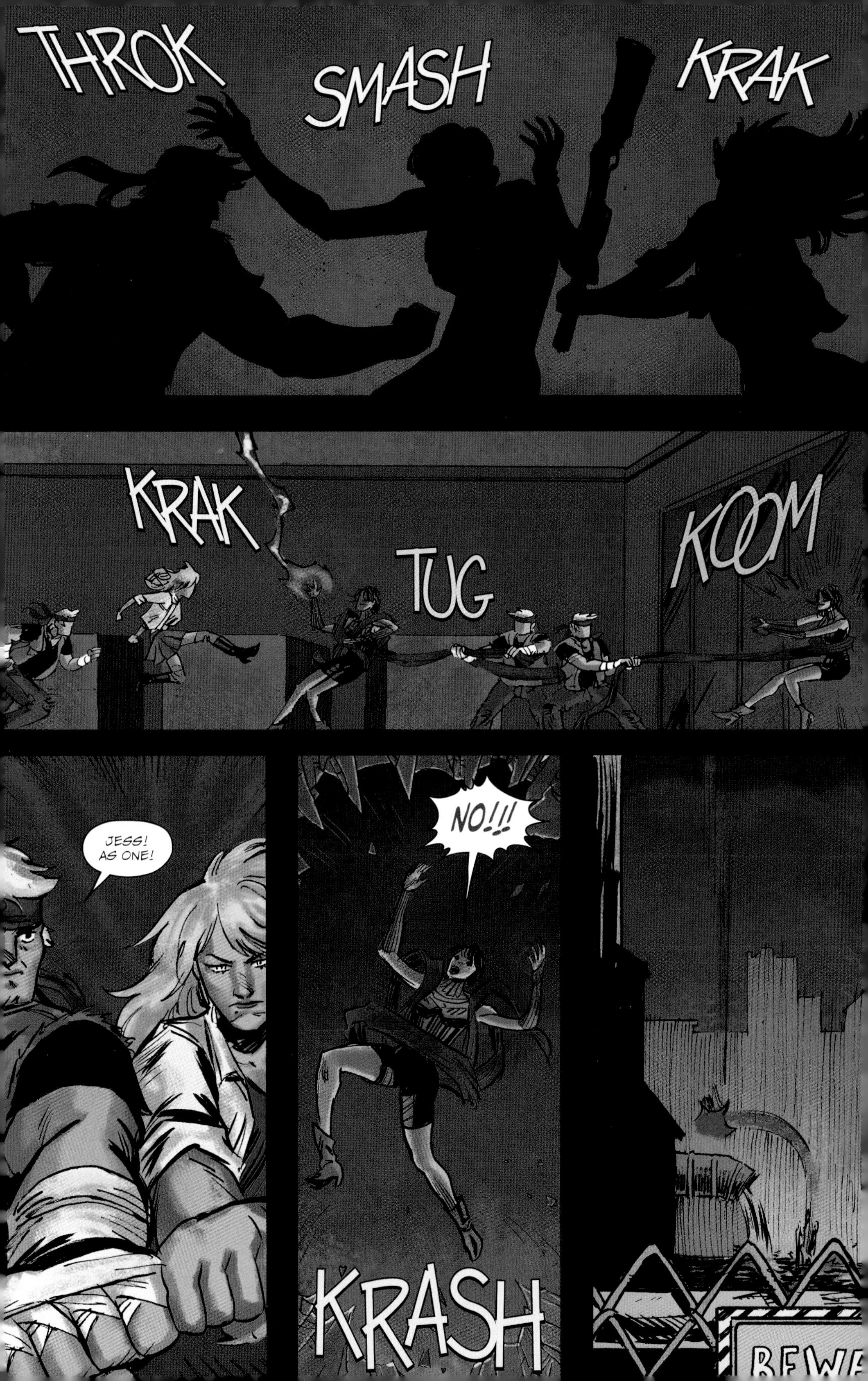
THROK
SMASH
KRAK
KRAK
TUG
KOOM
JESS! AS ONE!
NO!!!
KRASH
BEWA

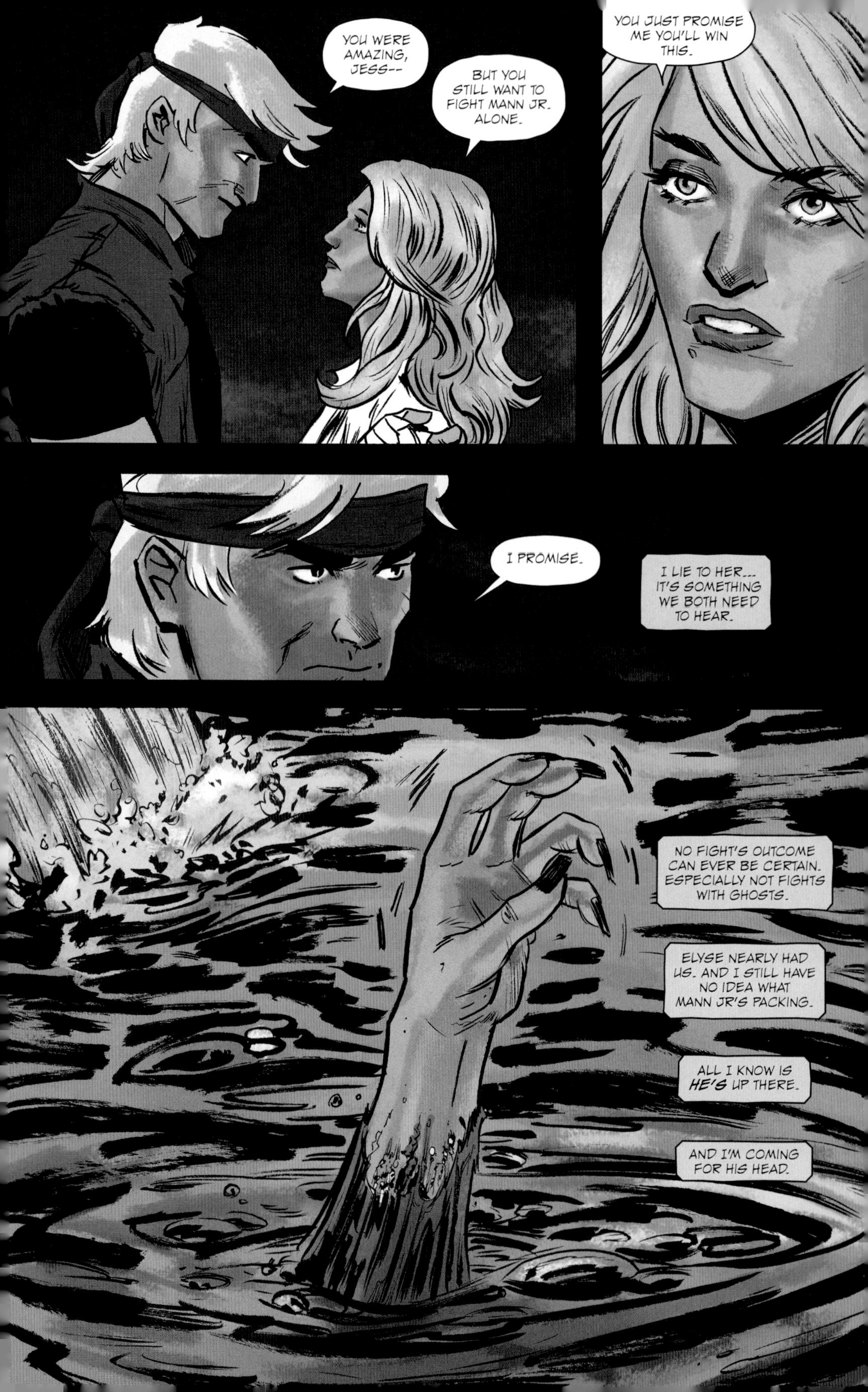
YOU WERE AMAZING, JESS--
BUT YOU STILL WANT TO FIGHT MANN JR. ALONE.
YOU JUST PROMISE ME YOU'LL WIN THIS.
I PROMISE.
I LIE TO HER... IT'S SOMETHING WE BOTH NEED TO HEAR.
NO FIGHT'S OUTCOME CAN EVER BE CERTAIN. ESPECIALLY NOT FIGHTS WITH GHOSTS.
ELYSE NEARLY HAD US. AND I STILL HAVE NO IDEA WHAT MANN JR'S PACKING.
ALL I KNOW IS HE'S UP THERE.
AND I'M COMING FOR HIS HEAD.

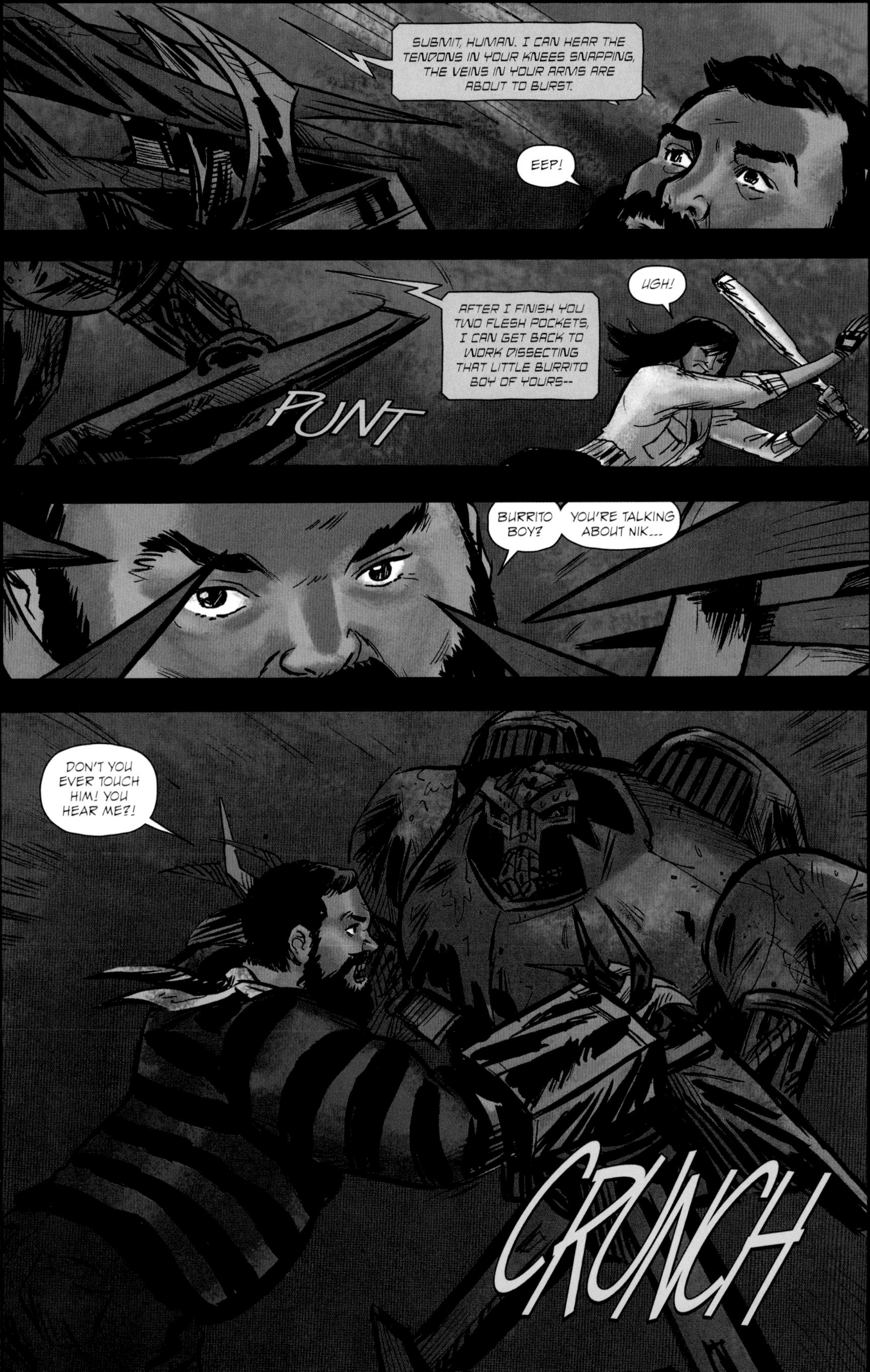
SUBMIT, HUMAN. I CAN HEAR THE TENDONS IN YOUR KNEES SNAPPING, THE VEINS IN YOUR ARMS ARE ABOUT TO BURST.
EEP!
UGH!
AFTER I FINISH YOU TWO FLESH POCKETS, I CAN GET BACK TO WORK DISSECTING THAT LITTLE BURRITO BOY OF YOURS--
PUNT
BURRITO BOY?
YOU'RE TALKING ABOUT NIK...
DON'T YOU EVER TOUCH HIM! YOU HEAR ME?!
CRUNCH

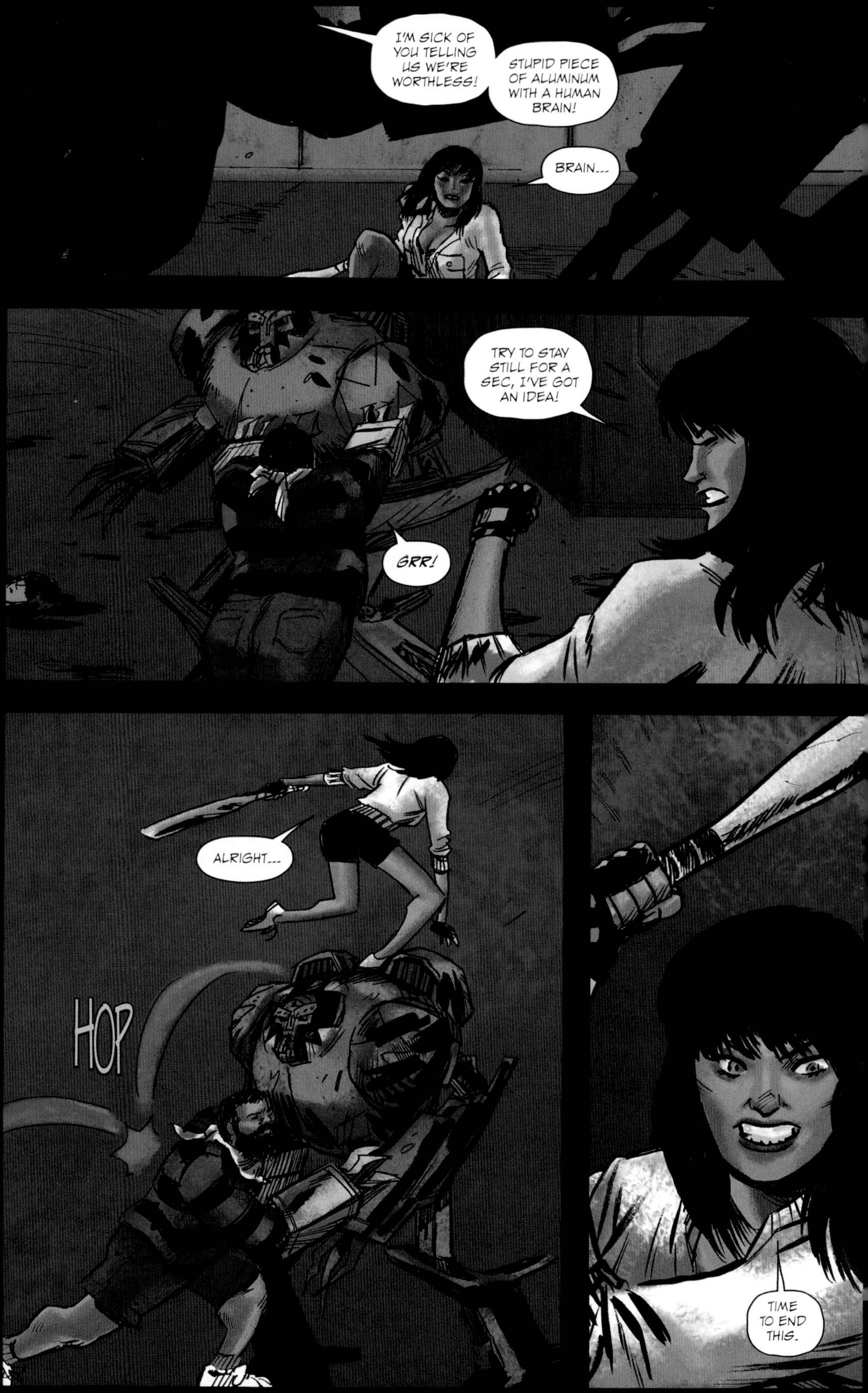
I'M SICK OF YOU TELLING US WE'RE WORTHLESS!
STUPID PIECE OF ALUMINUM WITH A HUMAN BRAIN!
BRAIN...
TRY TO STAY STILL FOR A SEC, I'VE GOT AN IDEA!
GRR!
ALRIGHT...
HOP
TIME TO END THIS.

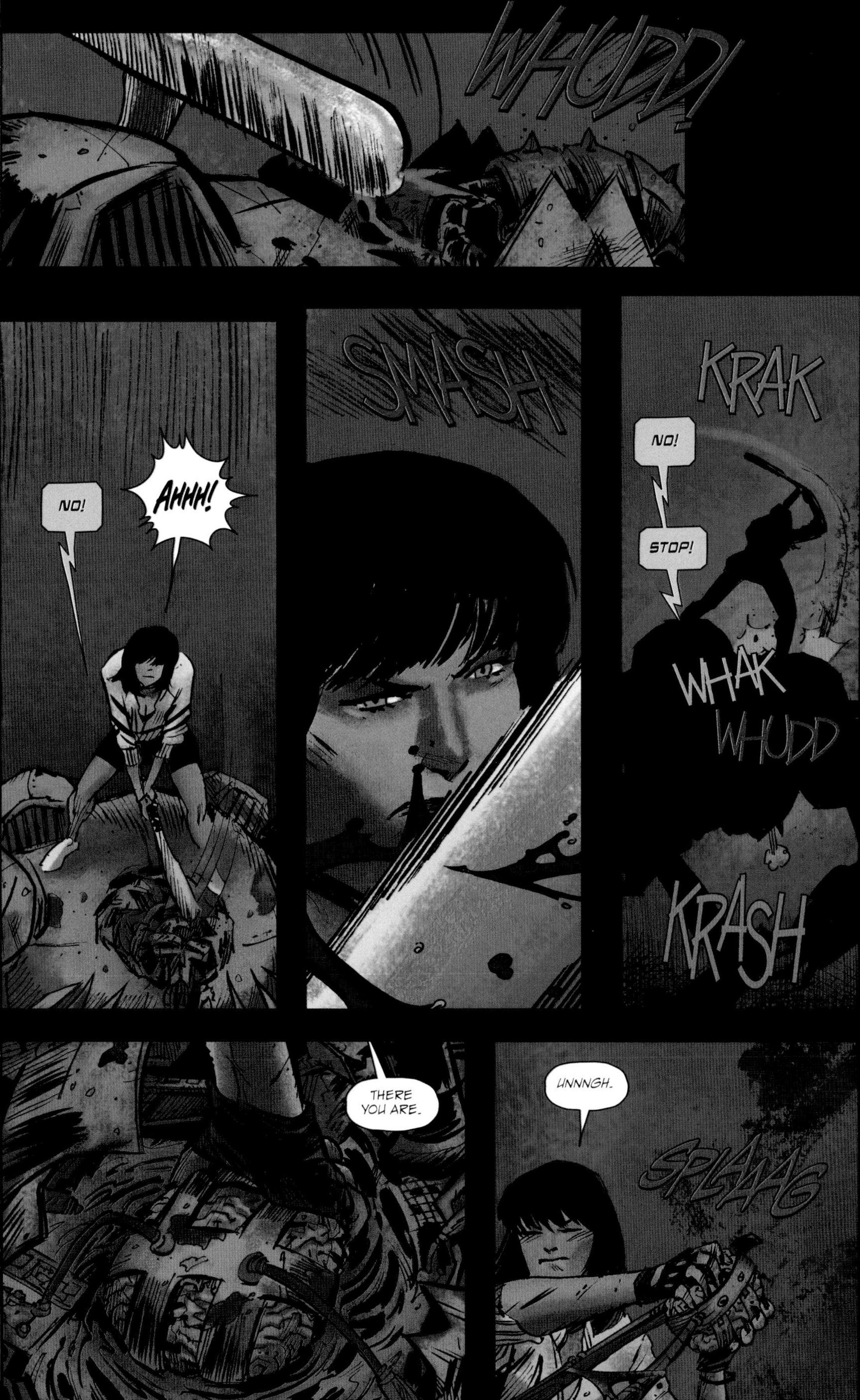
WHUDD!
NO!
AHHH!
SMASH
KRAK
NO!
STOP!
WHAK
WHUDD
KRASH
THERE YOU ARE.
UNNNGH.
SPLAAAG

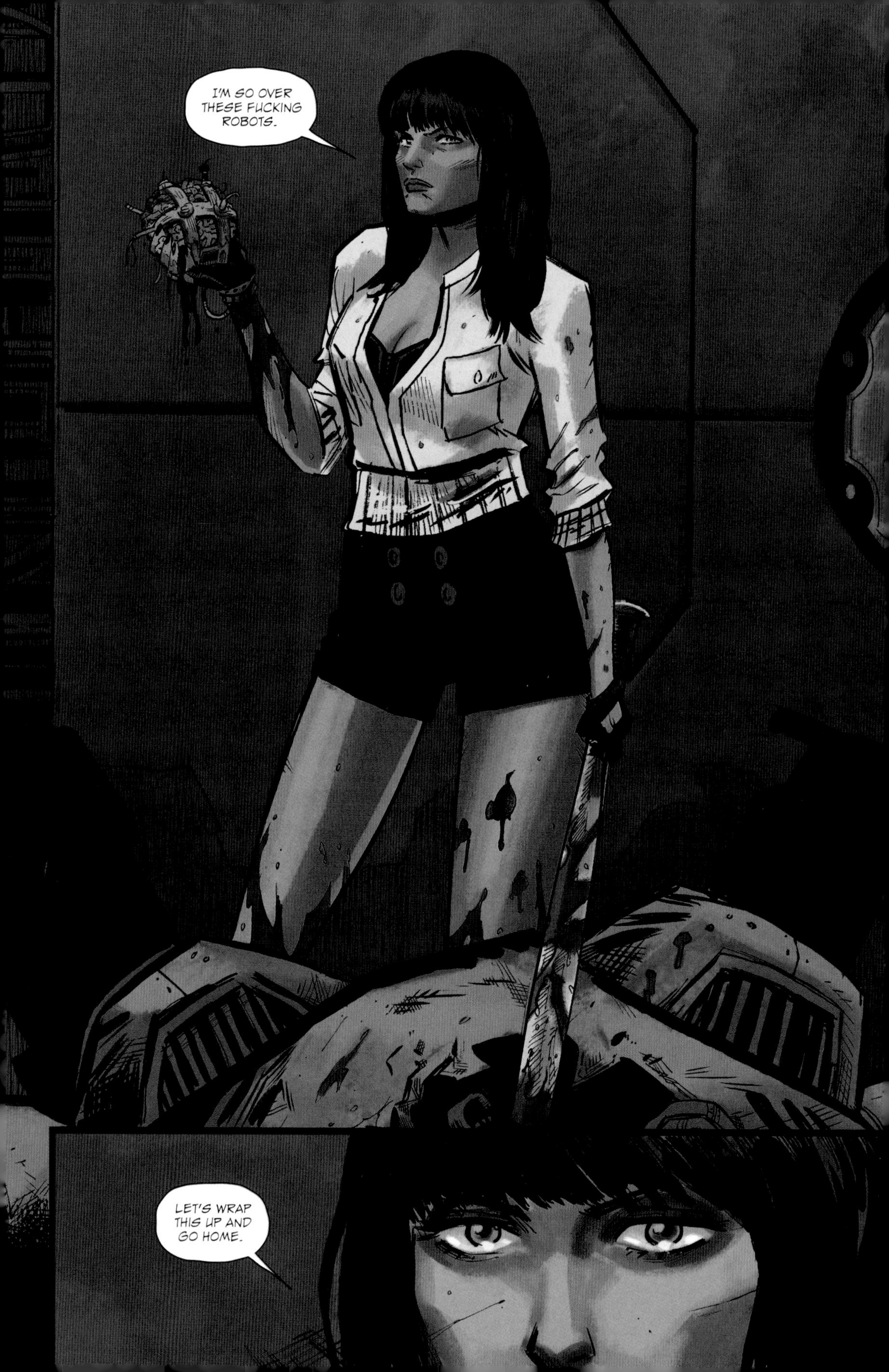
I'M SO OVER THESE FUCKING ROBOTS.
LET'S WRAP THIS UP AND GO HOME.

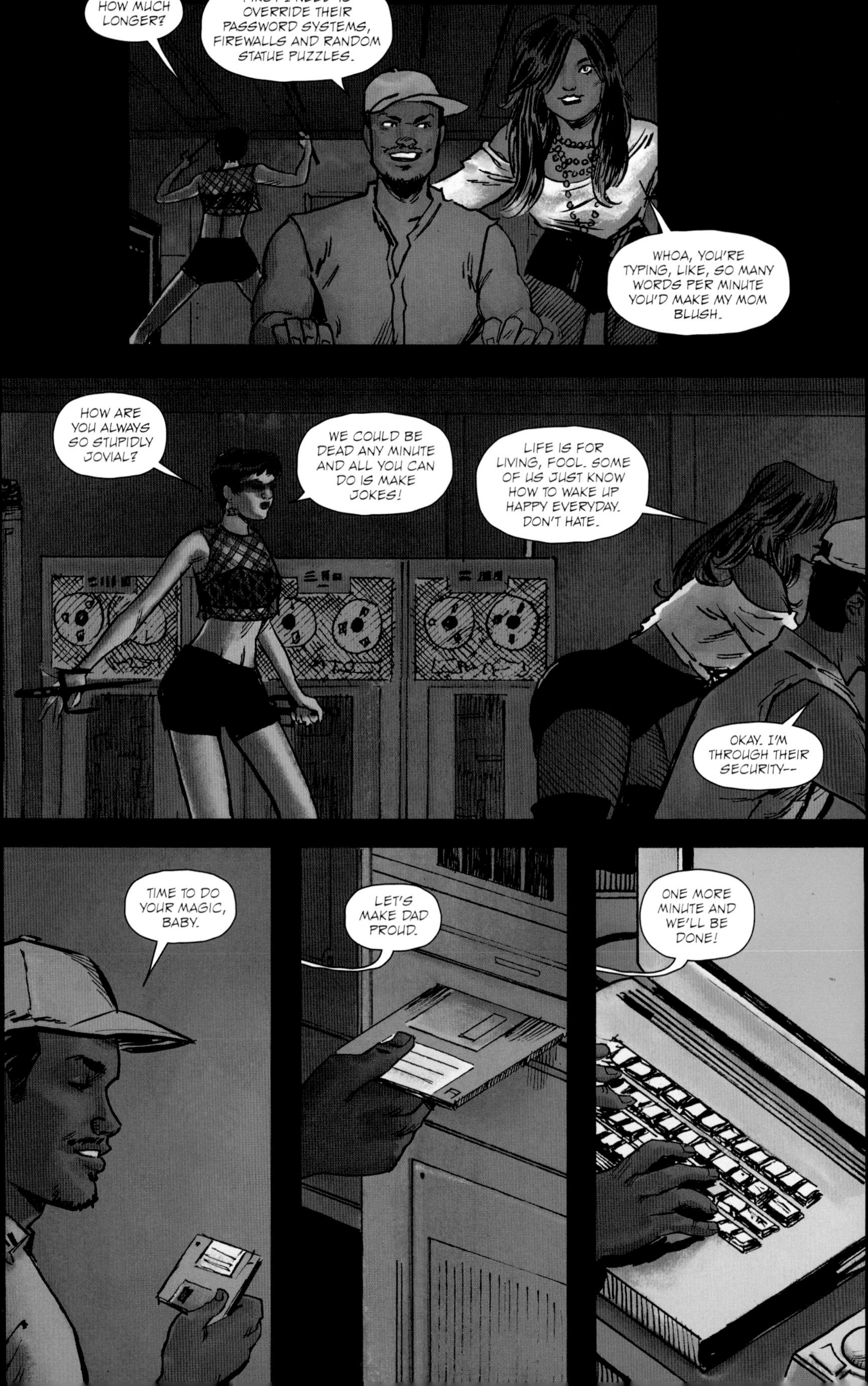
HOW MUCH LONGER?
FIRST I NEED TO OVERRIDE THEIR PASSWORD SYSTEMS, FIREWALLS AND RANDOM STATUE PUZZLES.
WHOA, YOU'RE TYPING, LIKE, SO MANY WORDS PER MINUTE YOU'D MAKE MY MOM BLUSH.
HOW ARE YOU ALWAYS SO STUPIDLY JOVIAL?
WE COULD BE DEAD ANY MINUTE AND ALL YOU CAN DO IS MAKE JOKES!
LIFE IS FOR LIVING, FOOL. SOME OF US JUST KNOW HOW TO WAKE UP HAPPY EVERYDAY. DON'T HATE.
OKAY. I'M THROUGH THEIR SECURITY--
TIME TO DO YOUR MAGIC, BABY.
LET'S MAKE DAD PROUD.
ONE MORE MINUTE AND WE'LL BE DONE!

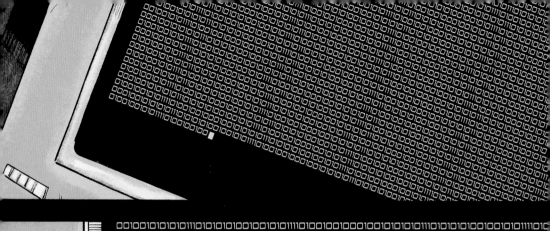

00100101010101110101010100100101011101001001001001010101011101010100100100101011101C
01001010101010111010101001001010111010100100100100101010111010101010010010010111011
00101000100101010111010010101010010101110101001010010101011101010100101001010101
11111001001001010111101001010100100101110101001001010101011101010100101011010101C
01011101001010101011101001010100100101110101001001010101010111010010101010010101
10101011110100100100010101011101010101110101001001001010111010101010100101010101
01001010101011101001001001010101111010100100101110101001010010101011101010101010101
01010010010101110111011101001001010100101011101001001010101010111010101010010010010
01010101010101011101010010010111010100100100100101010101110101010010010101001001001C
00101010101010101110101001010101001010101110101001001010101010111010010010010010111010
01011101001001010101111010010101010010101110101001010010101011101010101010101110100100100C

>MAINFRAME OVERRIDE COMPLETE. NETWORK FAILING. ALL SYSTEMS TERMINATED.

YES! THAT WASN'T EVEN THAT HARD!

YOU DID IT, CLINT! THAT WAS SICK--

BEEP!

PROPERTY-WIDE DETONATION IN T-MINUS

9 MINUTES 32 SECONDS...

SHIIIIIT...

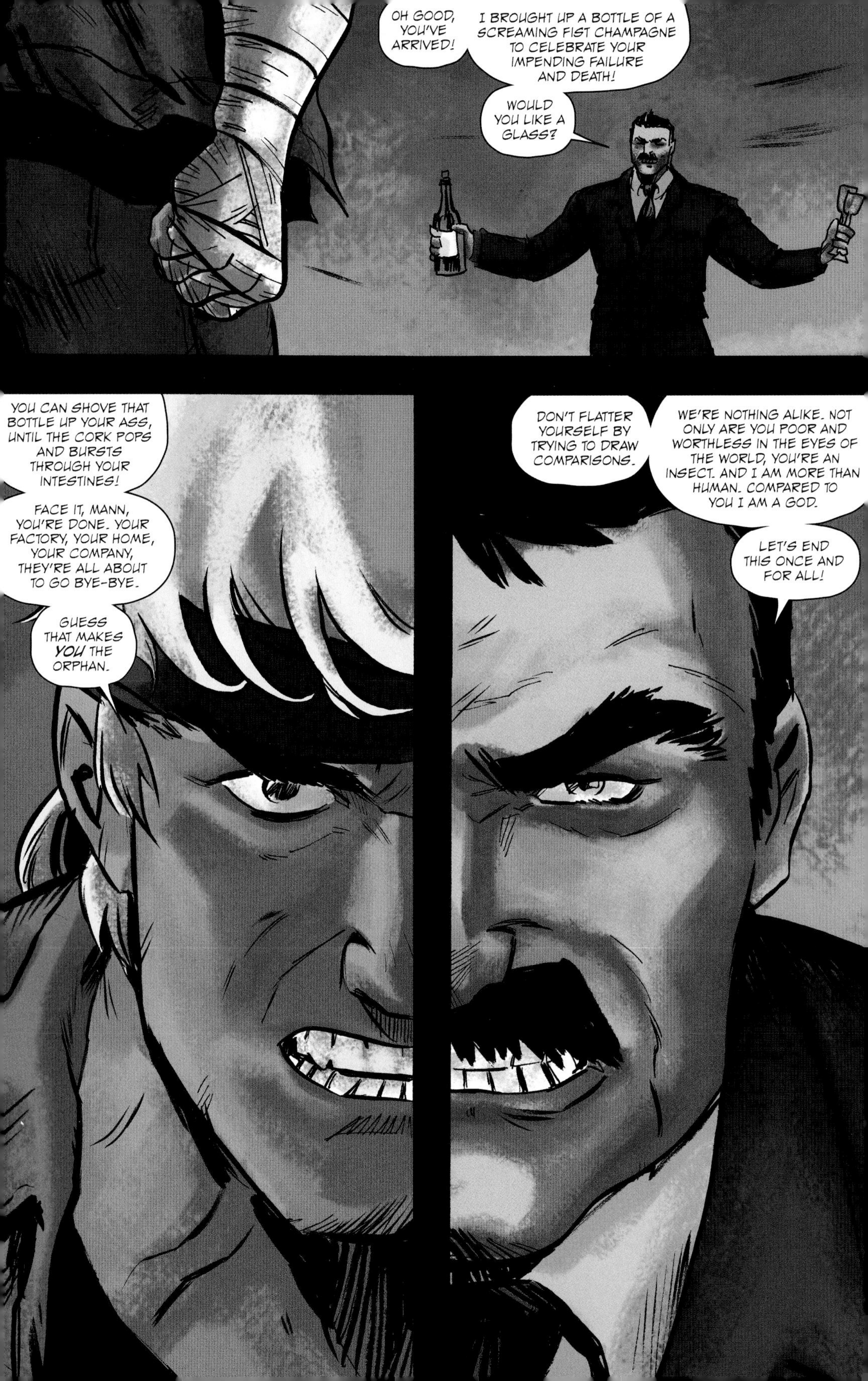
OH GOOD, YOU'VE ARRIVED!
I BROUGHT UP A BOTTLE OF A SCREAMING FIST CHAMPAGNE TO CELEBRATE YOUR IMPENDING FAILURE AND DEATH!
WOULD YOU LIKE A GLASS?
YOU CAN SHOVE THAT BOTTLE UP YOUR ASS, UNTIL THE CORK POPS AND BURSTS THROUGH YOUR INTESTINES!
FACE IT, MANN, YOU'RE DONE. YOUR FACTORY, YOUR HOME, YOUR COMPANY, THEY'RE ALL ABOUT TO GO BYE-BYE.
GUESS THAT MAKES *YOU* THE ORPHAN.
DON'T FLATTER YOURSELF BY TRYING TO DRAW COMPARISONS.
WE'RE NOTHING ALIKE. NOT ONLY ARE YOU POOR AND WORTHLESS IN THE EYES OF THE WORLD, YOU'RE AN INSECT. AND I AM MORE THAN HUMAN. COMPARED TO YOU I AM A GOD.
LET'S END THIS ONCE AND FOR ALL!

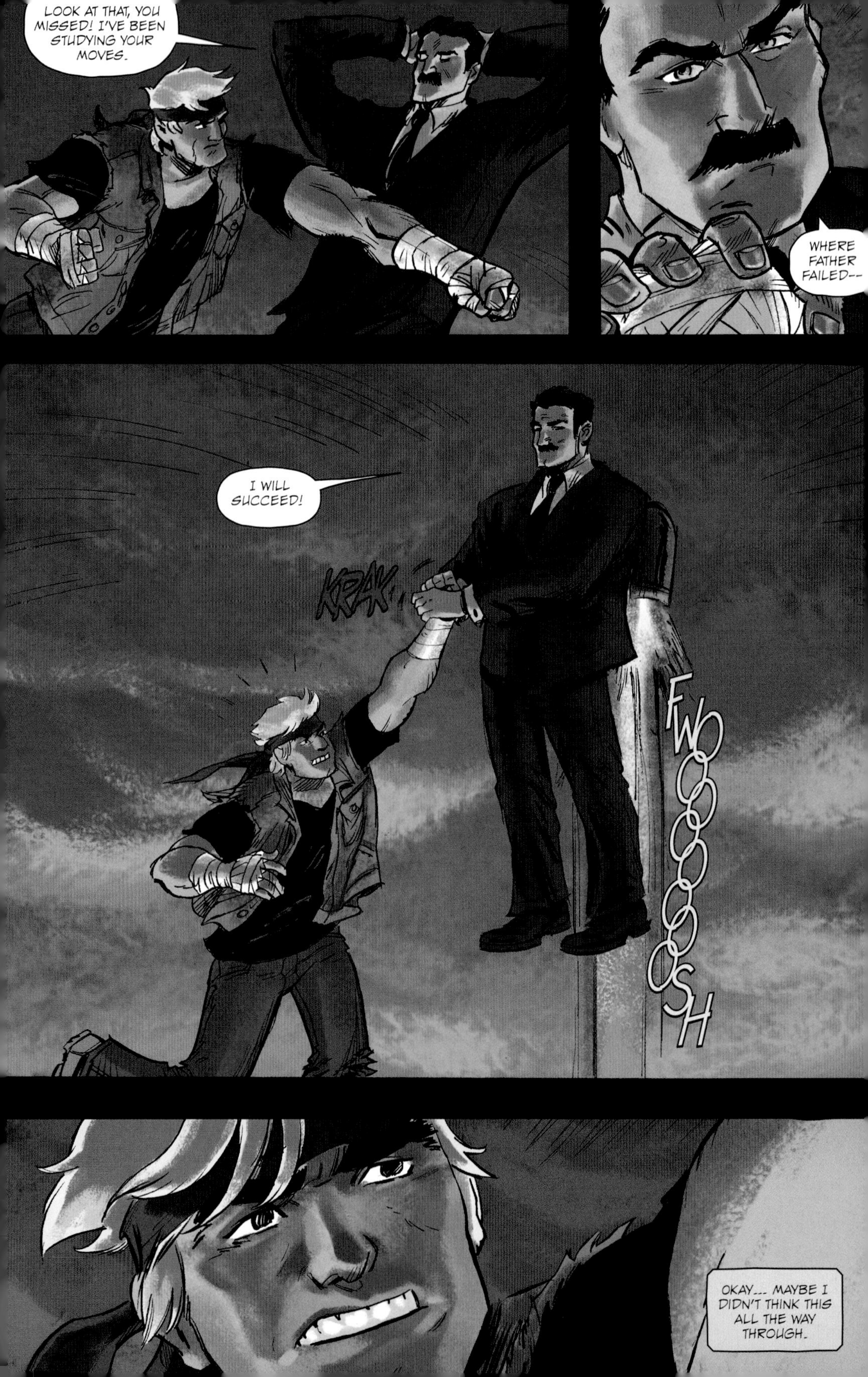
LOOK AT THAT, YOU MISSED! I'VE BEEN STUDYING YOUR MOVES.
WHERE FATHER FAILED--
I WILL SUCCEED!
KRAK
FWOOOOOOOSH
OKAY... MAYBE I DIDN'T THINK THIS ALL THE WAY THROUGH.

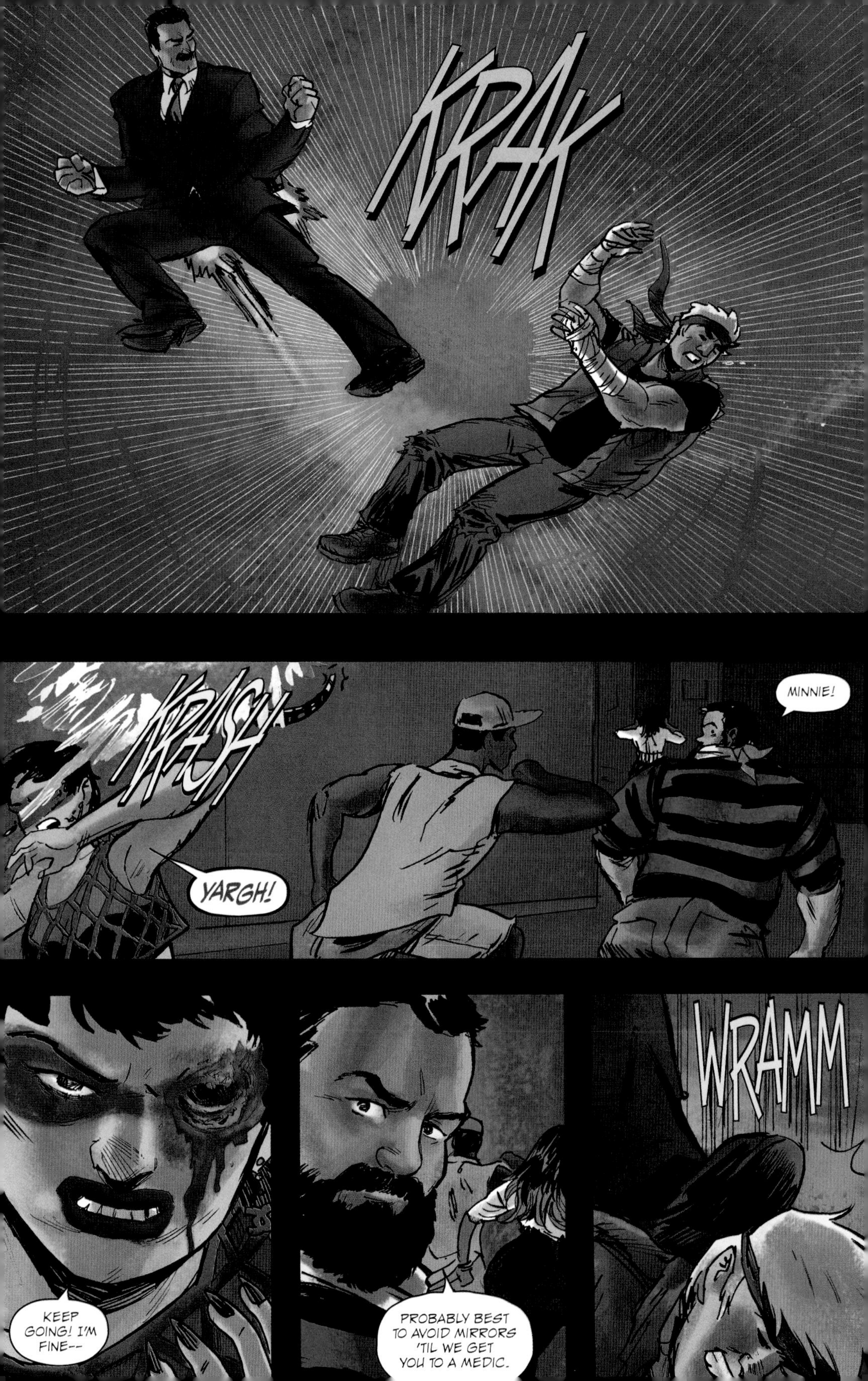
KRAK
KRASH
YARGH!
MINNIE!
KEEP GOING! I'M FINE--
PROBABLY BEST TO AVOID MIRRORS 'TIL WE GET YOU TO A MEDIC.
WRAMM

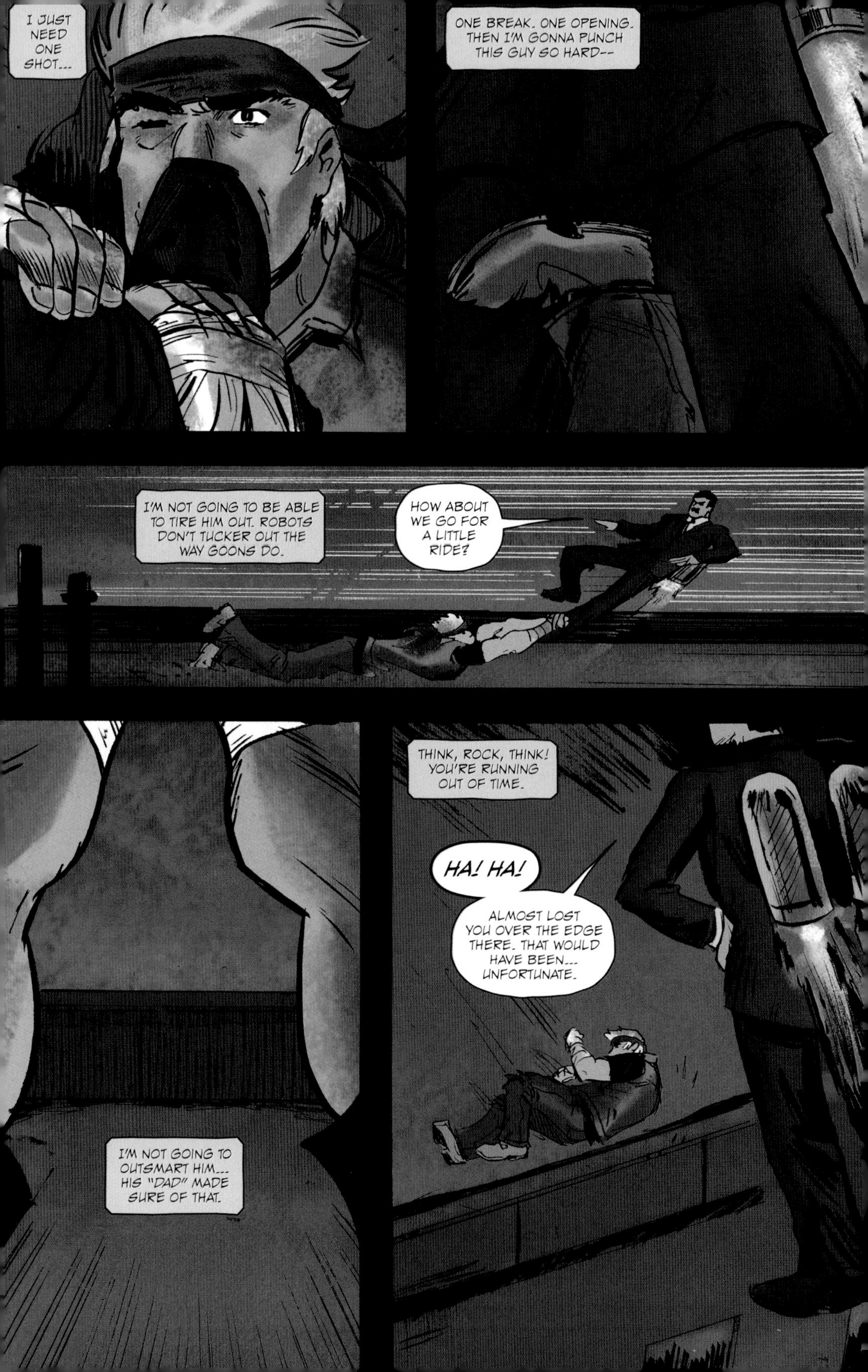

I JUST NEED ONE SHOT...
ONE BREAK. ONE OPENING. THEN I'M GONNA PUNCH THIS GUY SO HARD--
I'M NOT GOING TO BE ABLE TO TIRE HIM OUT. ROBOTS DON'T TUCKER OUT THE WAY GOONS DO.
HOW ABOUT WE GO FOR A LITTLE RIDE?
I'M NOT GOING TO OUTSMART HIM... HIS "DAD" MADE SURE OF THAT.
THINK, ROCK, THINK! YOU'RE RUNNING OUT OF TIME.
HA! HA!
ALMOST LOST YOU OVER THE EDGE THERE. THAT WOULD HAVE BEEN... UNFORTUNATE.

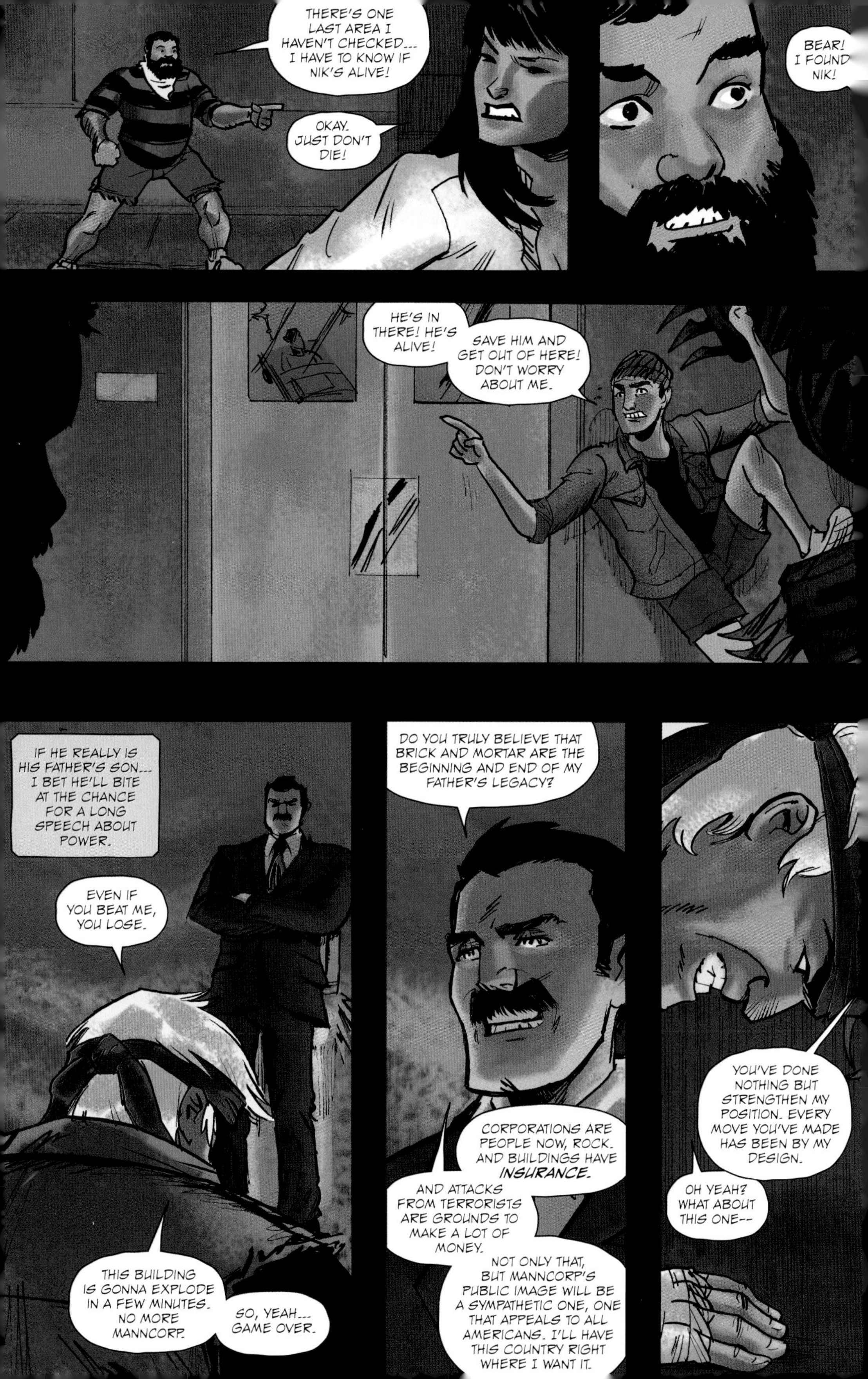
THERE'S ONE LAST AREA I HAVEN'T CHECKED... I HAVE TO KNOW IF NIK'S ALIVE!
OKAY. JUST DON'T DIE!
BEAR! I FOUND NIK!
HE'S IN THERE! HE'S ALIVE!
SAVE HIM AND GET OUT OF HERE! DON'T WORRY ABOUT ME.
IF HE REALLY IS HIS FATHER'S SON... I BET HE'LL BITE AT THE CHANCE FOR A LONG SPEECH ABOUT POWER.
EVEN IF YOU BEAT ME, YOU LOSE.
THIS BUILDING IS GONNA EXPLODE IN A FEW MINUTES. NO MORE MANNCORP.
SO, YEAH... GAME OVER.
DO YOU TRULY BELIEVE THAT BRICK AND MORTAR ARE THE BEGINNING AND END OF MY FATHER'S LEGACY?
CORPORATIONS ARE PEOPLE NOW, ROCK. AND BUILDINGS HAVE INSURANCE.
AND ATTACKS FROM TERRORISTS ARE GROUNDS TO MAKE A LOT OF MONEY.
NOT ONLY THAT, BUT MANNCORP'S PUBLIC IMAGE WILL BE A SYMPATHETIC ONE, ONE THAT APPEALS TO ALL AMERICANS. I'LL HAVE THIS COUNTRY RIGHT WHERE I WANT IT.
YOU'VE DONE NOTHING BUT STRENGTHEN MY POSITION. EVERY MOVE YOU'VE MADE HAS BEEN BY MY DESIGN.
OH YEAH? WHAT ABOUT THIS ONE--

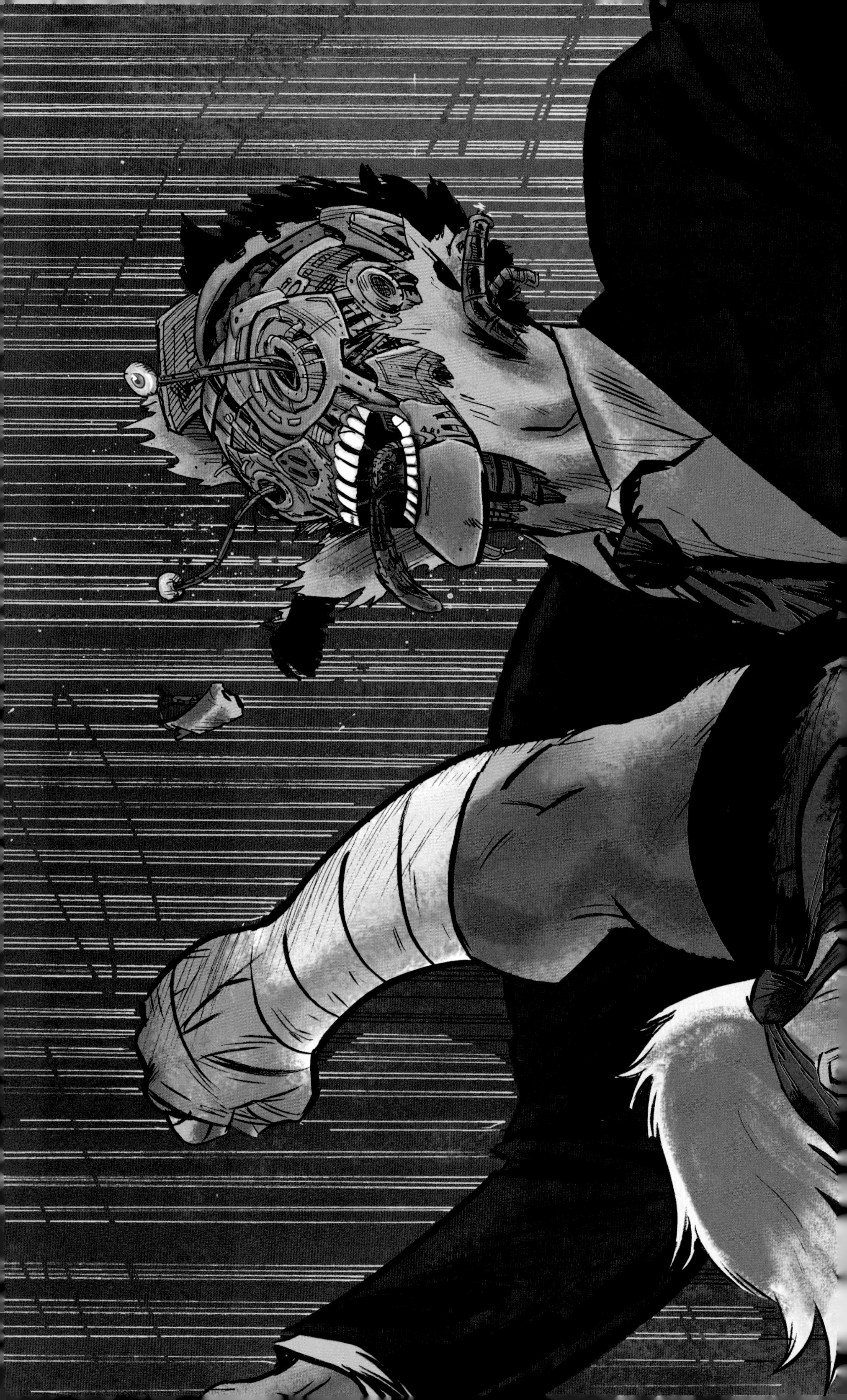

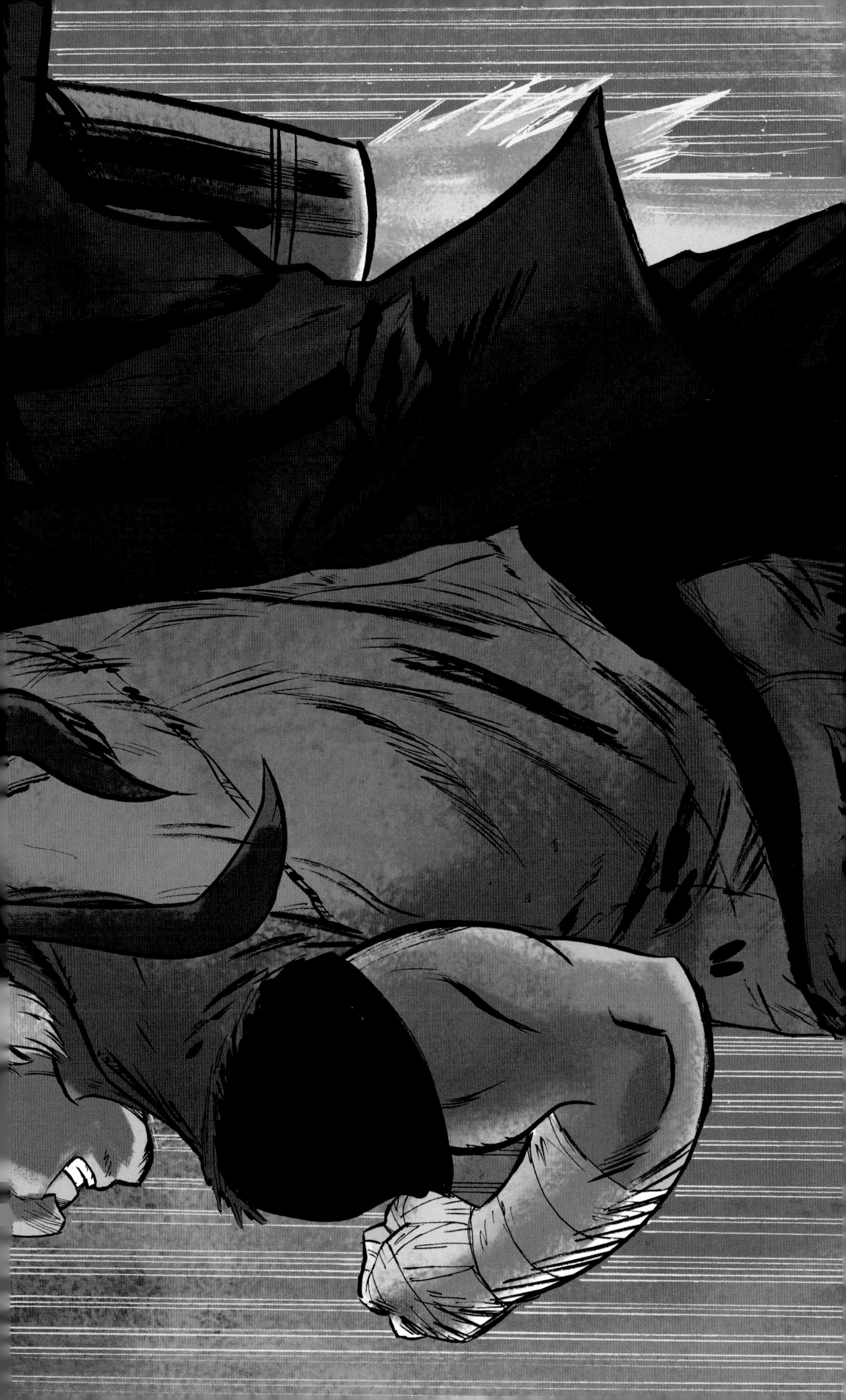

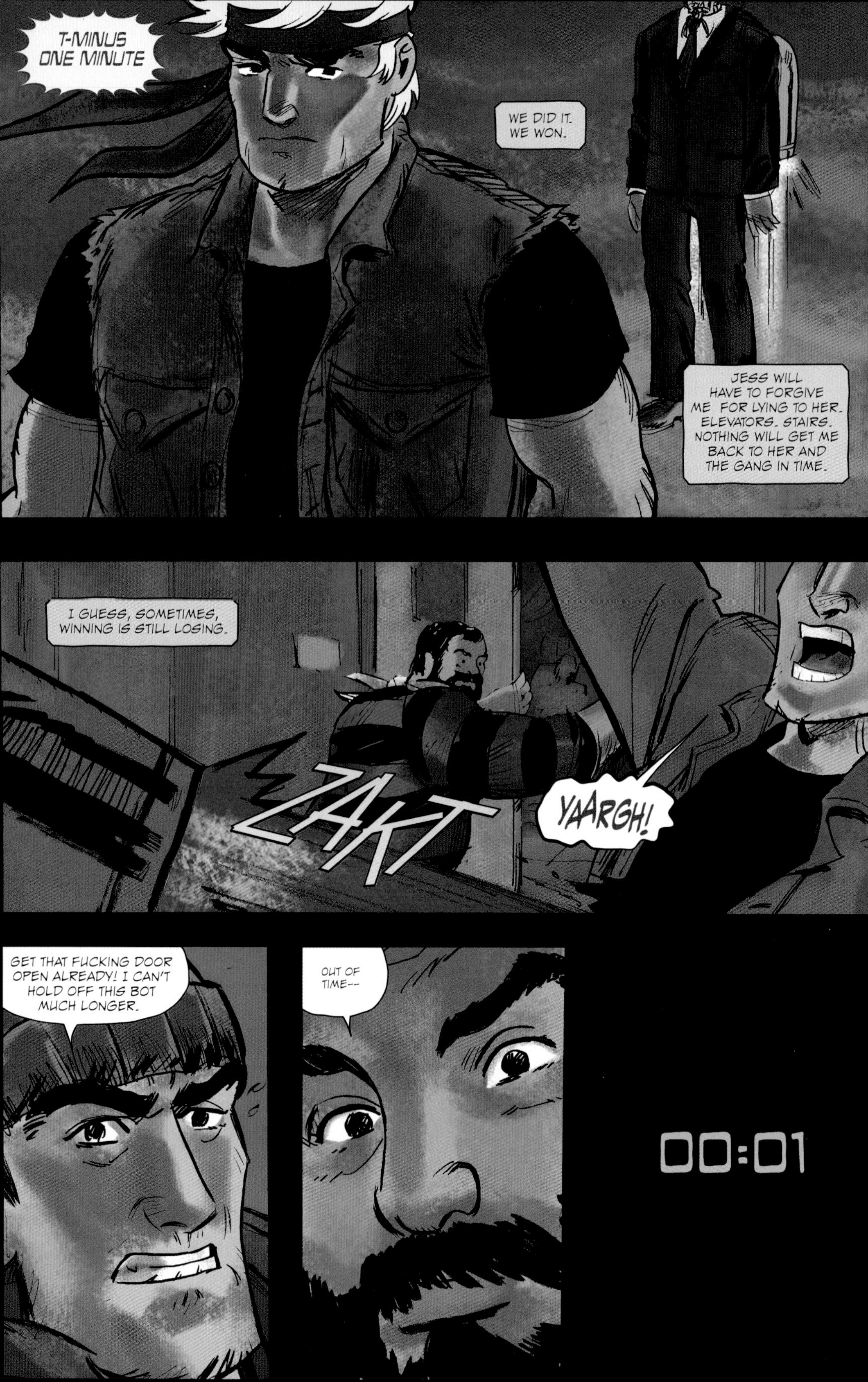
T-MINUS ONE MINUTE
WE DID IT. WE WON.
JESS WILL HAVE TO FORGIVE ME FOR LYING TO HER. ELEVATORS. STAIRS. NOTHING WILL GET ME BACK TO HER AND THE GANG IN TIME.
I GUESS, SOMETIMES, WINNING IS STILL LOSING.
ZAKT
YAARGH!
GET THAT FUCKING DOOR OPEN ALREADY! I CAN'T HOLD OFF THIS BOT MUCH LONGER.
OUT OF TIME--
00:01

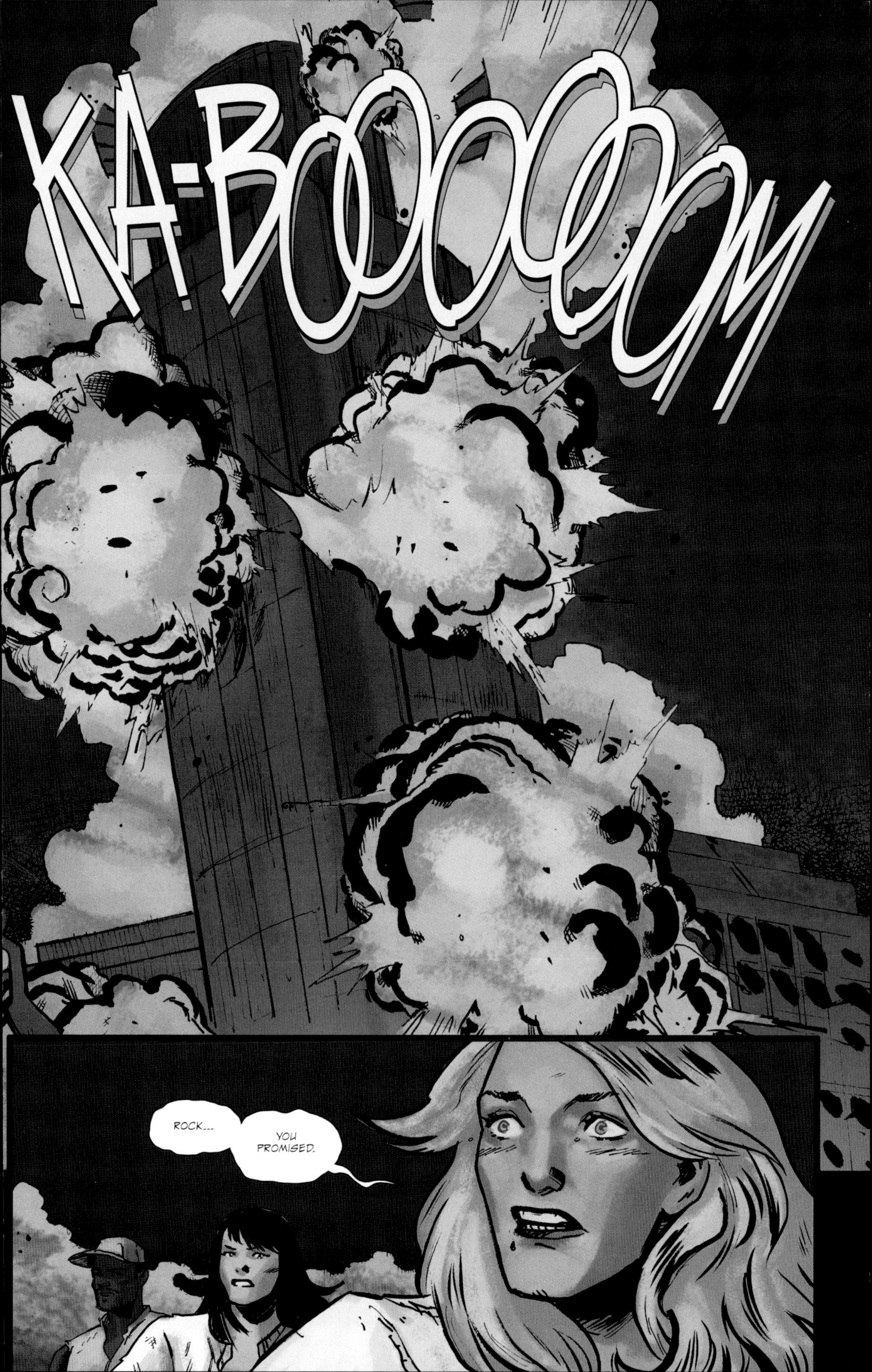
KA-BOOOOOOM
ROCK...
YOU PROMISED.

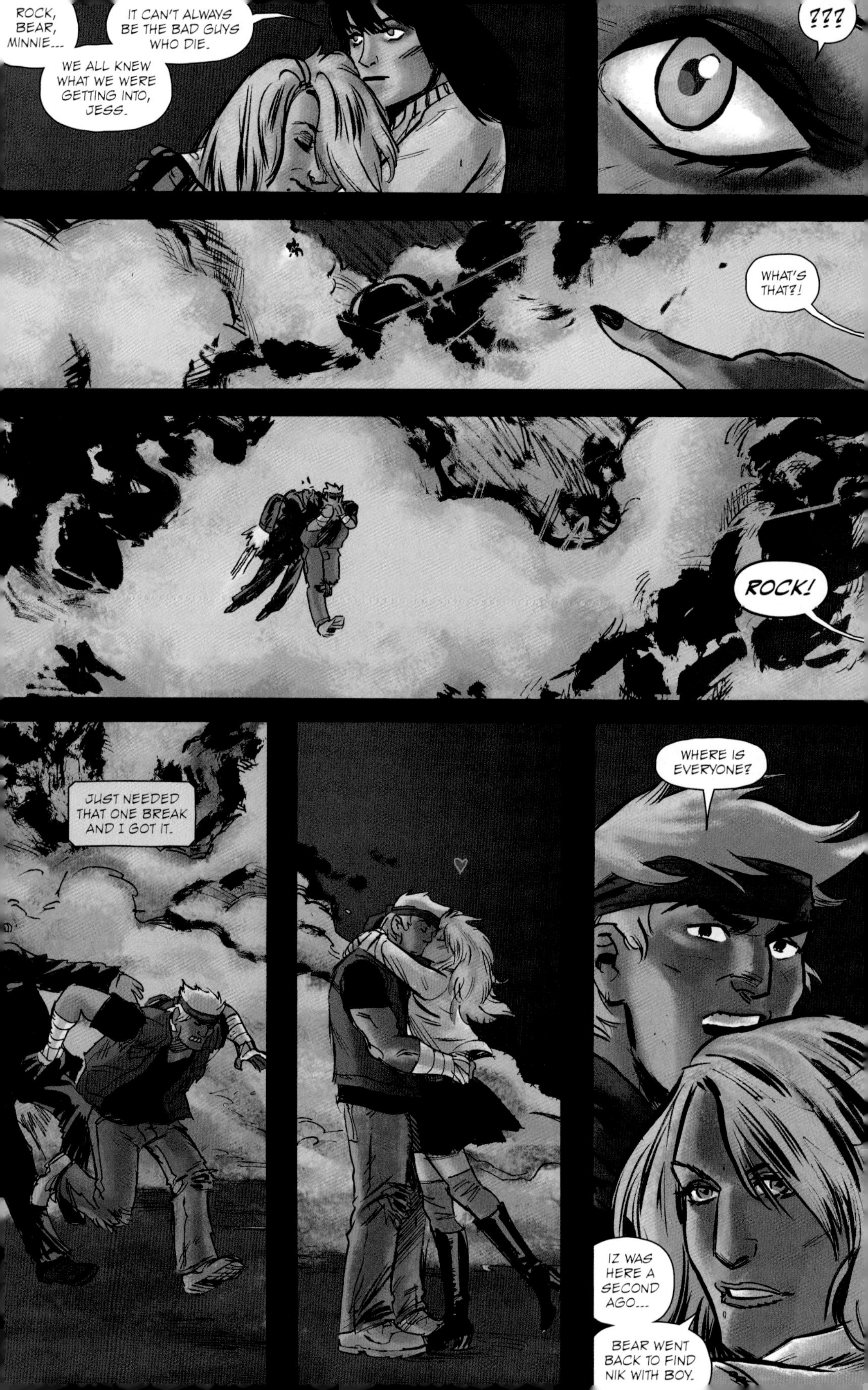
ROCK, BEAR, MINNIE...
IT CAN'T ALWAYS BE THE BAD GUYS WHO DIE.
WE ALL KNEW WHAT WE WERE GETTING INTO, JESS.
???
WHAT'S THAT?!
ROCK!
JUST NEEDED THAT ONE BREAK AND I GOT IT.
WHERE IS EVERYONE?
IZ WAS HERE A SECOND AGO...
BEAR WENT BACK TO FIND NIK WITH BOY.

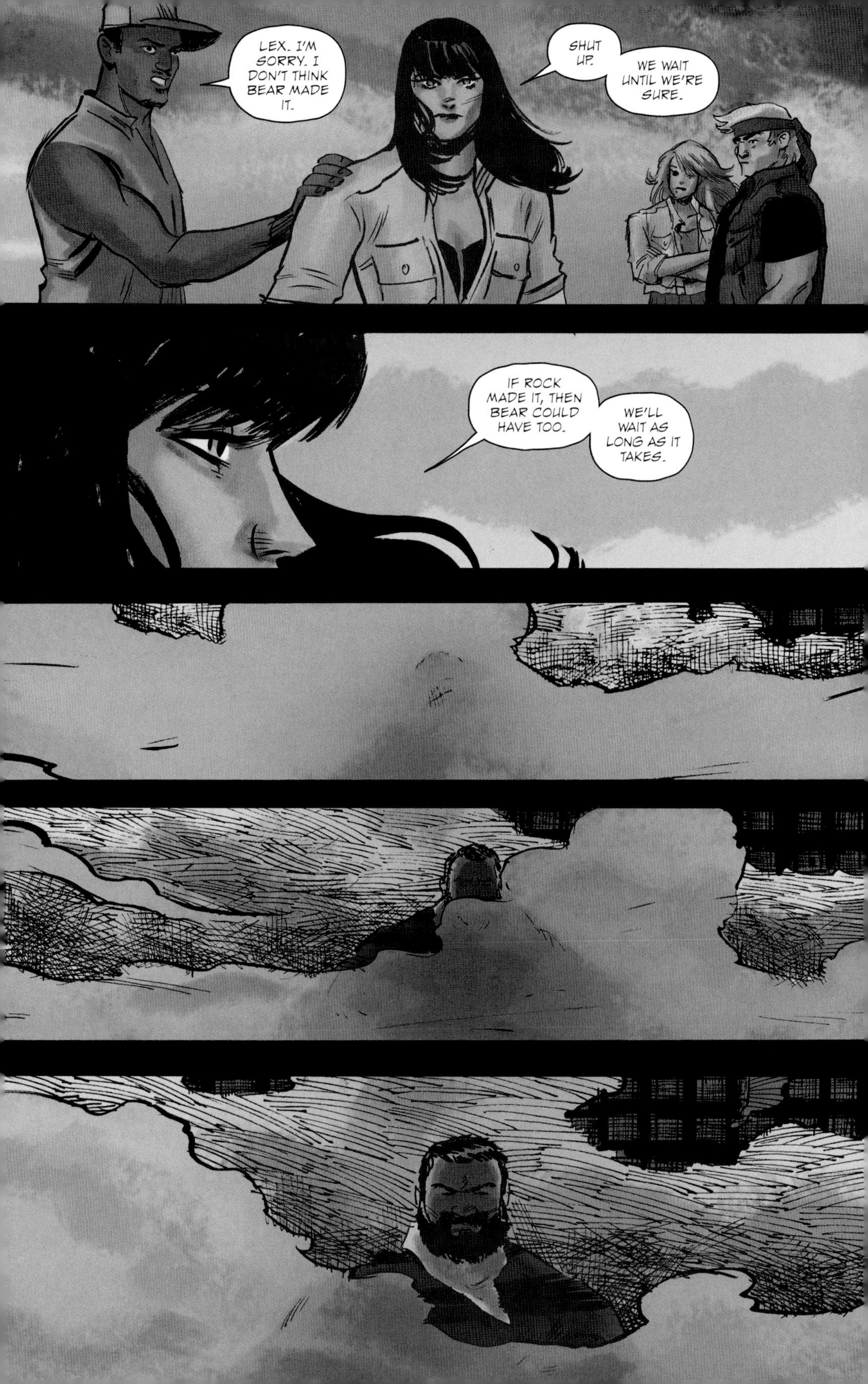
LEX. I'M SORRY. I DON'T THINK BEAR MADE IT.
SHUT UP.
WE WAIT UNTIL WE'RE SURE.
IF ROCK MADE IT, THEN BEAR COULD HAVE TOO.
WE'LL WAIT AS LONG AS IT TAKES.

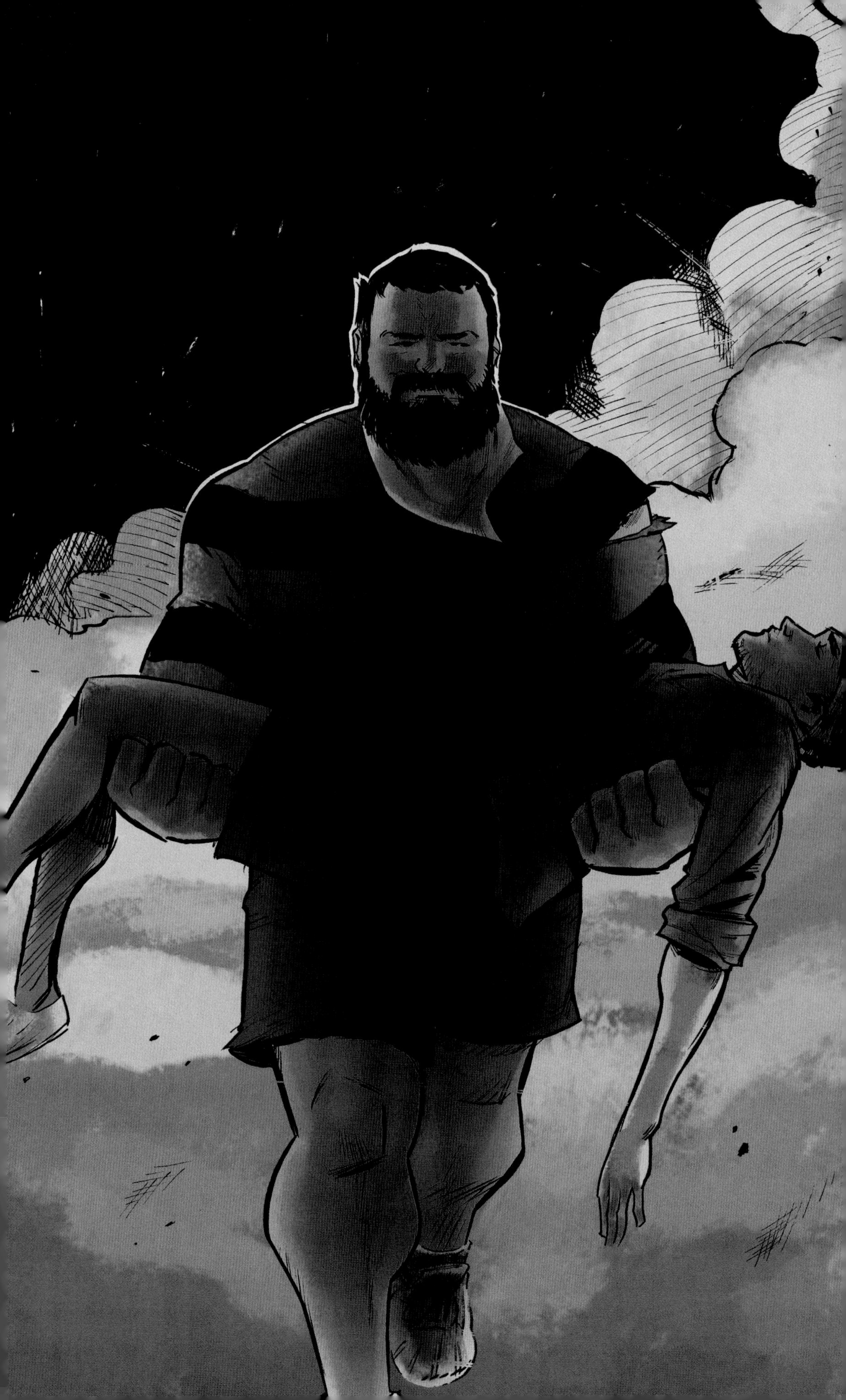

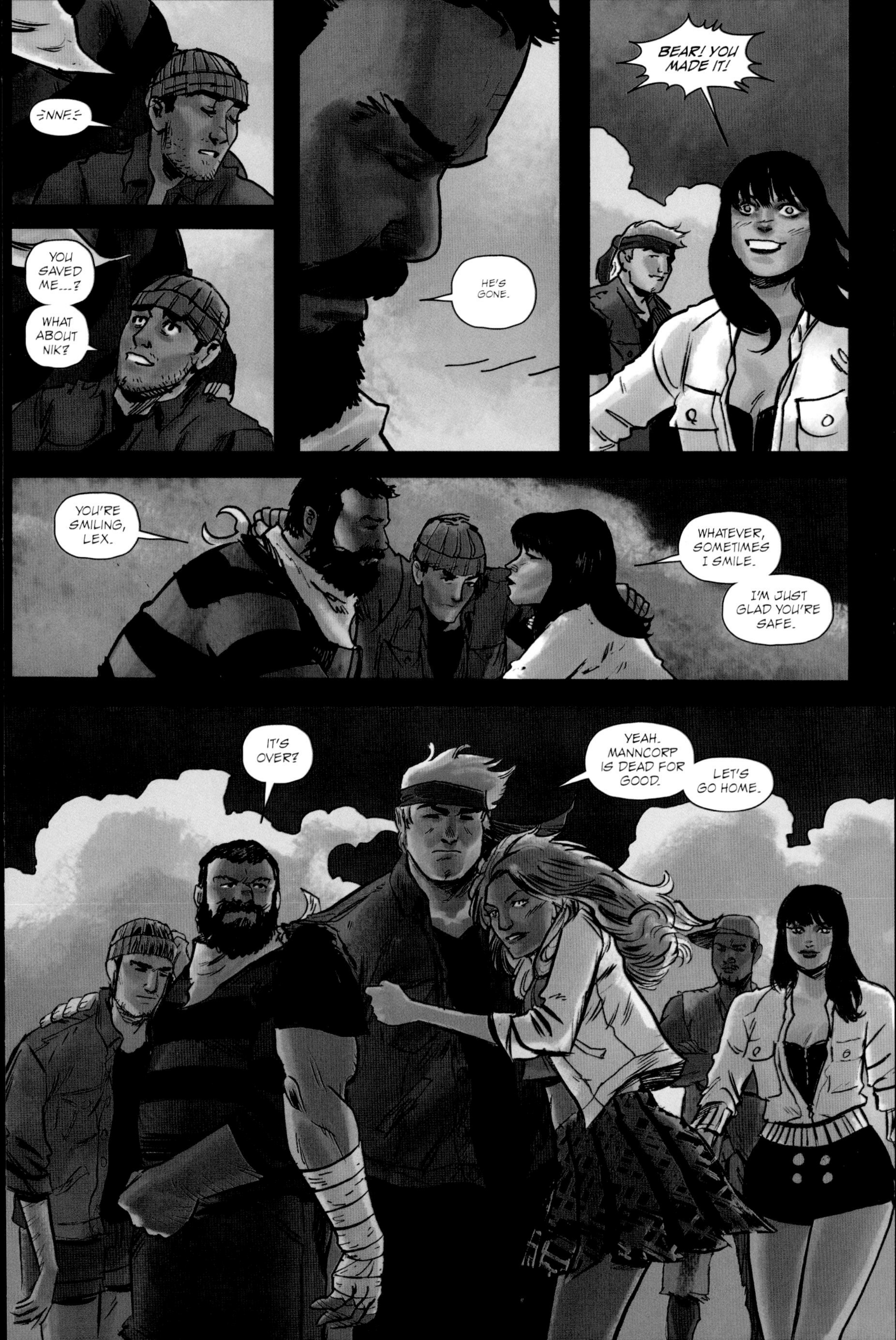

=NNF=
YOU SAVED ME...?
WHAT ABOUT NIK?
HE'S GONE.
BEAR! YOU MADE IT!
YOU'RE SMILING, LEX.
WHATEVER, SOMETIMES I SMILE.
I'M JUST GLAD YOU'RE SAFE.
IT'S OVER?
YEAH. MANNCORP IS DEAD FOR GOOD.
LET'S GO HOME.

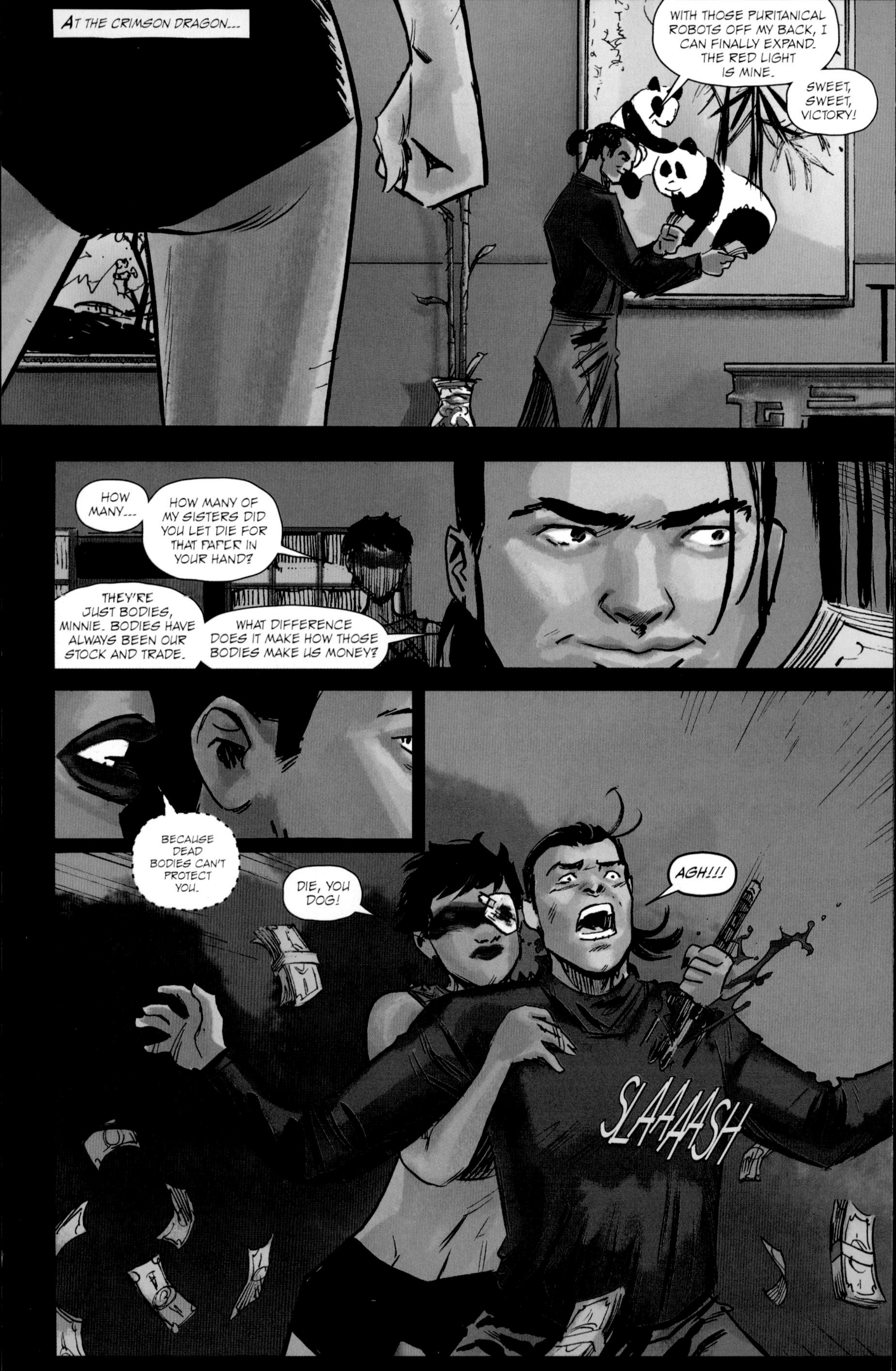
AT THE CRIMSON DRAGON...
WITH THOSE PURITANICAL ROBOTS OFF MY BACK, I CAN FINALLY EXPAND. THE RED LIGHT IS MINE.
SWEET, SWEET, VICTORY!
HOW MANY...
HOW MANY OF MY SISTERS DID YOU LET DIE FOR THAT PAPER IN YOUR HAND?
THEY'RE JUST BODIES, MINNIE. BODIES HAVE ALWAYS BEEN OUR STOCK AND TRADE.
WHAT DIFFERENCE DOES IT MAKE HOW THOSE BODIES MAKE US MONEY?
BECAUSE DEAD BODIES CAN'T PROTECT YOU.
DIE, YOU DOG!
AGH!!!
SLAAAASH

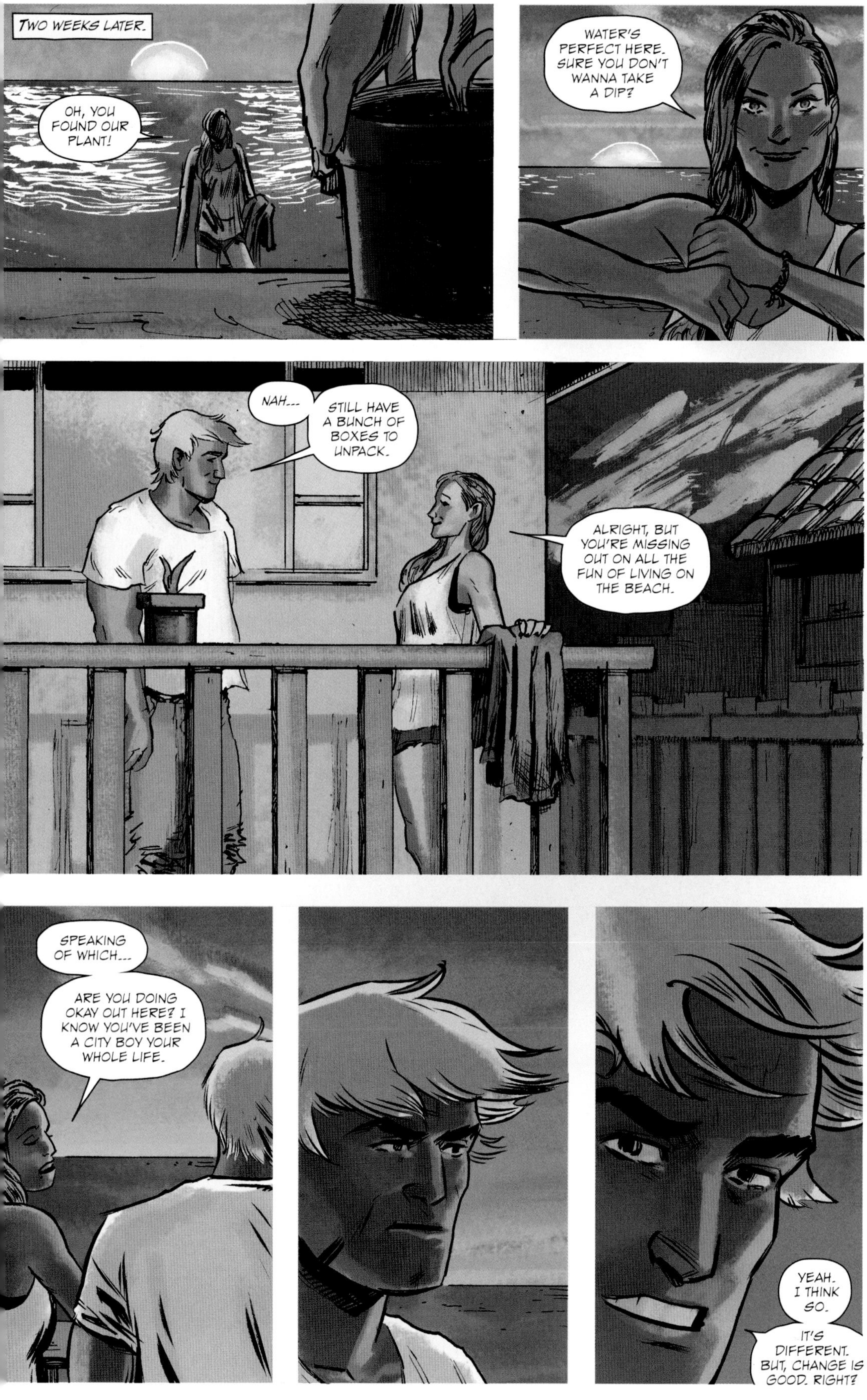
TWO WEEKS LATER.
OH, YOU FOUND OUR PLANT!
WATER'S PERFECT HERE. SURE YOU DON'T WANNA TAKE A DIP?
NAH...
STILL HAVE A BUNCH OF BOXES TO UNPACK.
ALRIGHT, BUT YOU'RE MISSING OUT ON ALL THE FUN OF LIVING ON THE BEACH.
SPEAKING OF WHICH...
ARE YOU DOING OKAY OUT HERE? I KNOW YOU'VE BEEN A CITY BOY YOUR WHOLE LIFE.
YEAH. I THINK SO.
IT'S DIFFERENT. BUT, CHANGE IS GOOD. RIGHT?

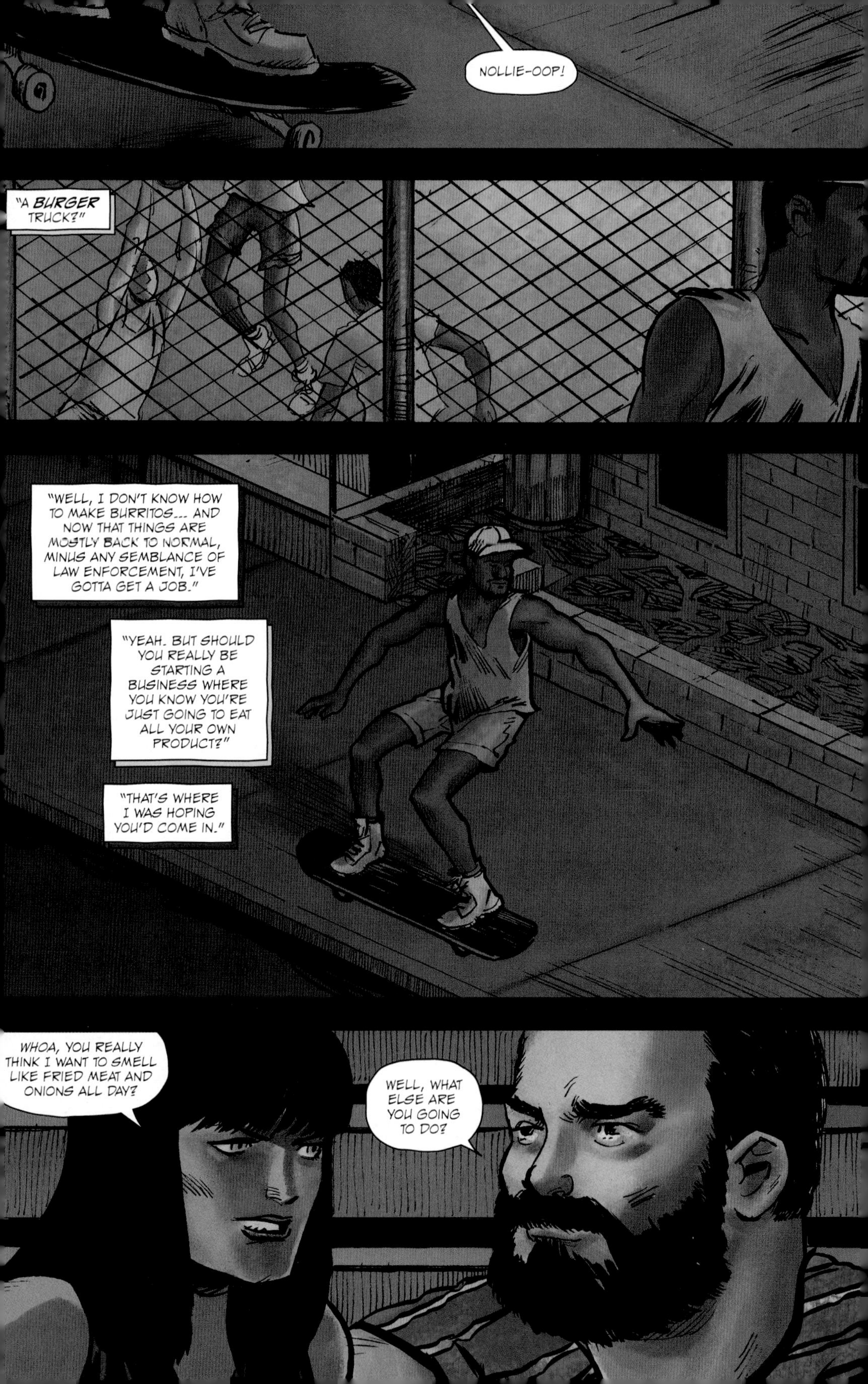
NOLLIE-OOP!
"A BURGER TRUCK?"
"WELL, I DON'T KNOW HOW TO MAKE BURRITOS... AND NOW THAT THINGS ARE MOSTLY BACK TO NORMAL, MINUS ANY SEMBLANCE OF LAW ENFORCEMENT, I'VE GOTTA GET A JOB."
"YEAH. BUT SHOULD YOU REALLY BE STARTING A BUSINESS WHERE YOU KNOW YOU'RE JUST GOING TO EAT ALL YOUR OWN PRODUCT?"
"THAT'S WHERE I WAS HOPING YOU'D COME IN."
WHOA, YOU REALLY THINK I WANT TO SMELL LIKE FRIED MEAT AND ONIONS ALL DAY?
WELL, WHAT ELSE ARE YOU GOING TO DO?

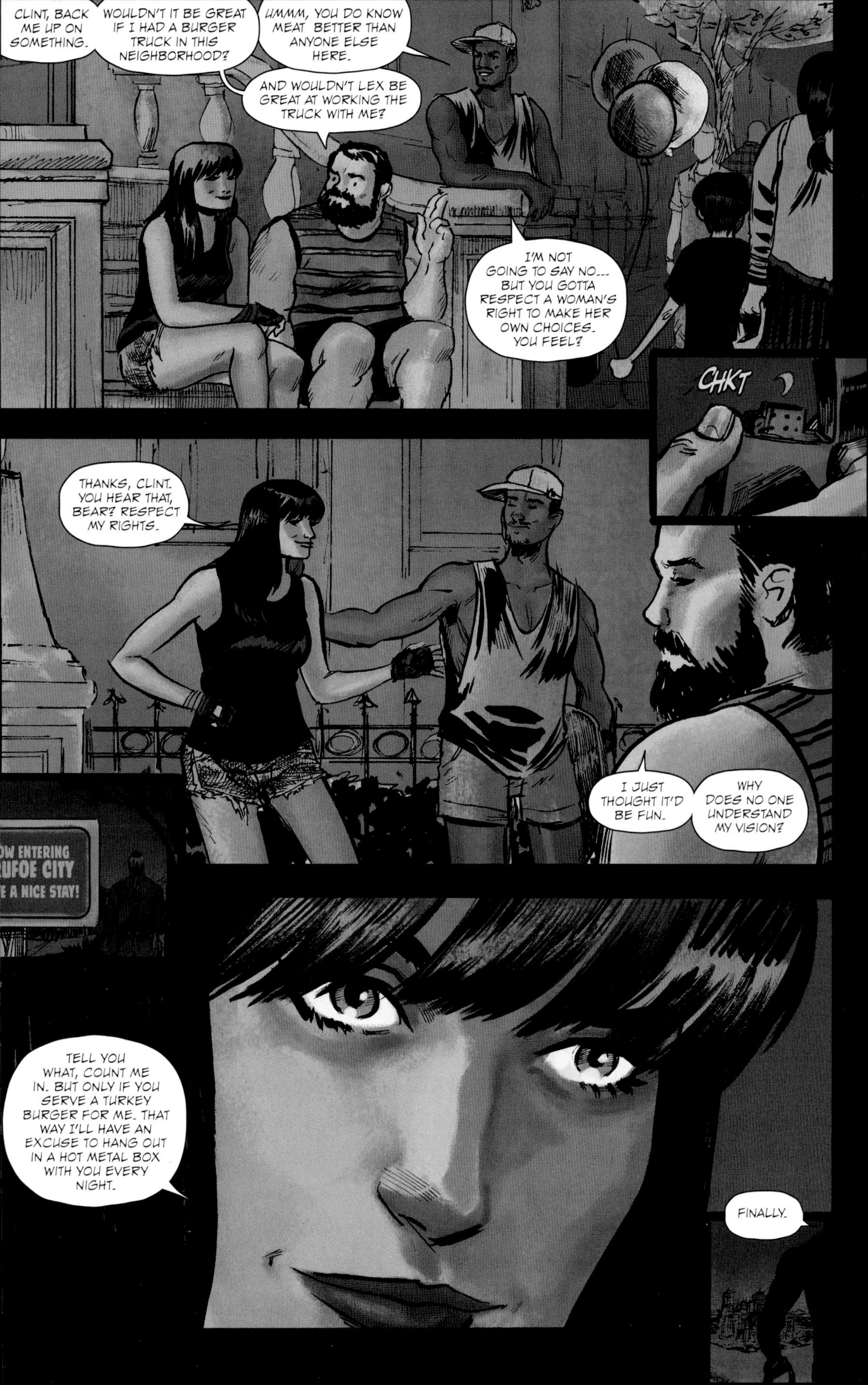
CLINT, BACK ME UP ON SOMETHING.
WOULDN'T IT BE GREAT IF I HAD A BURGER TRUCK IN THIS NEIGHBORHOOD?
UMMM, YOU DO KNOW MEAT BETTER THAN ANYONE ELSE HERE.
AND WOULDN'T LEX BE GREAT AT WORKING THE TRUCK WITH ME?
I'M NOT GOING TO SAY NO... BUT YOU GOTTA RESPECT A WOMAN'S RIGHT TO MAKE HER OWN CHOICES. YOU FEEL?
CHKT
THANKS, CLINT. YOU HEAR THAT, BEAR? RESPECT MY RIGHTS.
I JUST THOUGHT IT'D BE FUN.
WHY DOES NO ONE UNDERSTAND MY VISION?
OW ENTERING
RUFOE CITY
E A NICE STAY!
TELL YOU WHAT, COUNT ME IN. BUT ONLY IF YOU SERVE A TURKEY BURGER FOR ME. THAT WAY I'LL HAVE AN EXCUSE TO HANG OUT IN A HOT METAL BOX WITH YOU EVERY NIGHT.
FINALLY.

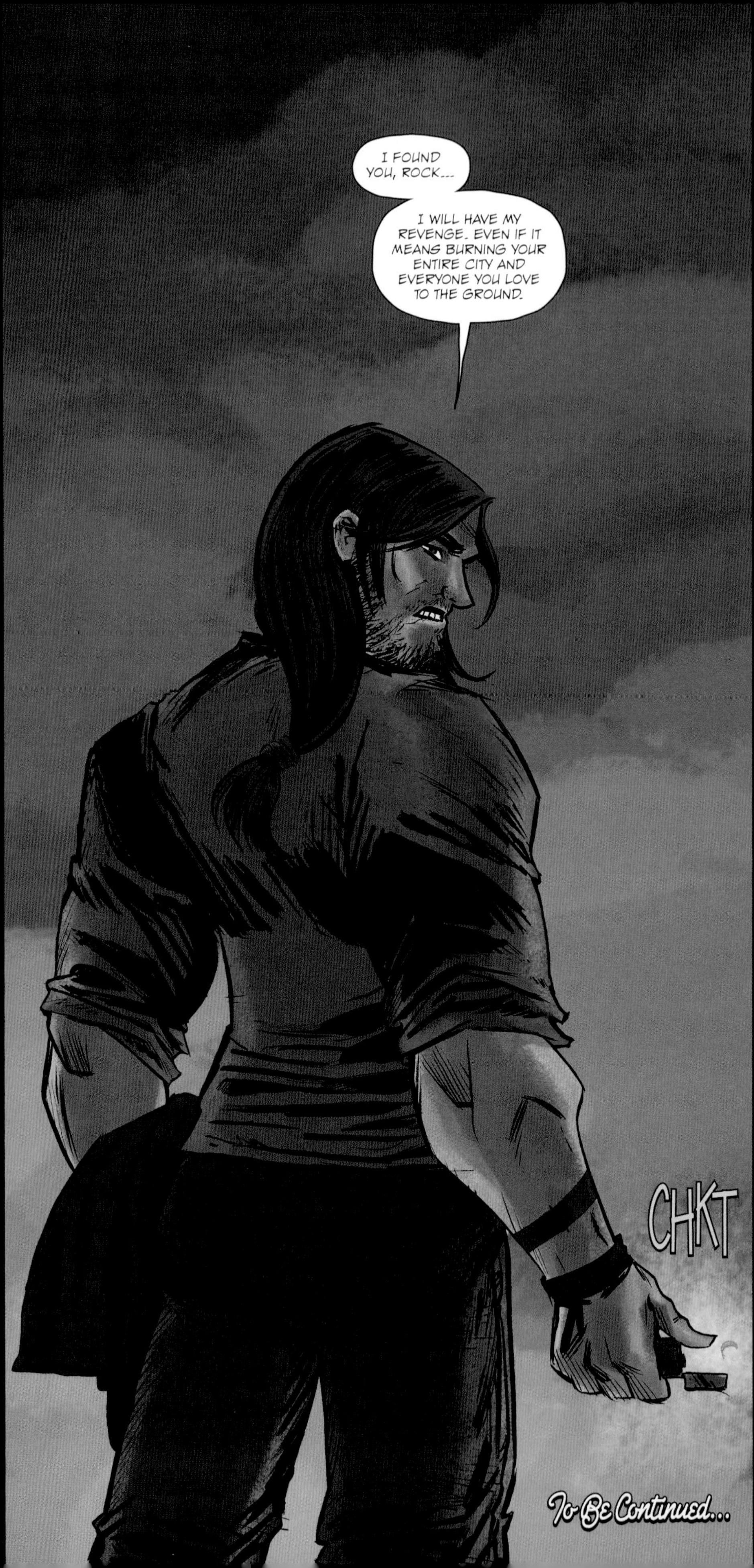
I FOUND YOU, ROCK...
I WILL HAVE MY REVENGE. EVEN IF IT MEANS BURNING YOUR ENTIRE CITY AND EVERYONE YOU LOVE TO THE GROUND.
CHKT
To Be Continued...

COVER GALLERY

REIGN OF TERROR #1 COVER B
ANDY BELANGER
REIGN OF TERROR # 1 MAXIMUM COMICS EXCLUSIVE
JEFF LEMIRE
REIGN OF TERROR # 2 COVER B
EMI LENOX
REIGN OF TERROR #3 COVER B
MALACHI WARD & MATT SHEEAN
REIGN OF TERROR # 4 COVER B
ED LUCE
REIGN OF TERROR #5 COVER B
SETH DAMOOSE & SHAUN STEVEN STRUBLE

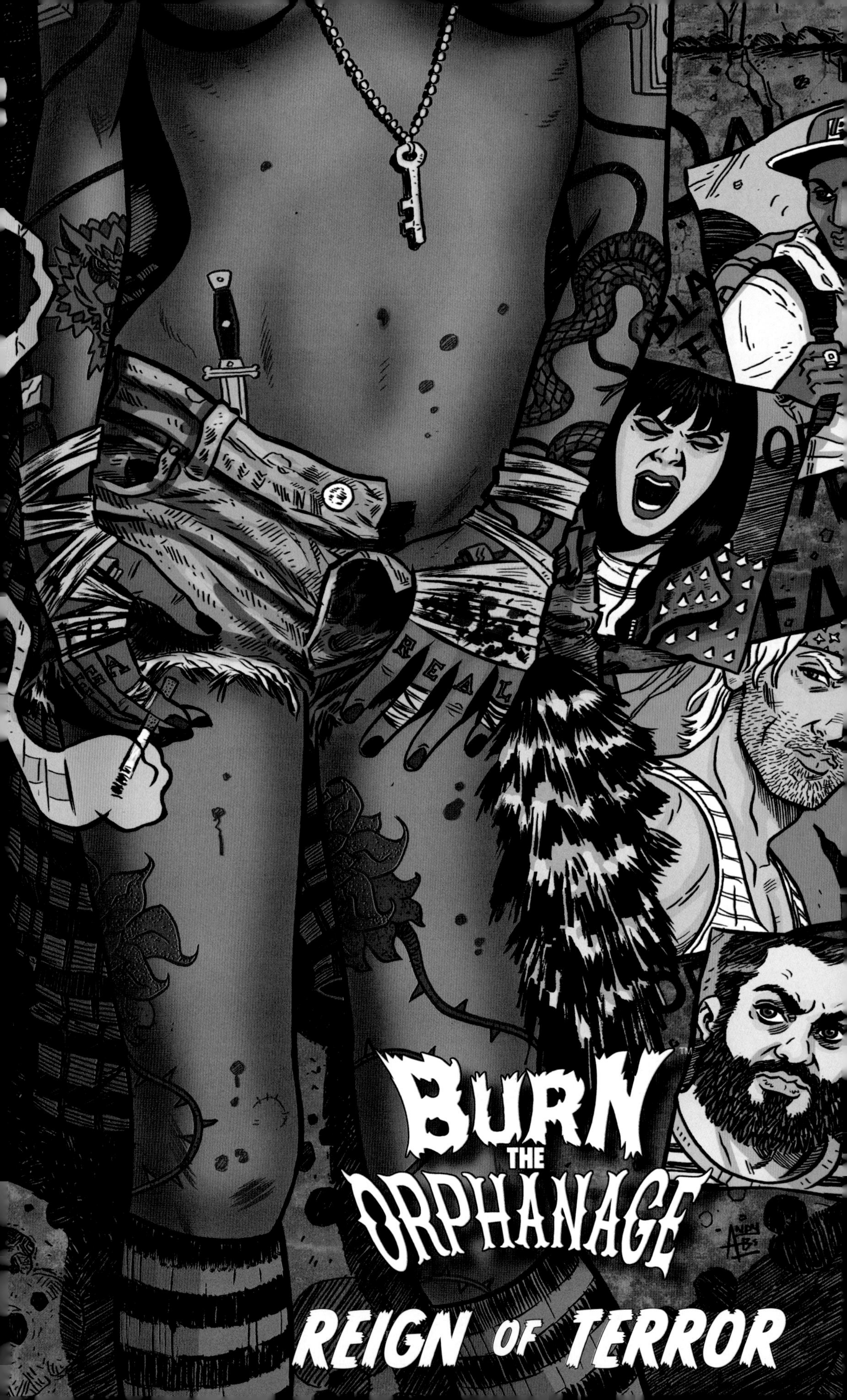
BURN THE ORPHANAGE™
REIGN OF TERROR

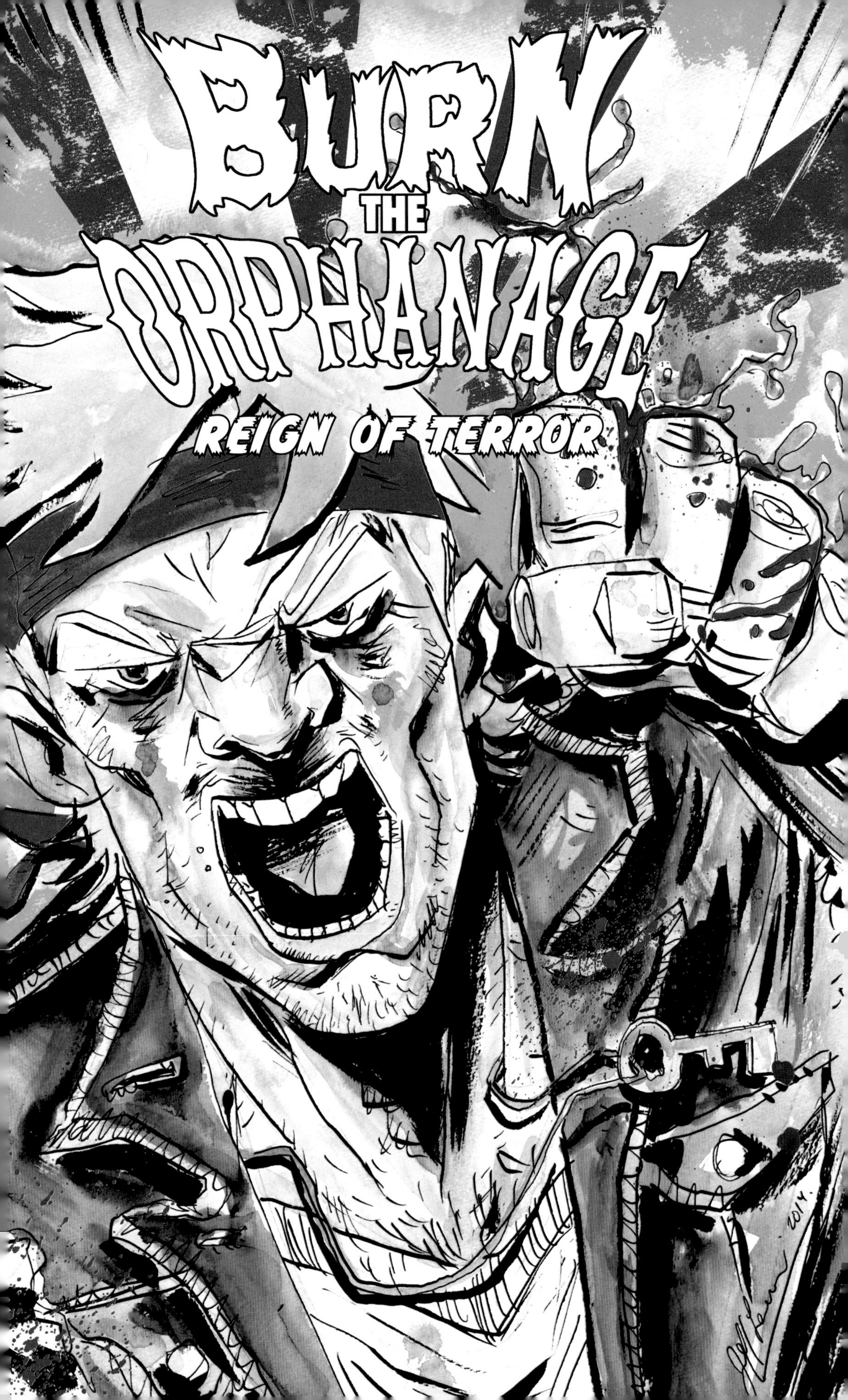
BURN™
THE
ORPHANAGE
REIGN OF TERROR

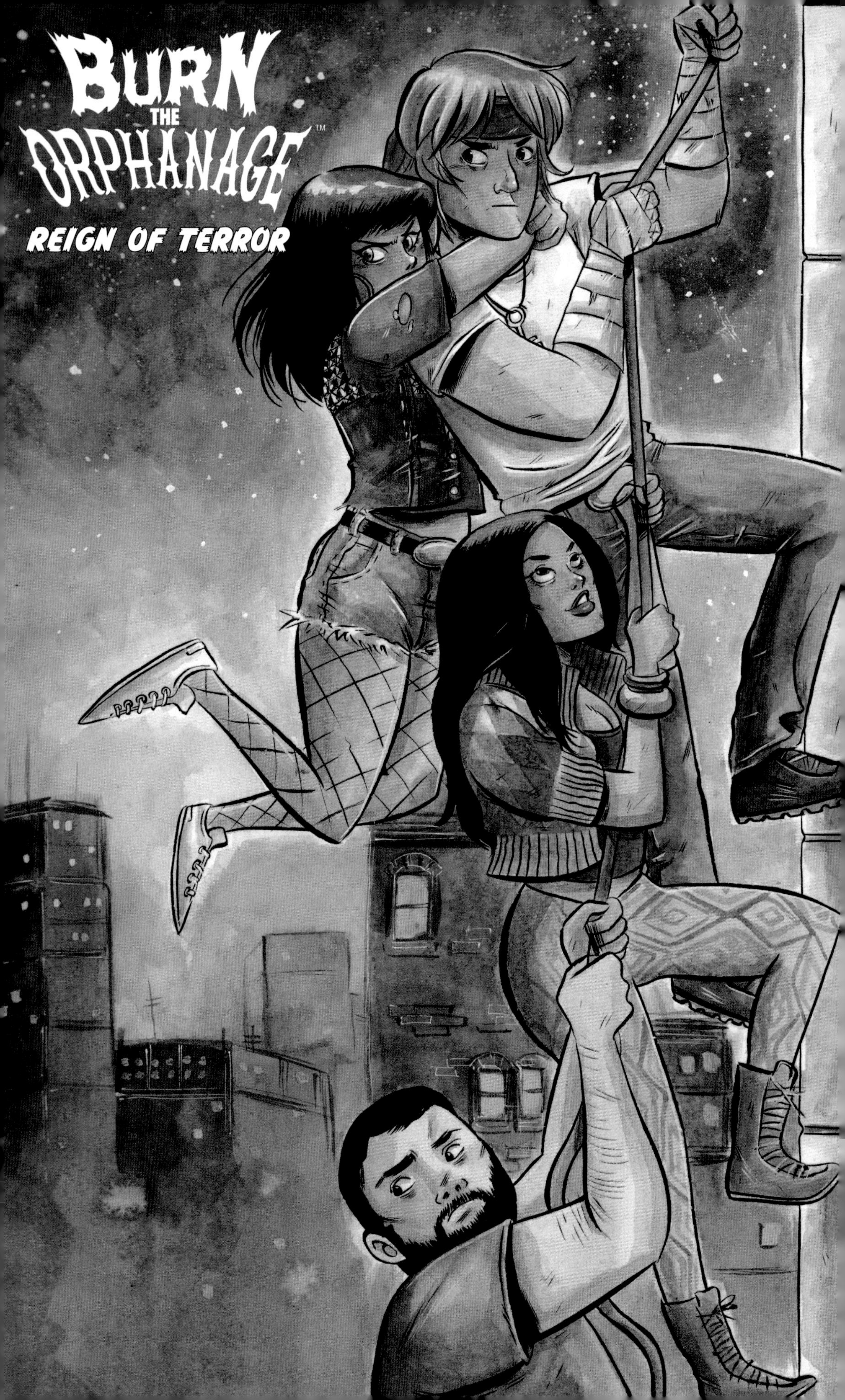
BURN THE ORPHANAGE™
REIGN OF TERROR

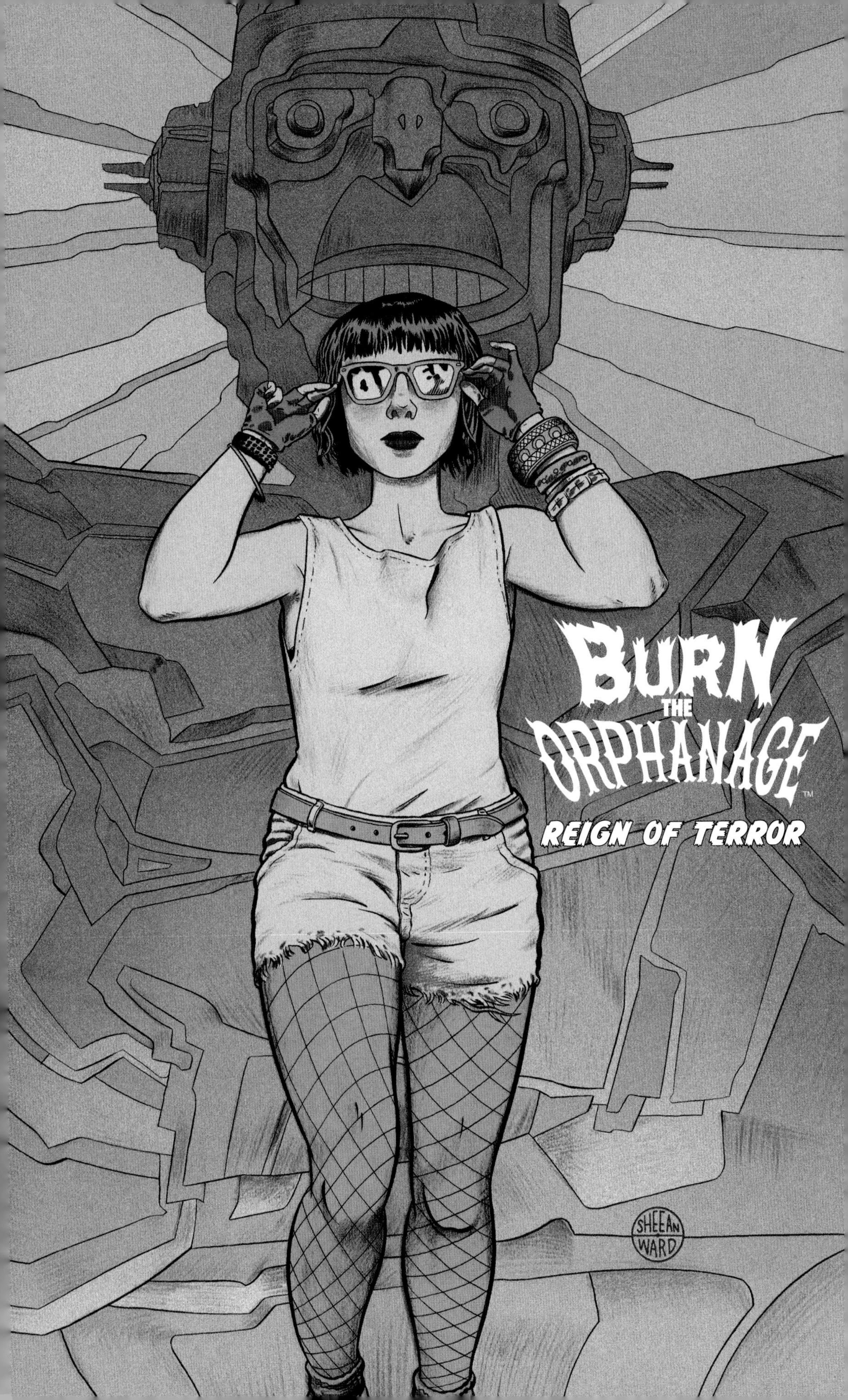
BURN THE ORPHANAGE™
REIGN OF TERROR
SHEEAN WARD

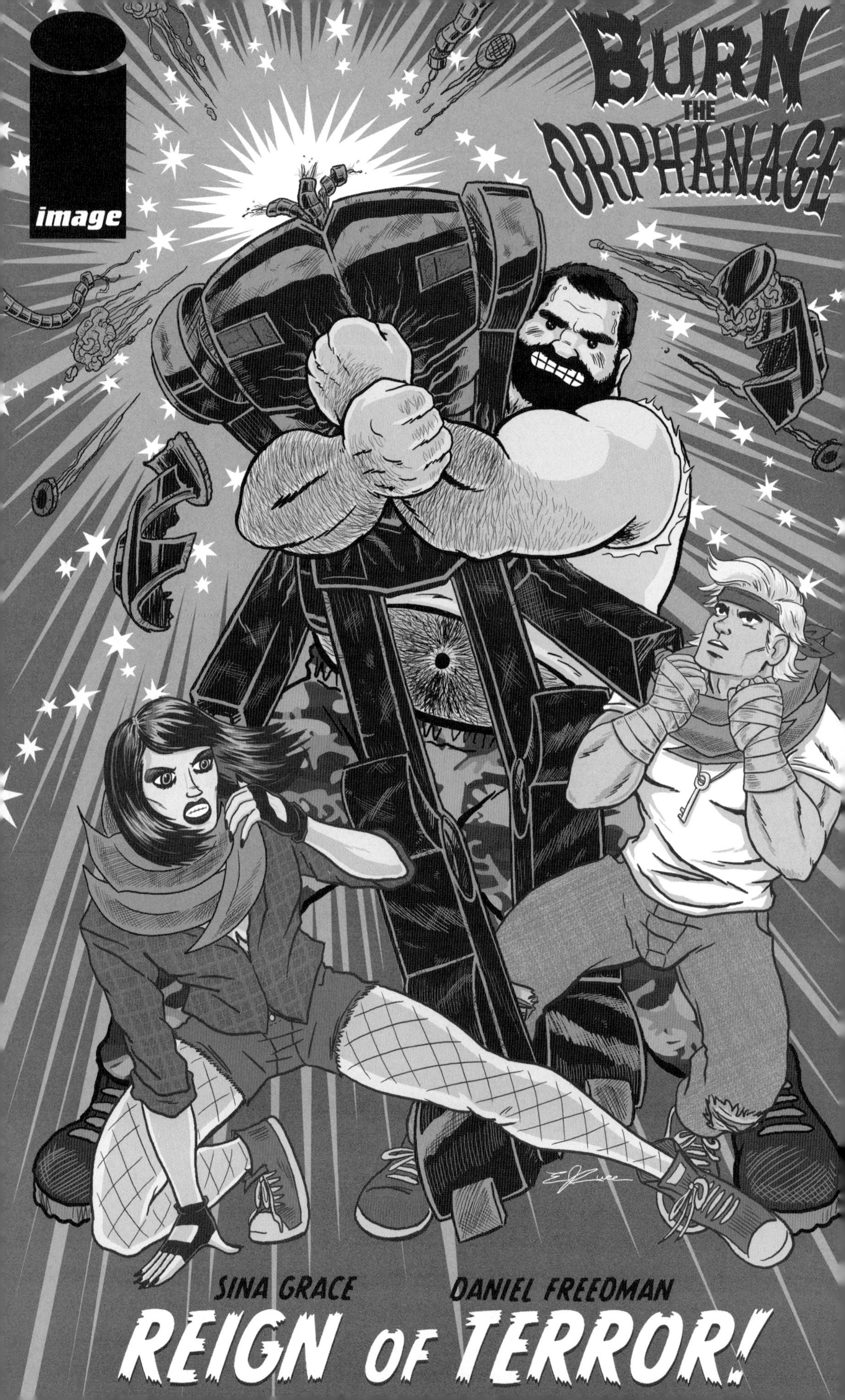
image
BURN THE ORPHANAGE
SINA GRACE
DANIEL FREEDMAN
REIGN OF TERROR!

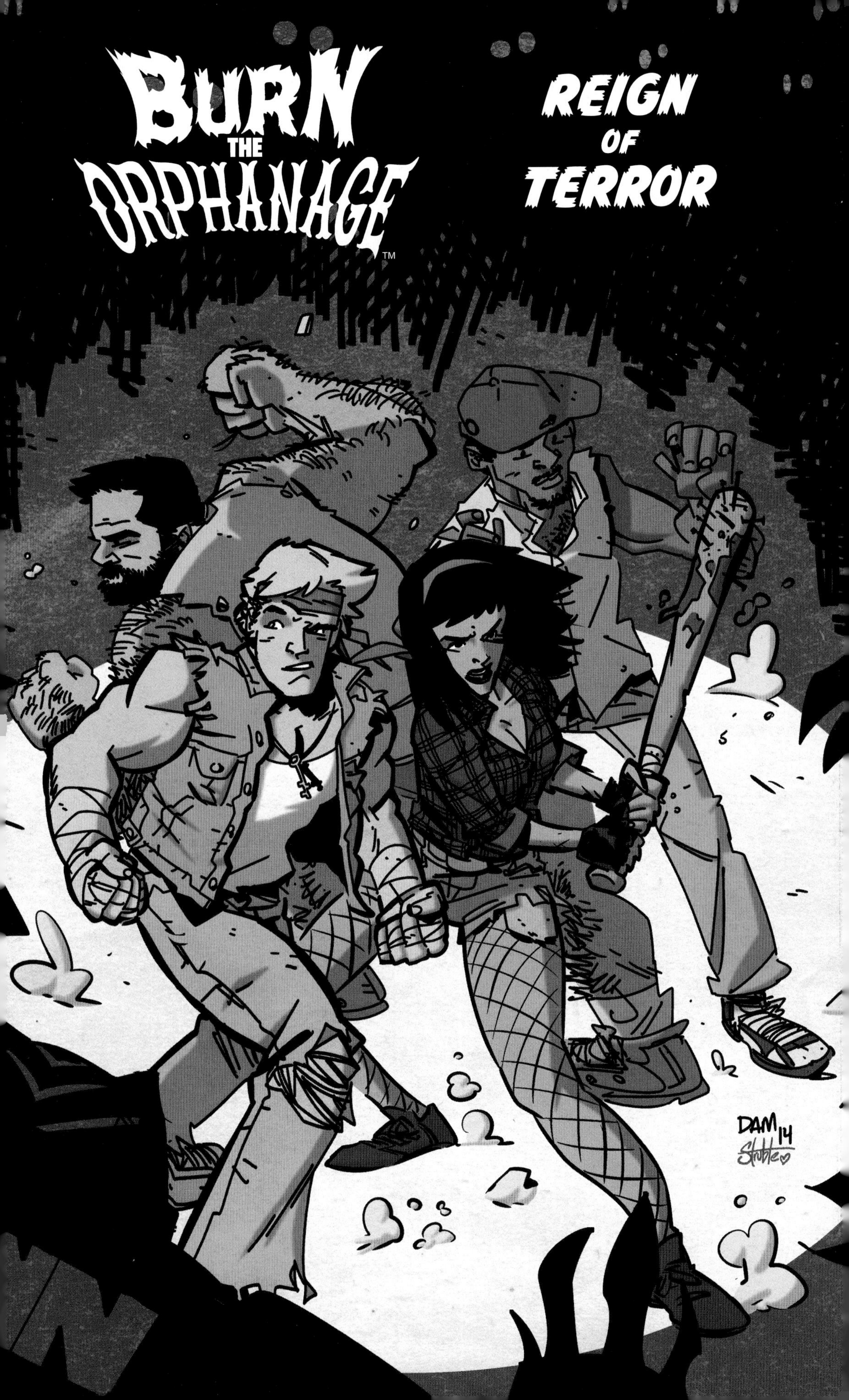
BURN THE ORPHANAGE™
REIGN OF TERROR
DAM 14
Struble

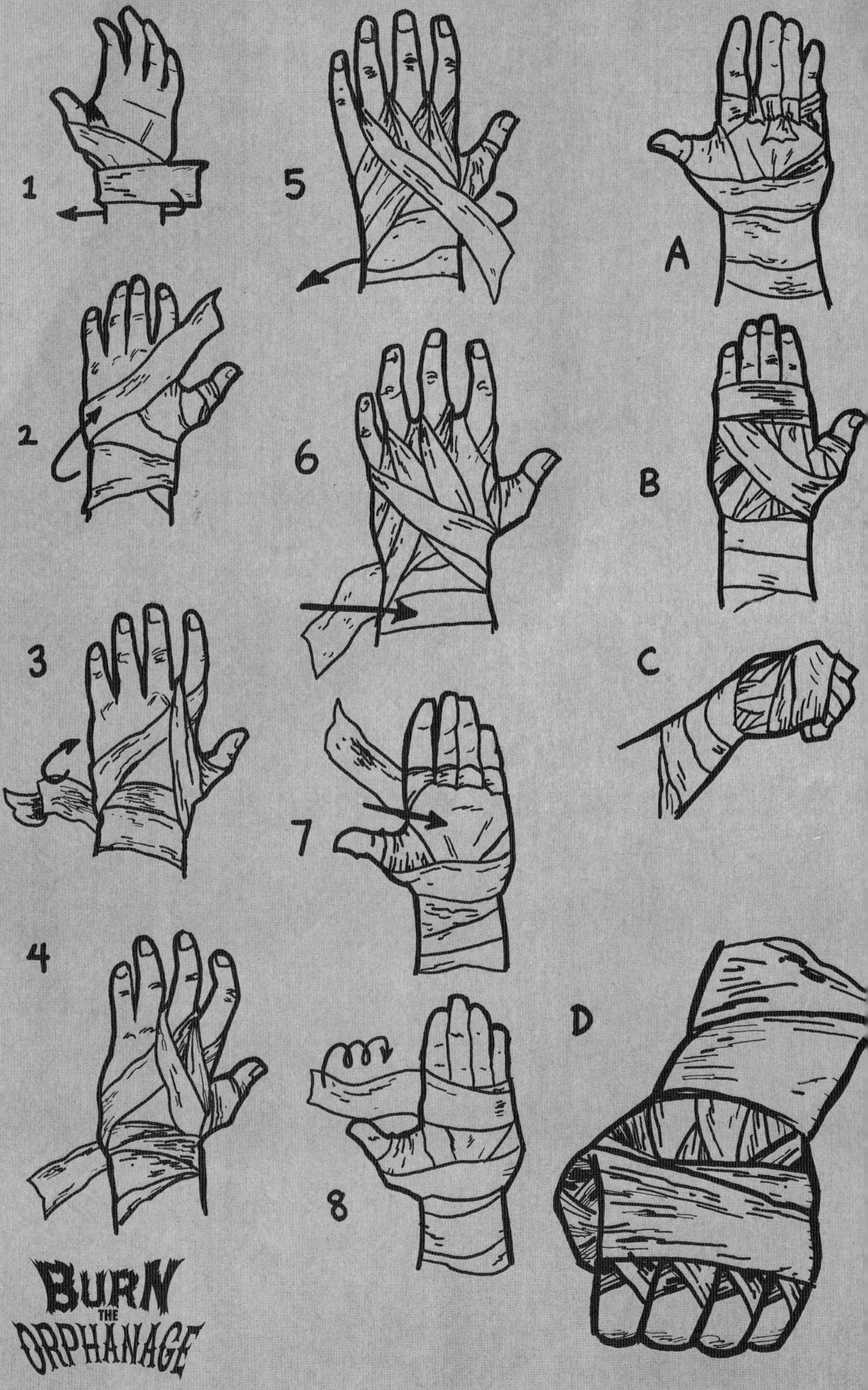
1
2
3
4
5
6
7
8
A
B
C
D

BURN THE ORPHANAGE

PROMOTIONAL ART

ROCK'S PIE-LATTE'S BYCYCLE EXCERCISE

STEP 1. EAT PIE. THEN LIE DOWN WITH YOUR CORE TUCKED. RAISE LEGS. ARMS STRAIGHT OUT. PALMS UP.

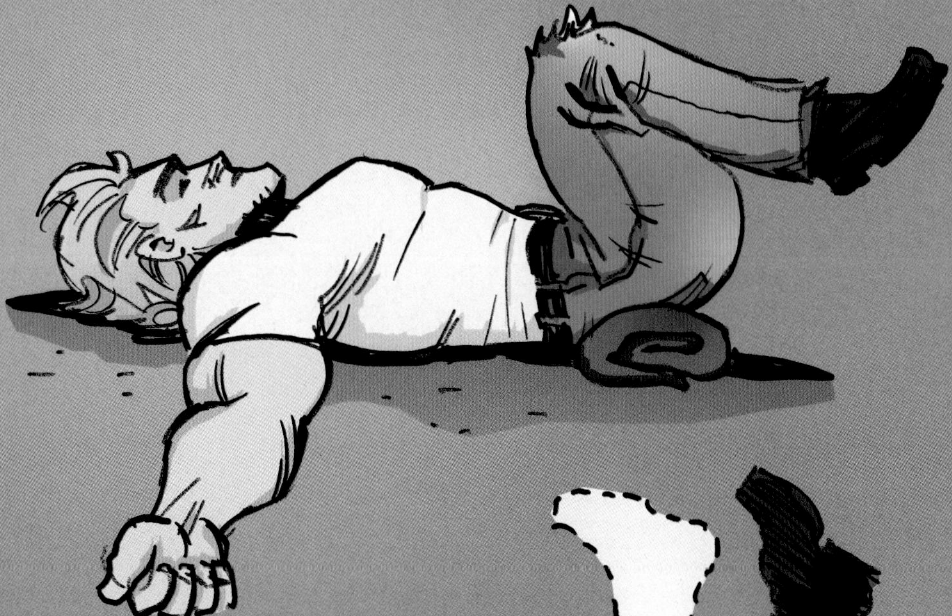

STEP 2. KEEPING ARMS DOWN AND WITHOUT LIFTING YOUR BACK, ROTATE EACH FOOT IN A BYCYCLE MOTION BY STRAIGHTENING ONE LEG AND BENDING THE OPPOSITE KNEE TO YOUR CHEST. AFTER ROTATATING LEGS 10 TIMES ONE WAY, REVERSE AND DO 10 MORE.

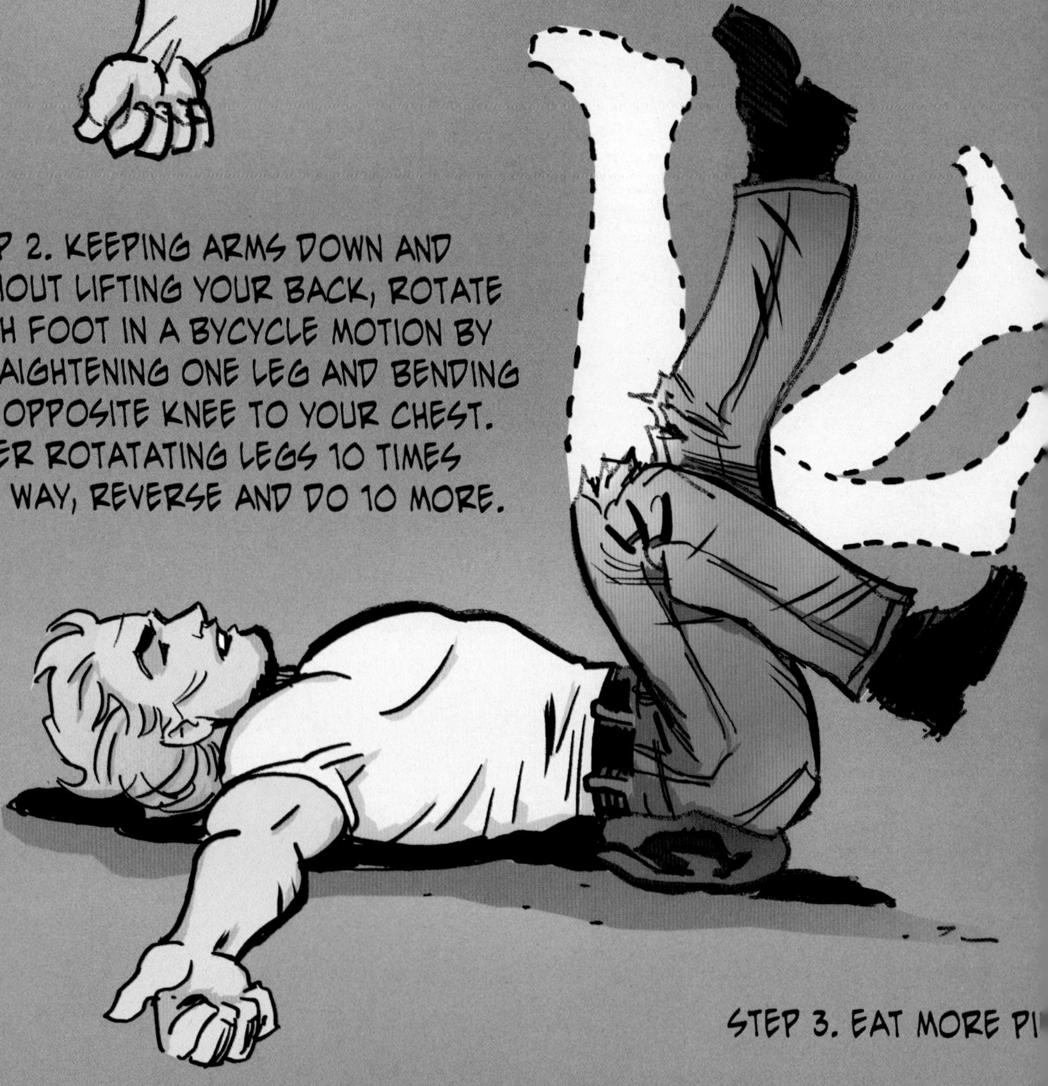

STEP 3. EAT MORE PI

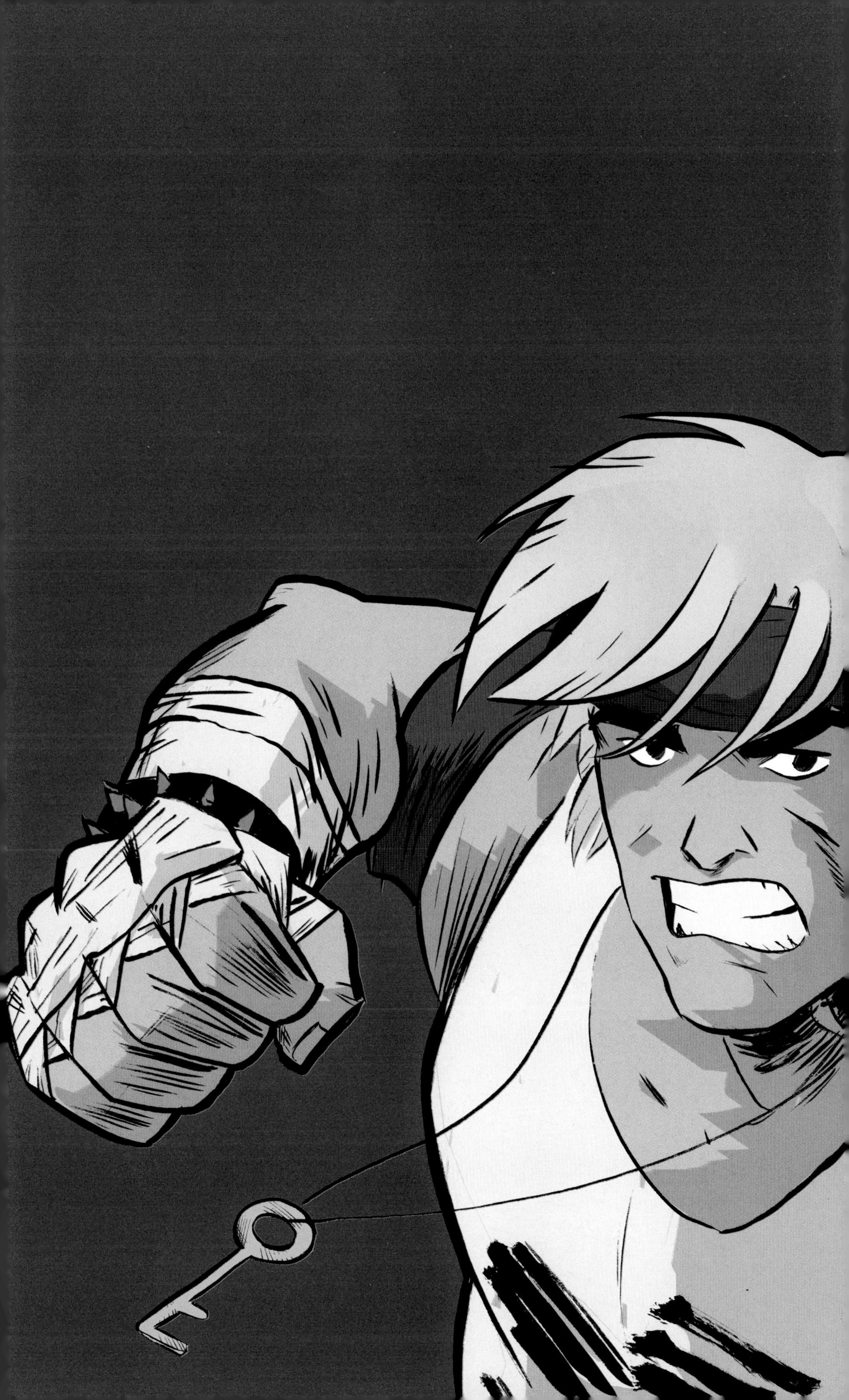

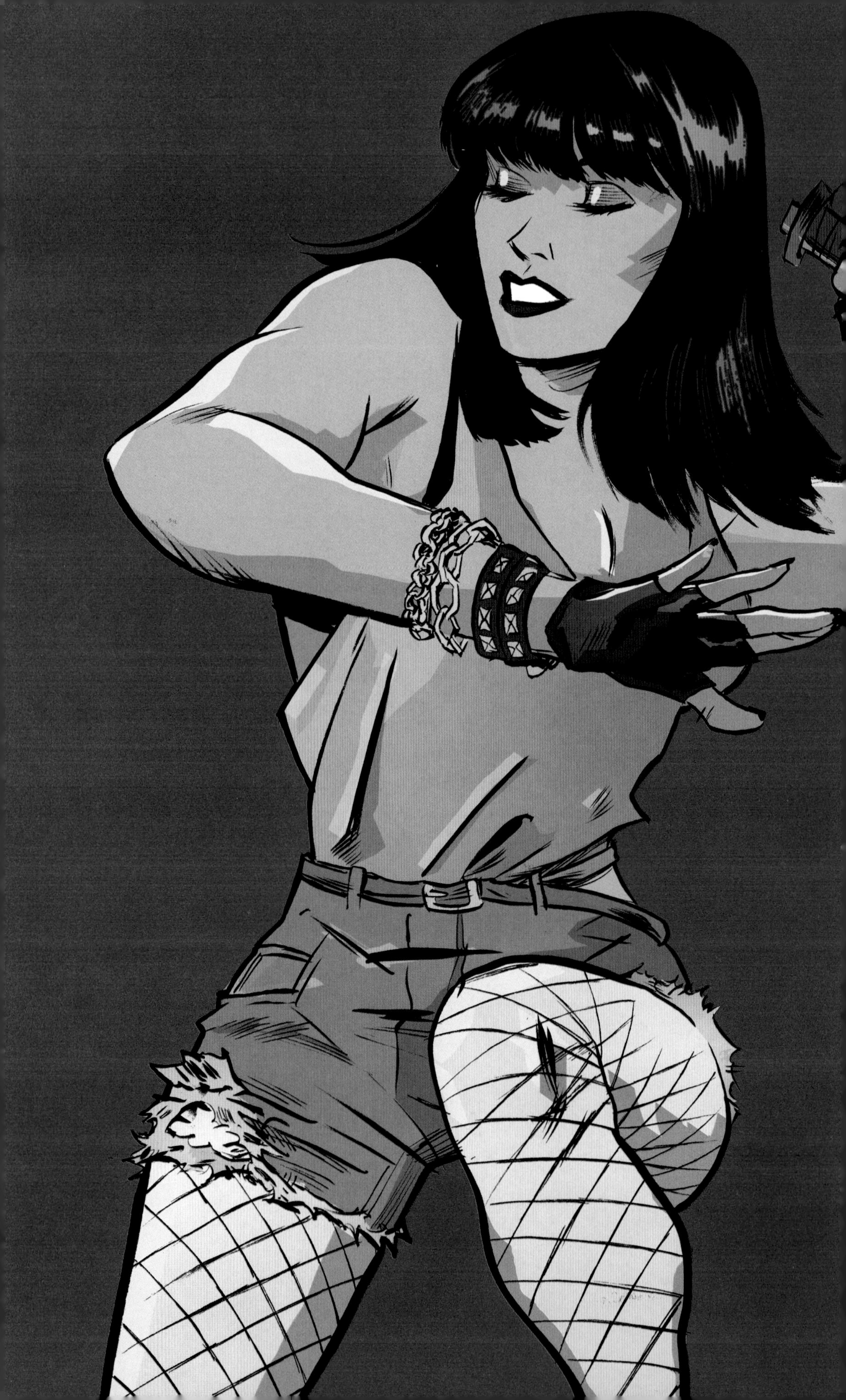

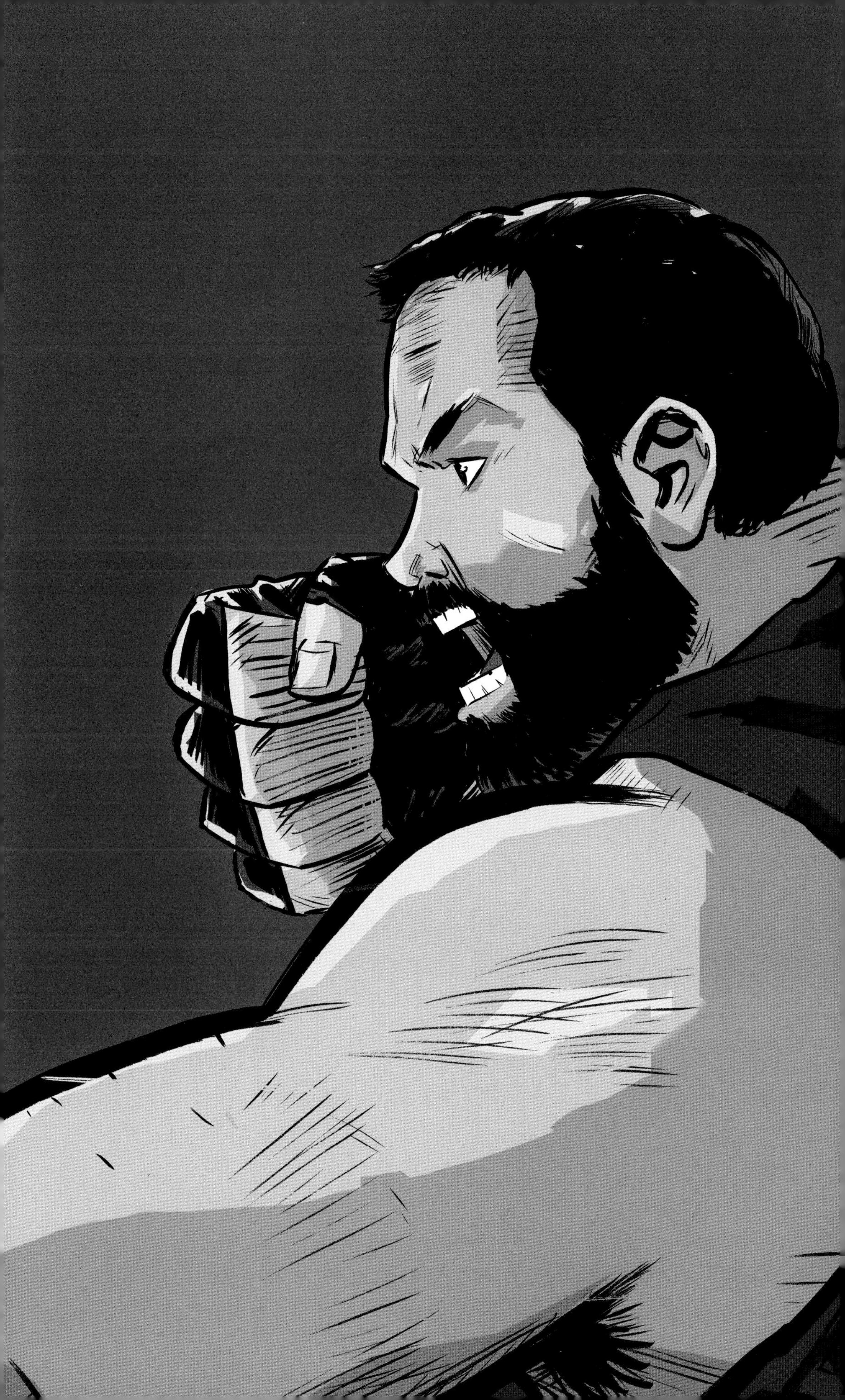

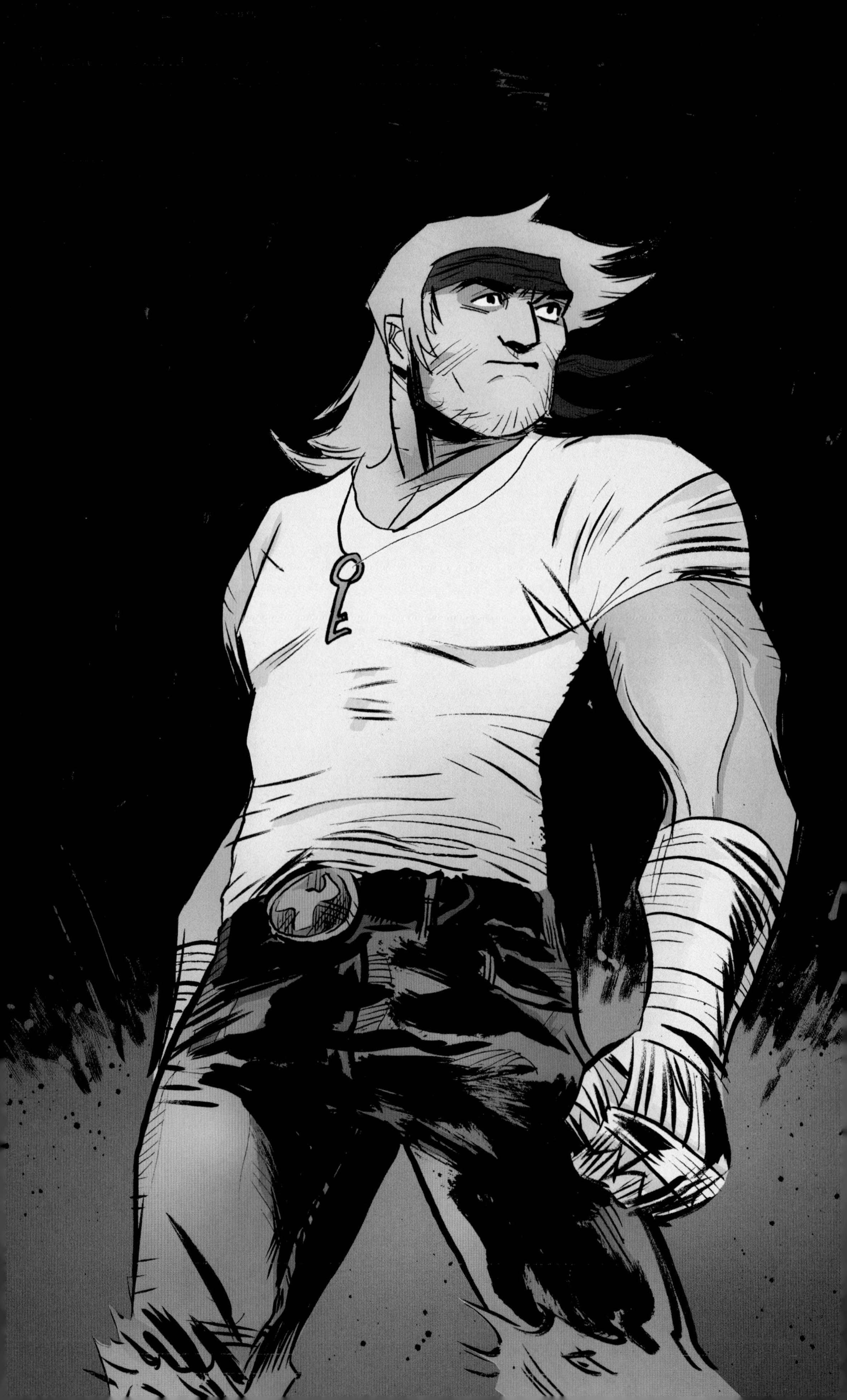

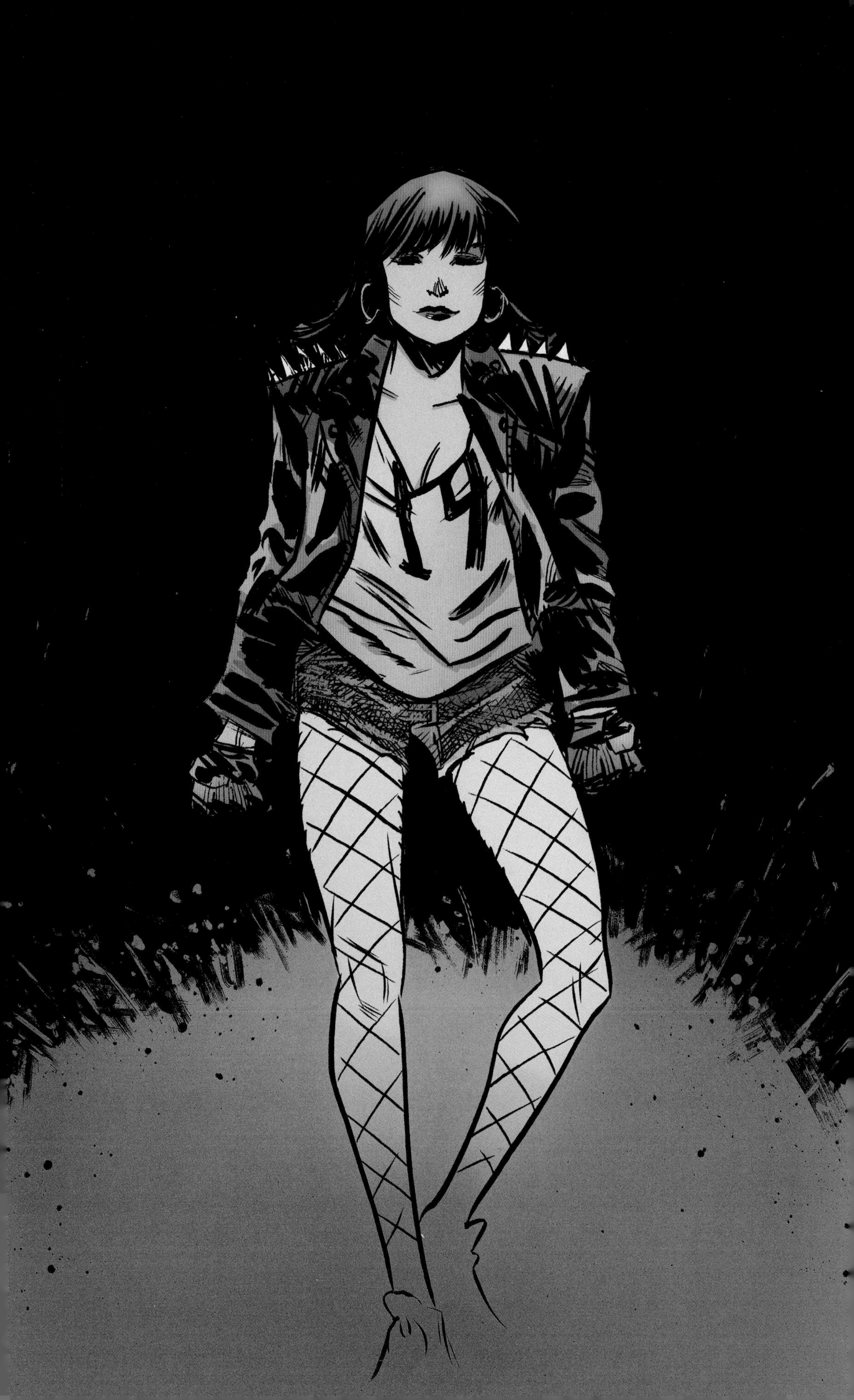

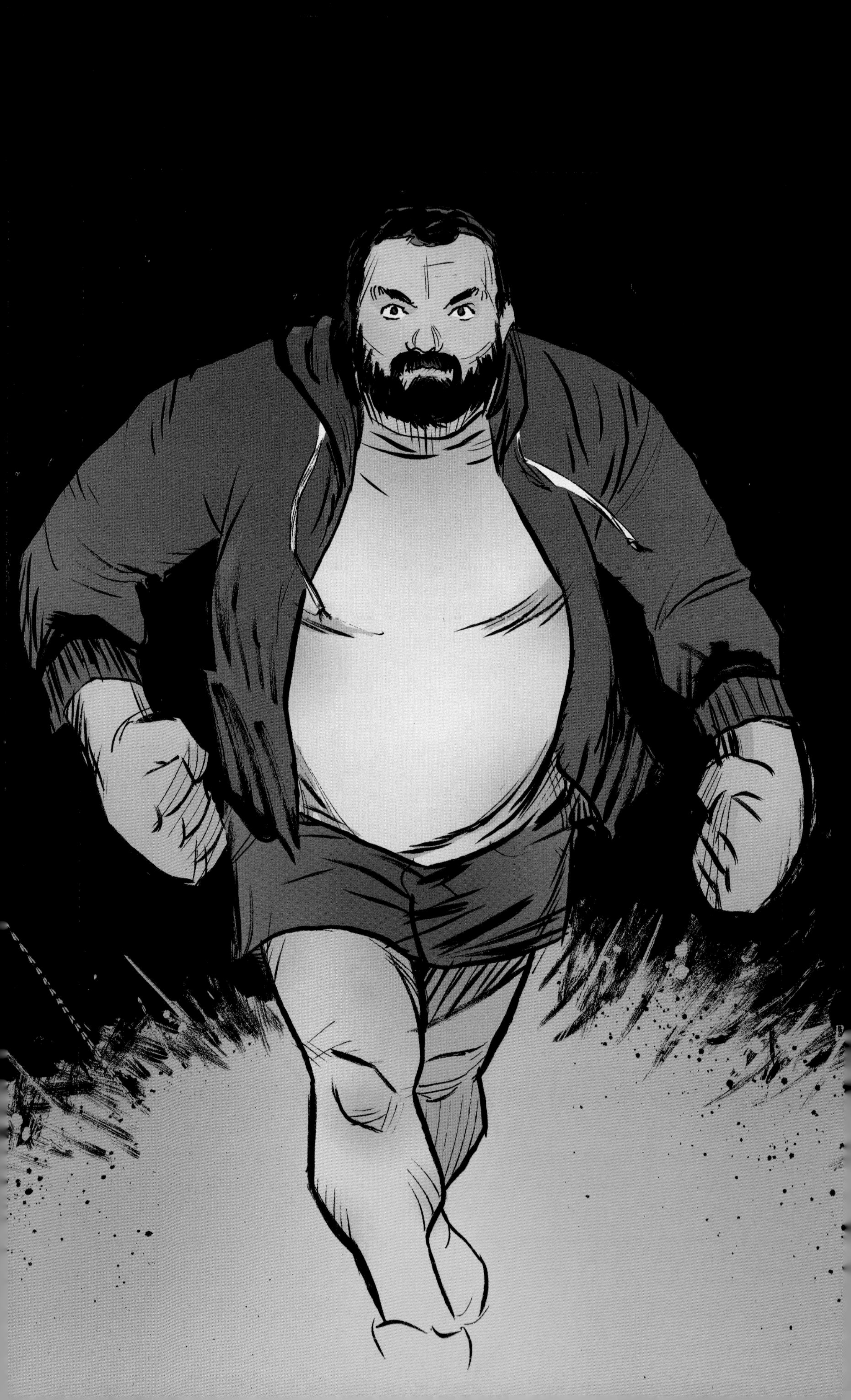

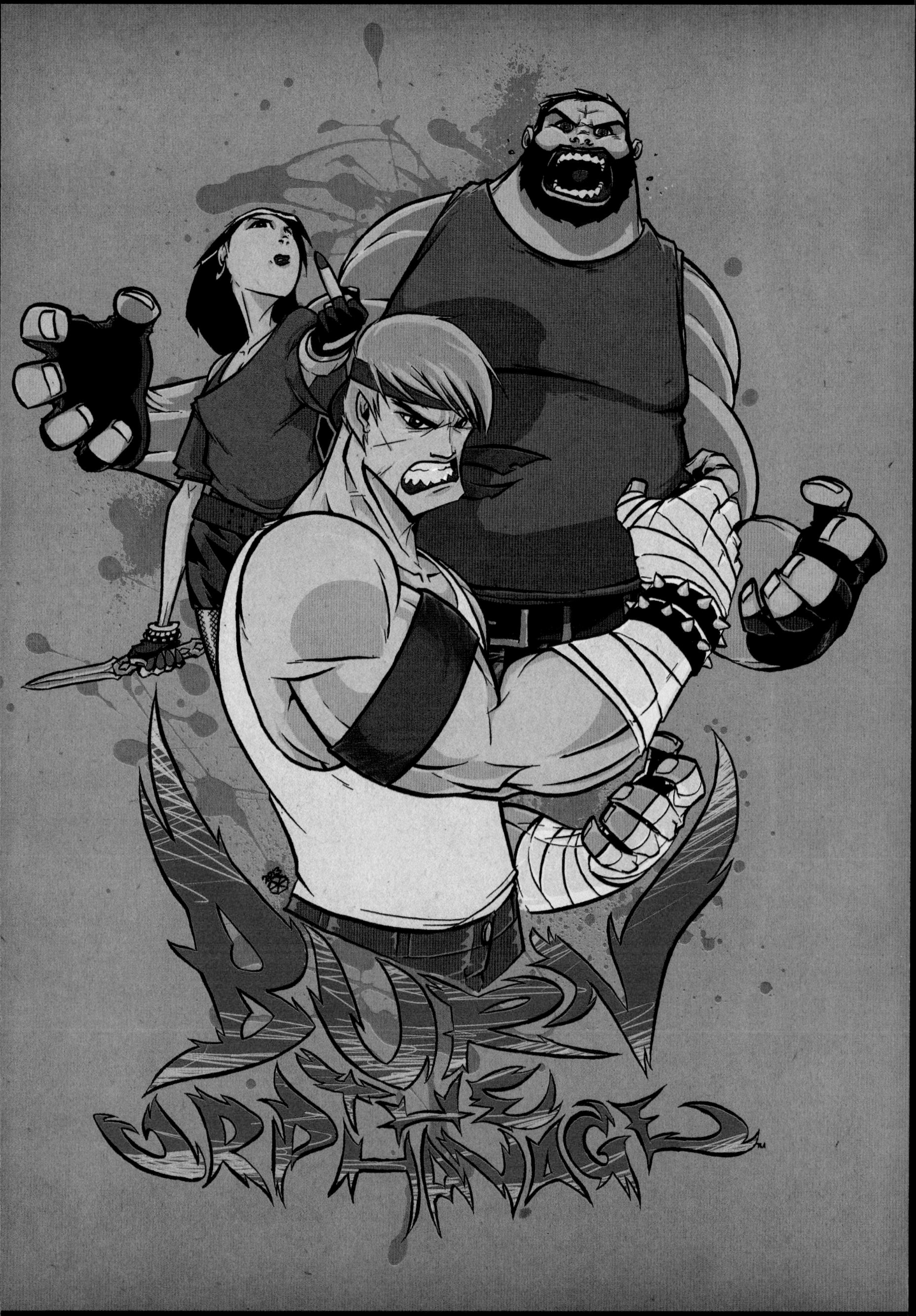

ARTWORK BY VINCENT KUKUA

VINCENTKUKUA.DEVIANTART.COM

TWITTER: @HAWAIIANPUNCH

INSTAGRAM: @VKUKUA

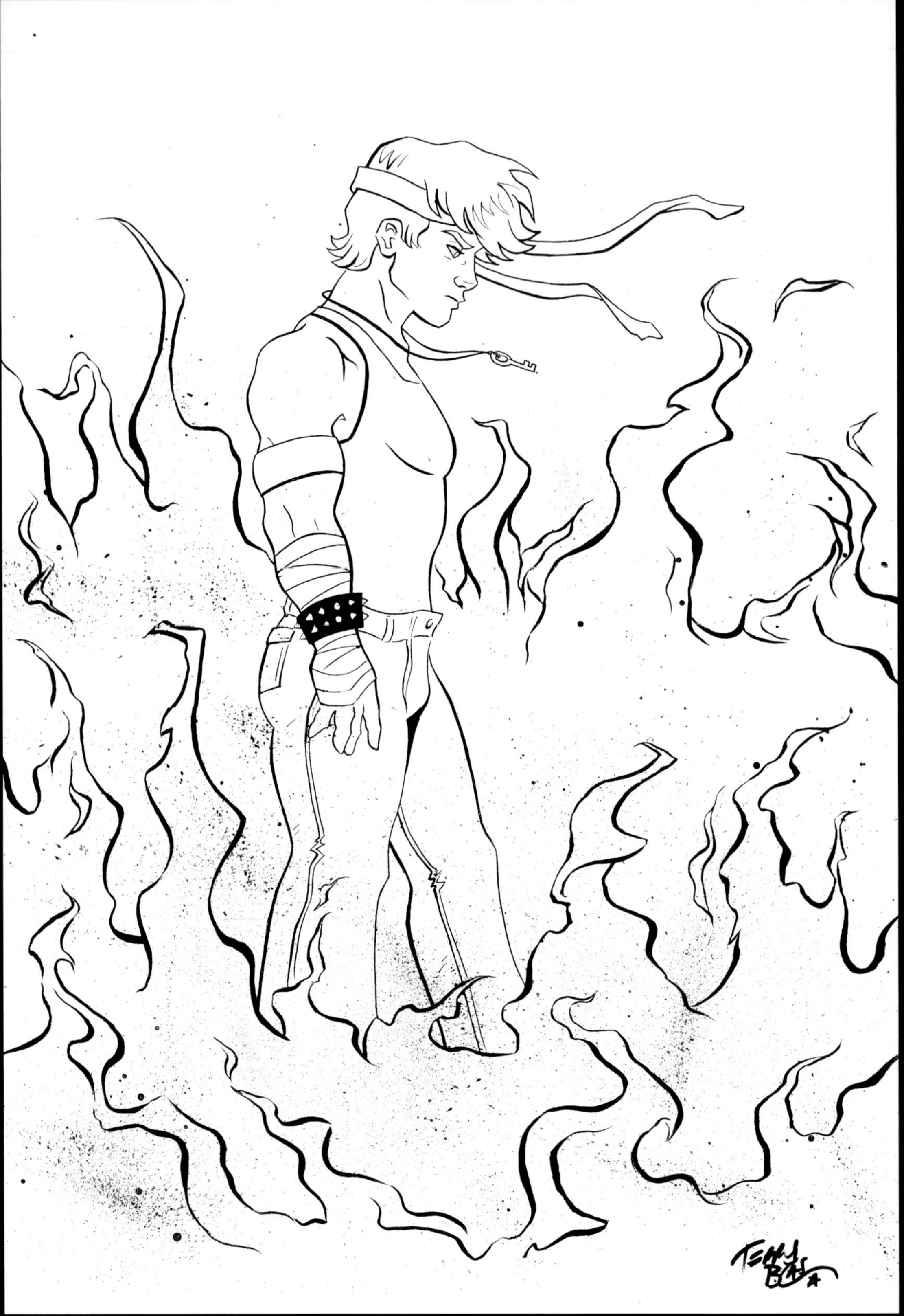

ILLUSTRATION BY TERRY BLAS
TERRYBLAS.COM
TWITTER/ INSTAGRAM: @TERRYBLAS

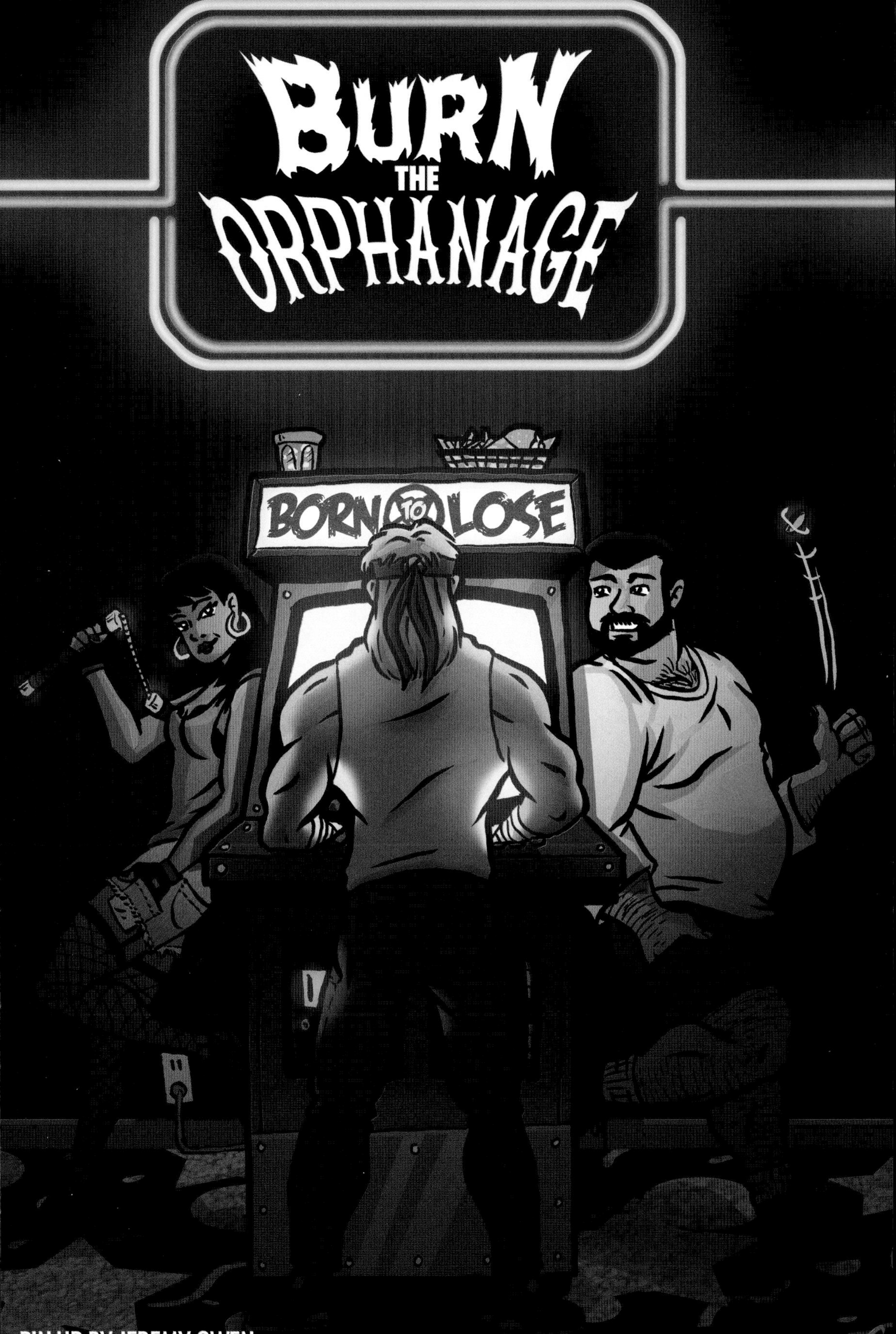
BURN
THE
ORPHANAGE
BORN TO LOSE

PIN-UP BY JEREMY OWEN

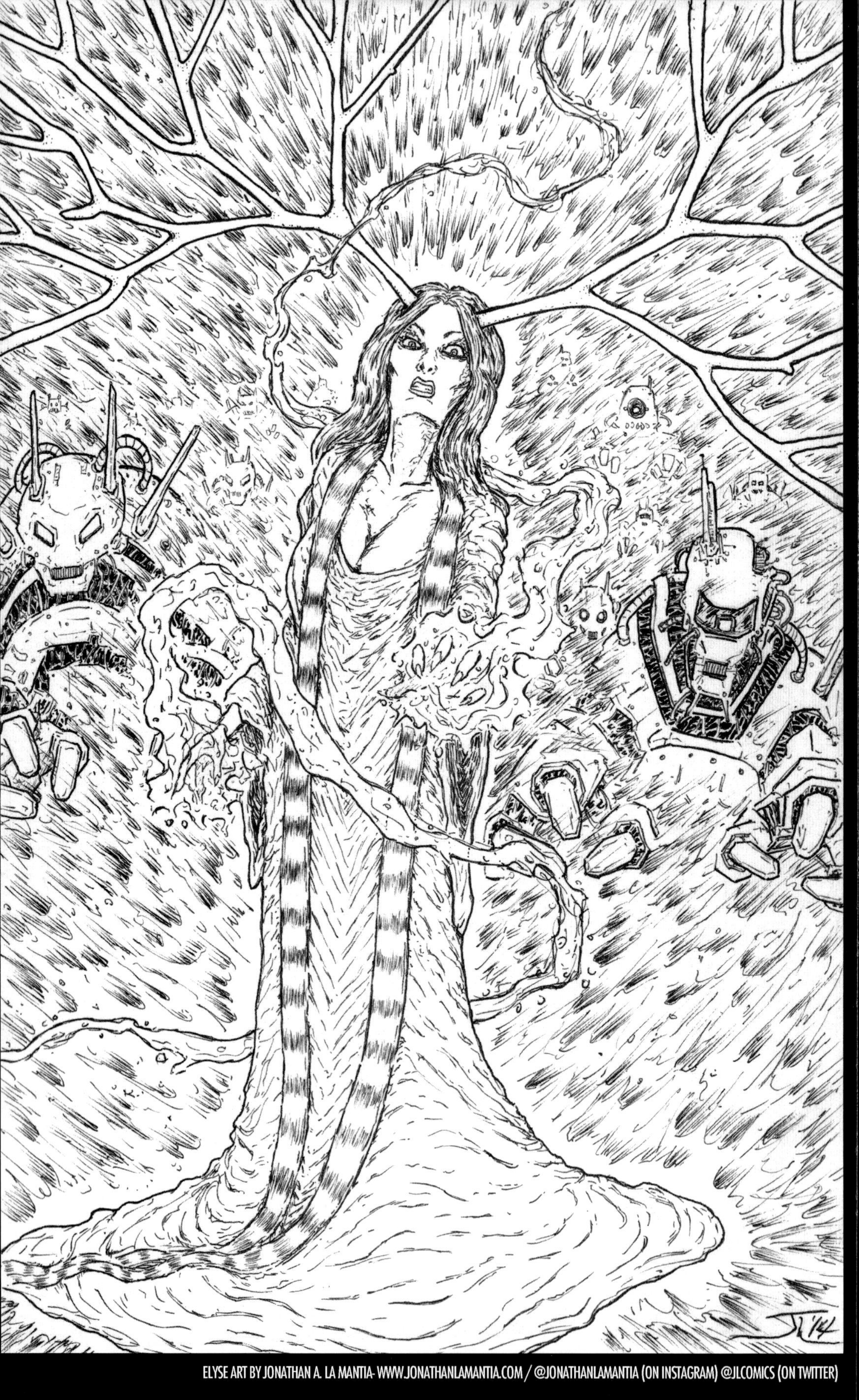
JL'14

ELYSE ART BY JONATHAN A. LA MANTIA- WWW.JONATHANLAMANTIA.COM / @JONATHANLAMANTIA (ON INSTAGRAM) @JLCOMICS (ON TWITTER)

BONUS MATERIAL

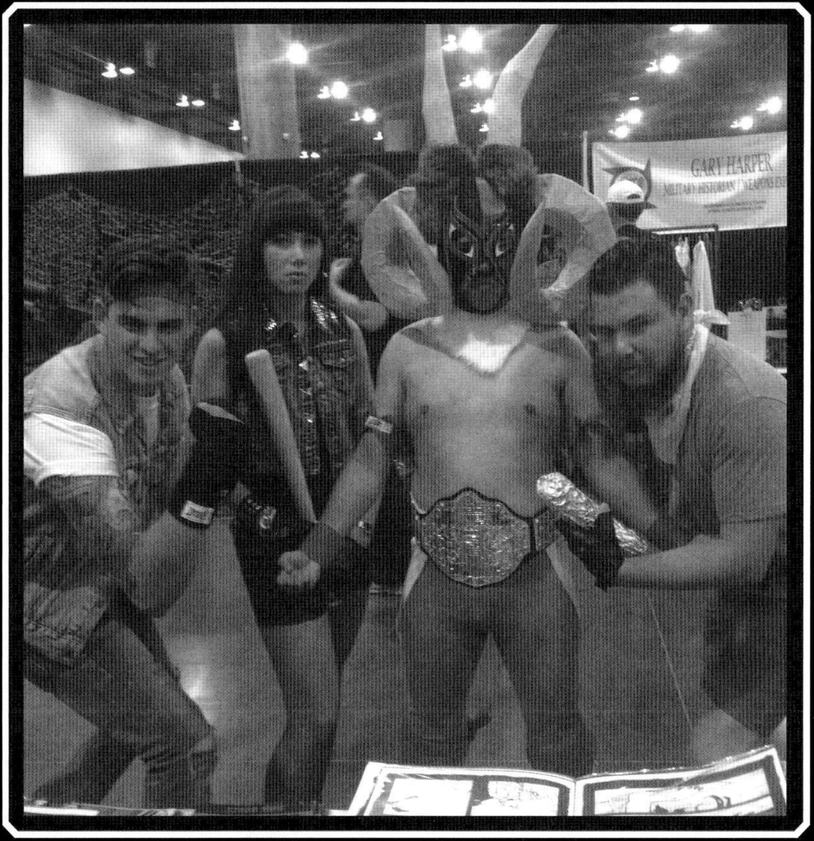
GARY HARPER

(Instagram homies @stephencam, @mell2ls, @alexlacson, & @chris_earth616 crushing the cosplay at Phoenix Comic-Con)

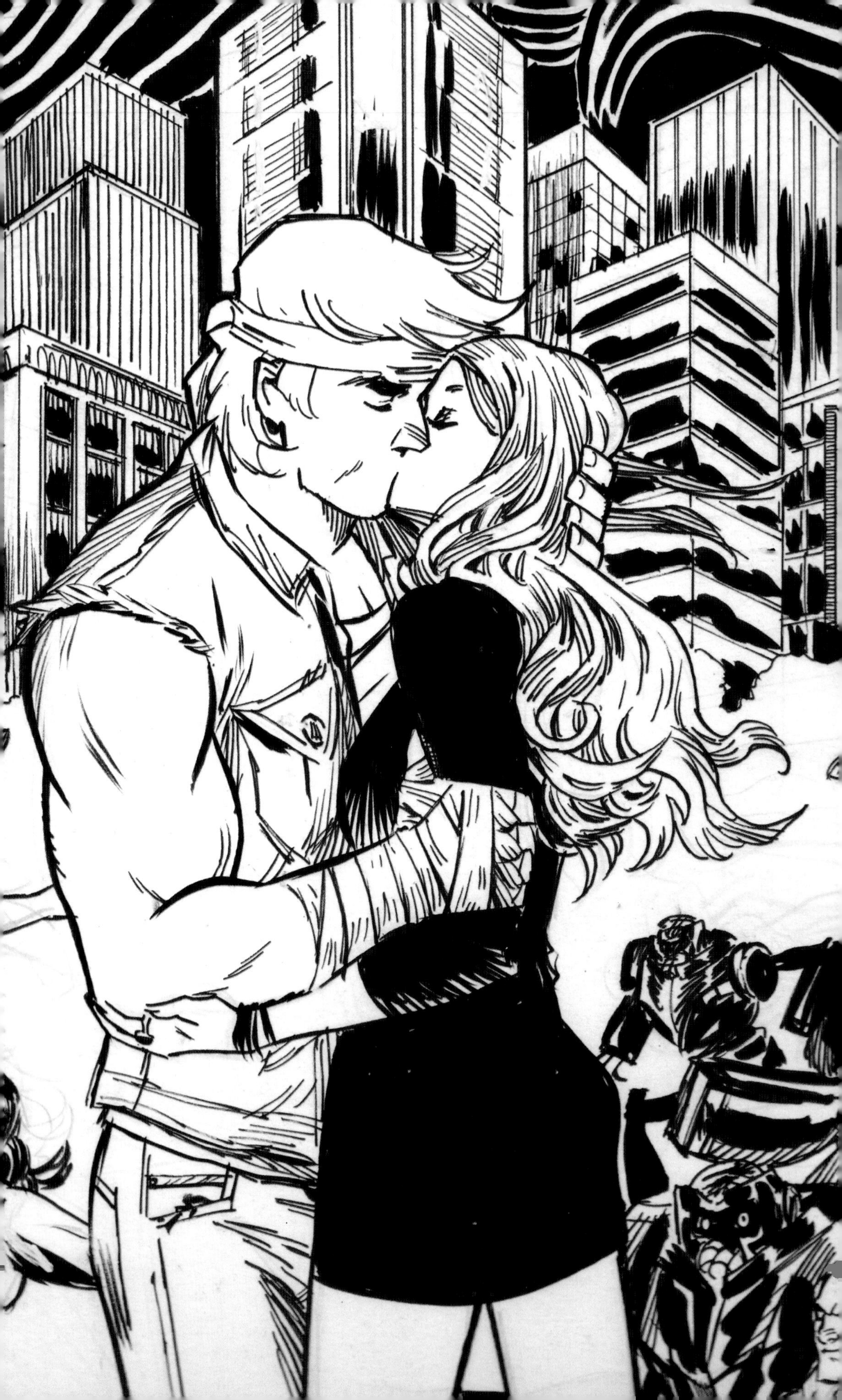

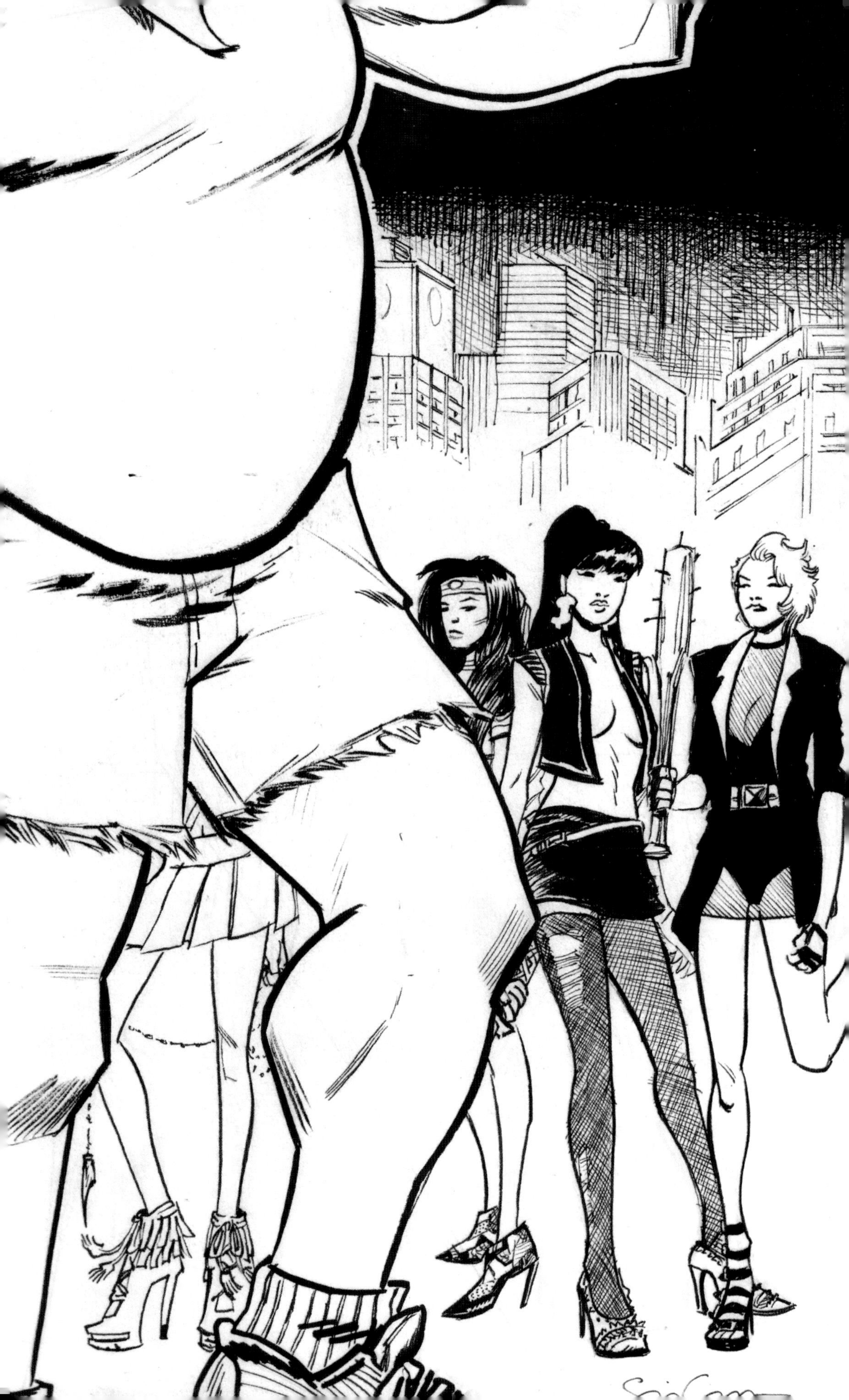

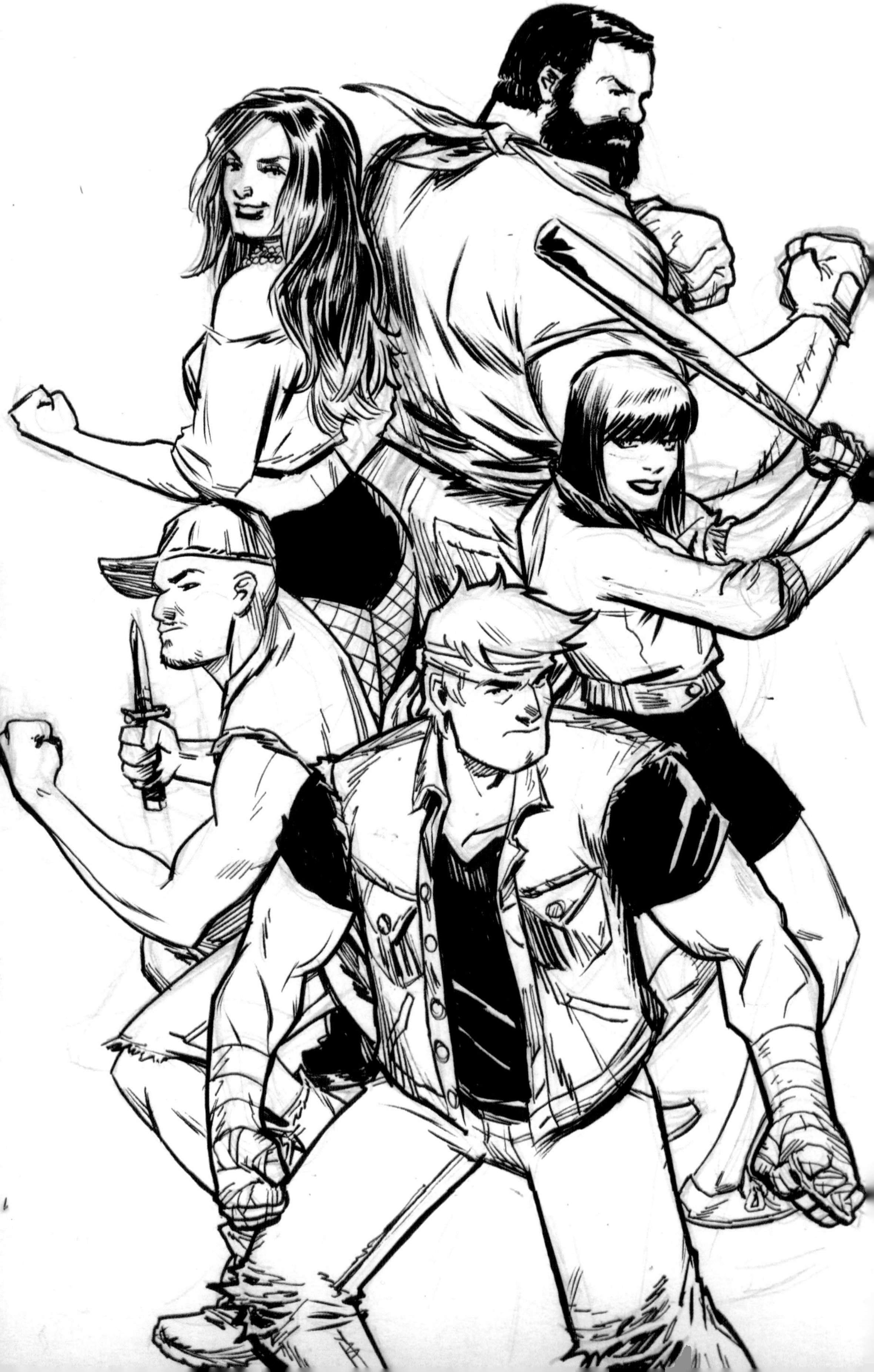

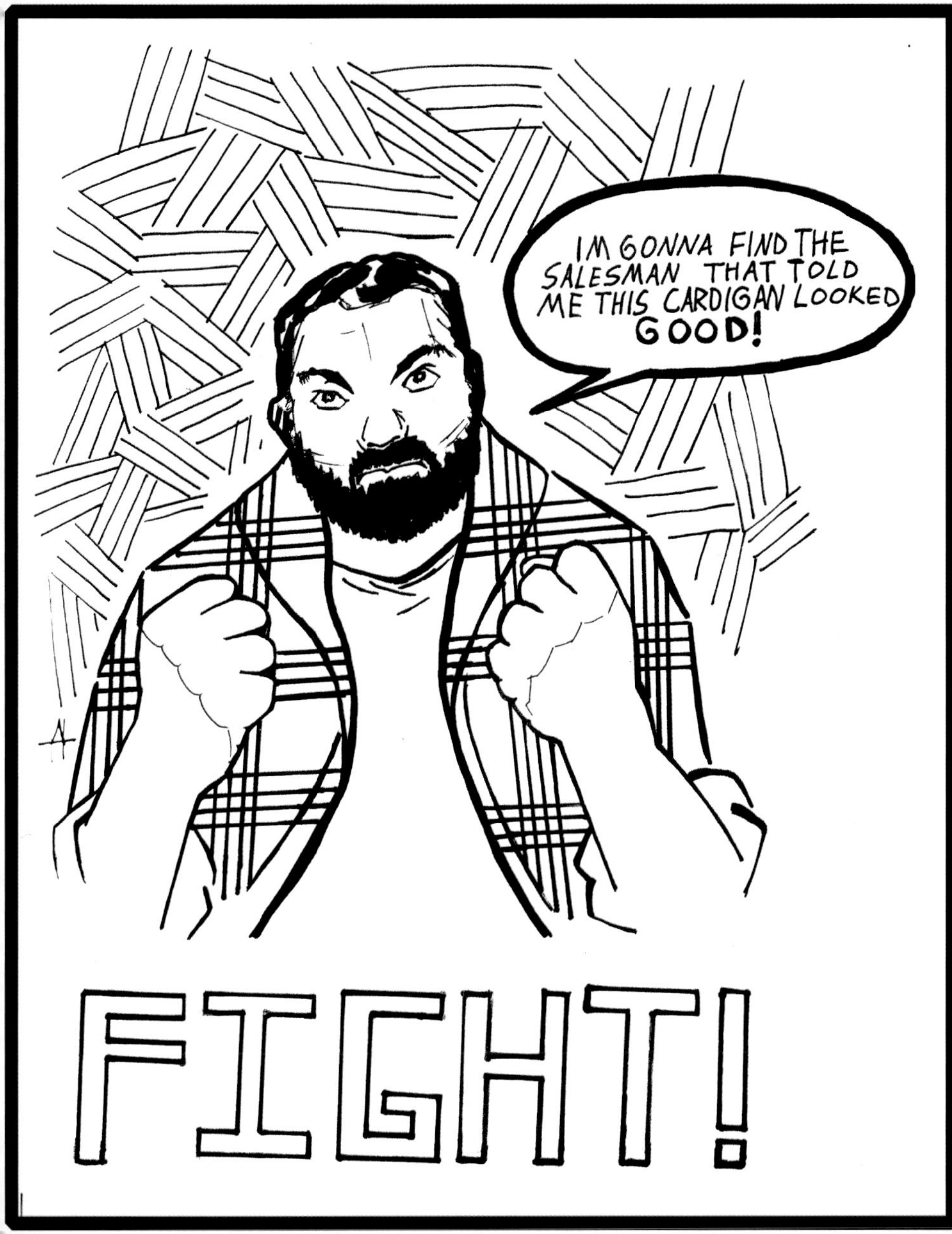
IM GONNA FIND THE SALESMAN THAT TOLD ME THIS CARDIGAN LOOKED GOOD!
FIGHT!

ʇunter Ardehali hooked us up with this cool drawing of
ʒear at our Golden Apple signing a while back.
ʂina is not taking it personally that Hunter thinks Bear hates
he cardigan.
@HunterArdehali on twitter/ instagram
ıunterardehali.deviantart.com

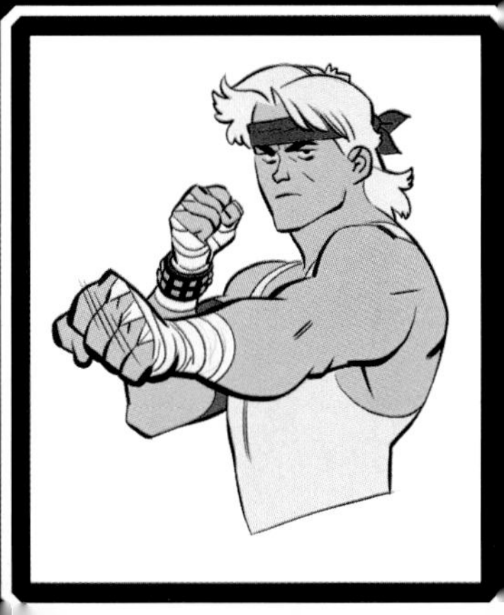

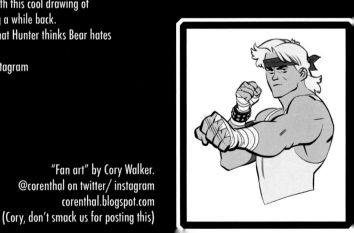

"Fan art" by Cory Walker.
@corenthal on twitter/ instagram
corenthal.blogspot.com
(Cory, don't smack us for posting this)

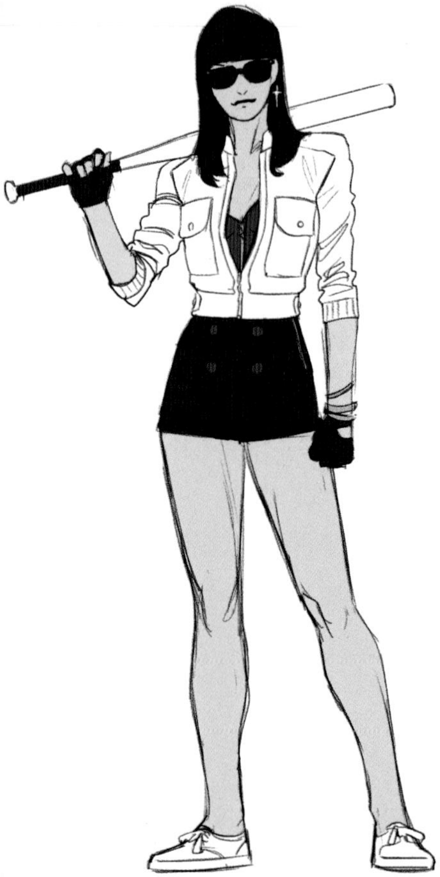

Above: Kris Anka making Lex harder and sleeker
kristaferanka.tumblr.com / TWITTER & INSTAGRAM: @kristaferanka

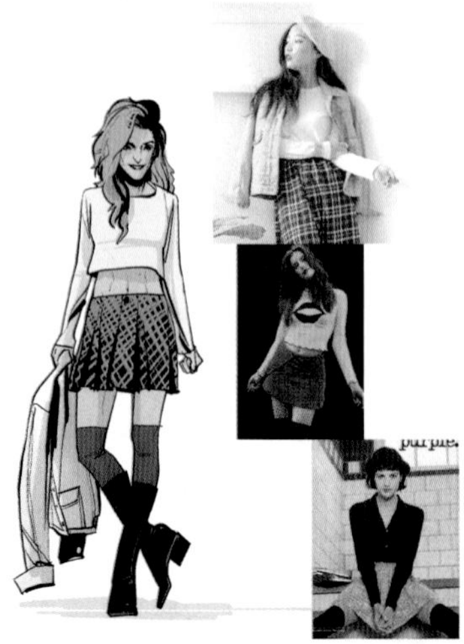

Above: Fiona Staples giving Jess some '90s love
fionastaples.tumblr.com/ Twitter & Instagram: @fionastaples

With everyone trapped at the Crimson Dragon, we thought it would b refreshing to put the ladies in new duds, courtesy of the topless stripper ninjas.

At its heart, Burn the Orphanage is about that time when you and yo friends met at the arcade, or hit the multi-player option on an at-hor console... coming together and collaborating with our artist friends t make funny books is our version of that.

Thanks so much to Kris Anka, Fiona Staples, W. Scott Forbes and Ming Doyle for coming up with bad-ass outfits for the BTO ladies to rock in issues four and five.

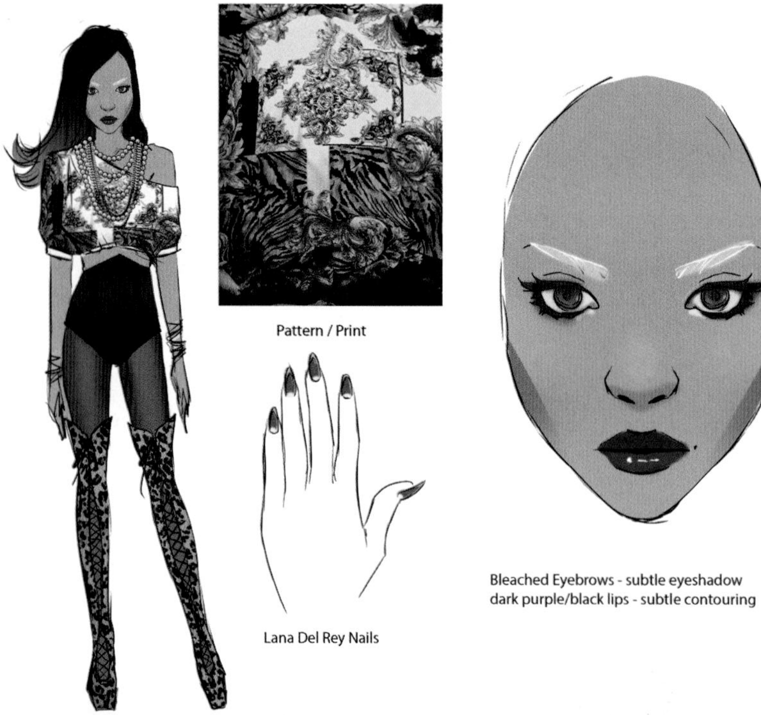
Pattern / Print
Lana Del Rey Nails
Bleached Eyebrows - subtle eyeshadow
dark purple/black lips - subtle contouring

This side: W. Scott Forbes doing a bombastic head-to-toe reimagining of Iz, all the way down to her nails

wscottforbes.com
TWITTER: @scottforbes
INSTAGRAM: @wscottforbes

Next Page: Ming Doyle making Elyse that much more intense

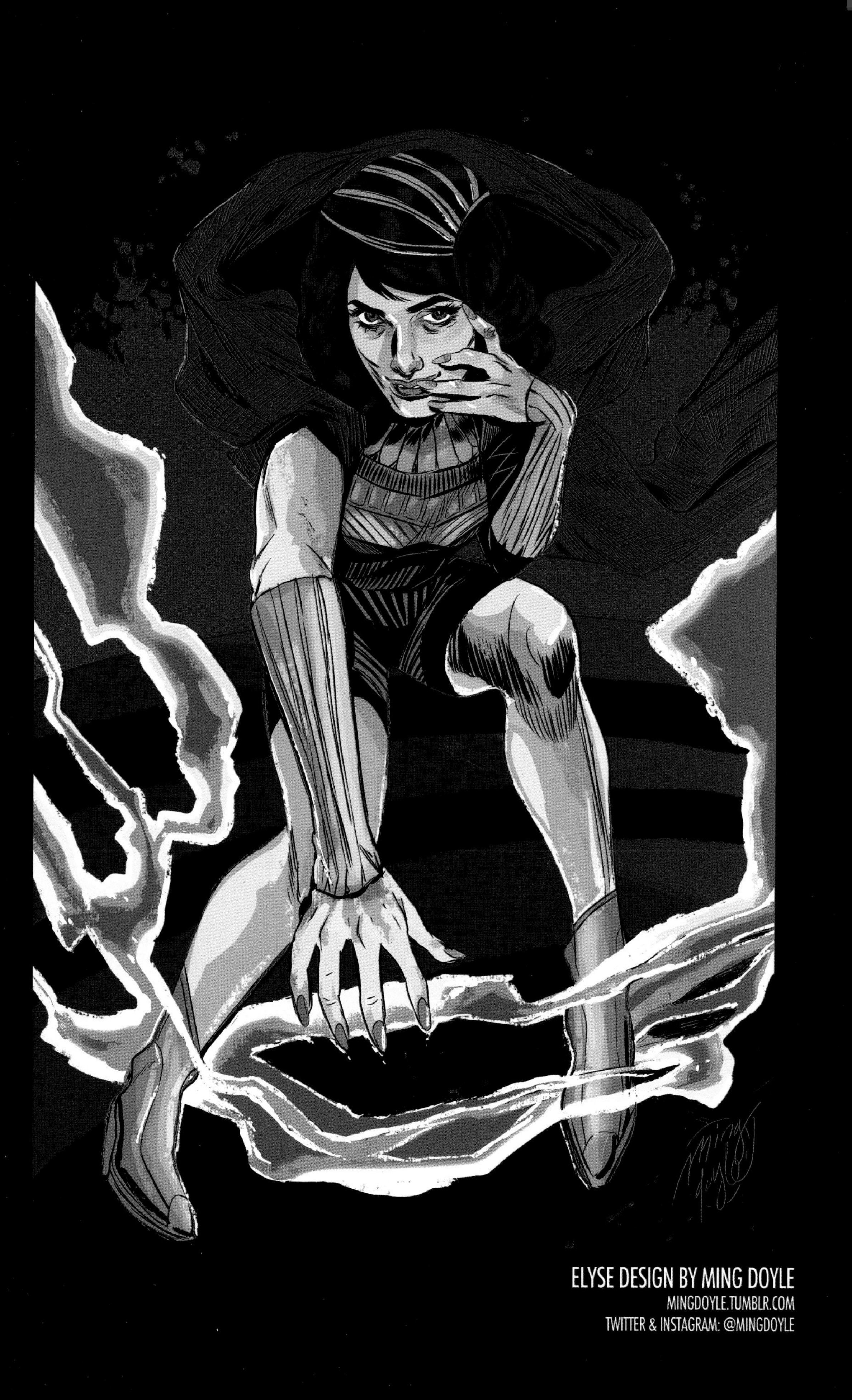

ELYSE DESIGN BY MING DOYLE
MINGDOYLE.TUMBLR.COM
TWITTER & INSTAGRAM: @MINGDOYLE

Illustration by Aaron Carrillo - instagram.com/elbow_mcshreddz

Amber (@Cheebidee- twitter/ @_Cheebidee on insta) cosplaying as Lex alongside IRL Bear and Iz during our Meltdown Comics kickoff.

Artwork by Earl Yi
tumblr, Society 6 & deviantART:
s133pDEADart

Illustration by Derek Pashano Dirtysavage84.deviantart.com & Facebook.com/Derek.pashano

Daniel Renee, and Sina signing at Meltdown Comics in Los Angeles, CA.

Rock by Luis Calderon (@spacebaystudios) & Andy Manley (@andymanley

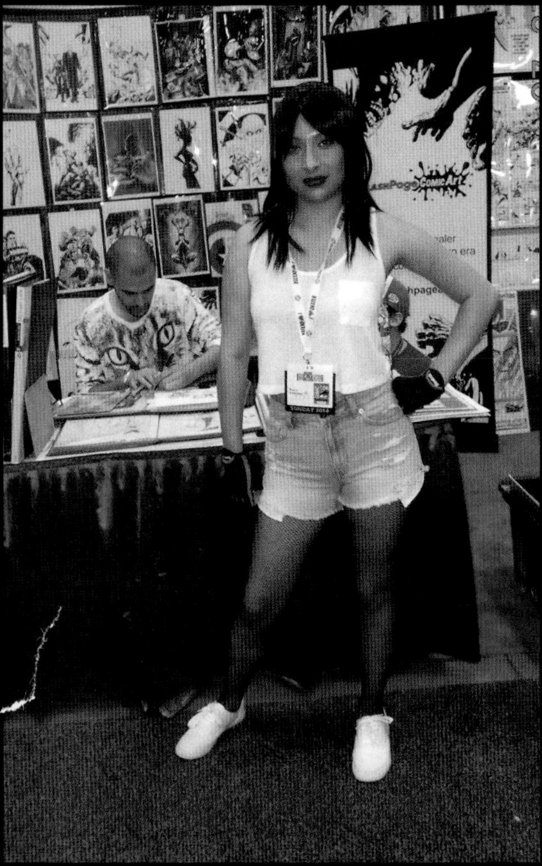

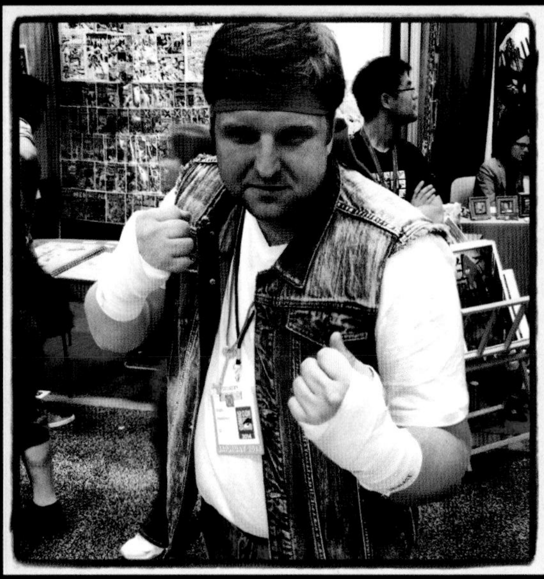

ABOVE: @DOUGIEDONUTS SHOWING US SOME TRUE GRIT AT SAN DIEGO COMIC-CON AS CLASSIC ROCK.

LEFT: ROSANA BUSTAMANTE (@ROSANAB1031) CAME CORRECT AS LEX. SHE WENT THROUGH TWO WIGS AND MADE SURE TO KILL IT IN WHITE KEDS. (SINA'S IN THE BACKGROUND WEARING A CAT SWEATER)

COSPLAY RULES

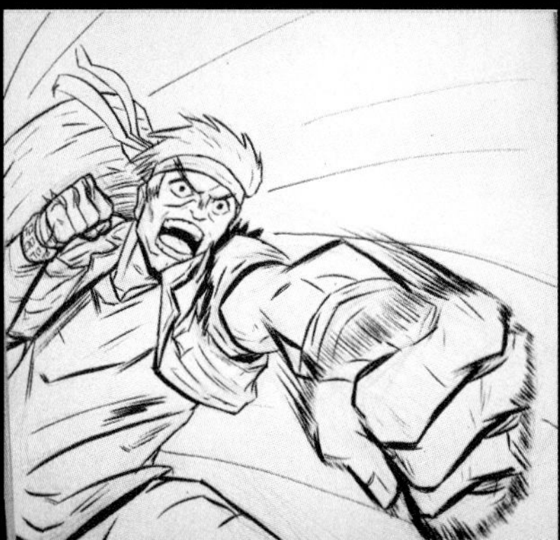

BONUS!!!
WARM-UP ROCK SKETCH BY BRANDON HANKINS (@BRANDONLHANKINS)

YOU CAN COSPLAY TOO!

@BEARTURNEDZOMBIE POSTED A SHOT ON INSTAGRAM OF HIS AT-HOME BEAR COSPLAY, AND HE NAILED IT!

THANKS AGAIN TO EVERYONE WHO MADE THE SUMMER CONVENTIONS SO MUCH FUN FOR US! YOUR SUPPORT PUTS THE BIGGEST GRINS ON OUR FACES.

FEEL FREE TO KEEP ON COSPLAYING, DRAWING, AND LOVING BTO!

- DF & SG

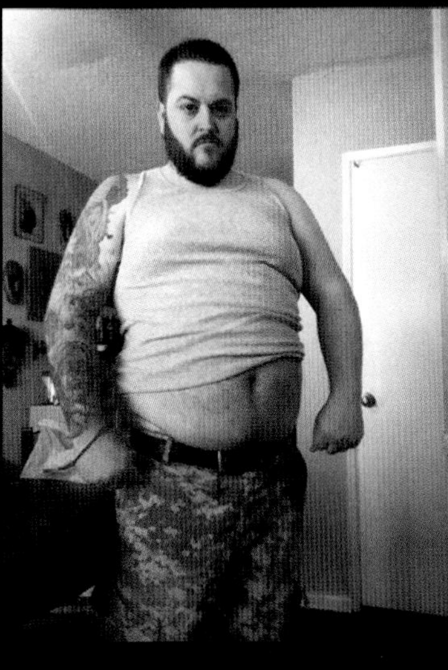

DANIEL FREEDMAN

Daniel Freedman was born and raised in Los Angeles. After proudly dropping out of two prestigious art schools he went to work writing for page and screen. Daniel co-created, wrote and colored the Image Comics mini-series UNDYING LOVE with Tomm Coker. He has edited award-winning documentaries like DIRTY HANDS: The Art and Crimes of David Choe, as well as edited a multitude of music videos, shorts and features.

To see more of Daniel's work, check out: www.bandit-town.com
On Twitter: _DanielFreedman
On Instagram: @NotDanielFreedman

SINA GRACE

Sina Grace draws kids books comics books and adult books in coffee shops all over Los Angeles. Known for his art contributions to the cult-classic THE LI'L DEPRESSED BOY, Grace has released several works of his own at Image Comics, including the gothic-tinged retail hell graphic novel NOT MY BAG, and the humorous follow-up, SELF-OBSESSED. He has served at the Editorial Director at Robert Kirkman's Skybound imprint, and still gets confused for a girl.

To see more of Sina's work, check out: www.sinagrace.com
On all social media: @SinaGrace